CONSPIRACY NARRATIVES
FROM POSTCOLONIAL AFRICA

CONSPIRACY NARRATIVES FROM POSTCOLONIAL AFRICA

Freemasonry, Homosexuality, and Illicit Enrichment

ROGERS OROCK AND
PETER GESCHIERE

The University of Chicago Press
CHICAGO AND LONDON

The University of Chicago Press, Chicago 60637
The University of Chicago Press, Ltd., London
© 2024 by The University of Chicago
Published 2024

33 32 31 30 29 28 27 26 25 24   1 2 3 4 5

ISBN-13: 978-0-226-83584-6 (cloth)
ISBN-13: 978-0-226-83586-0 (paper)
ISBN-13: 978-0-226-83585-3 (e-book)
DOI: https://doi.org/10.7208/chicago/9780226835853.001.0001

Library of Congress Cataloging-in-Publication Data

Names: Orock, Rogers (Rogers Tabe Egbe), author. | Geschiere, Peter, author.
Title: Conspiracy narratives from postcolonial Africa : Freemasonry, homosexuality, and illicit
enrichment / Rogers Orock and Peter Geschiere.
Description: Chicago ; London : The University of Chicago Press, 2024. | Includes
bibliographical references and index.
Identifiers: LCCN 2024016376 | ISBN 9780226835846 (cloth) | ISBN 9780226835860
(paperback) | ISBN 9780226835853 (e-book)
Subjects: LCSH: Conspiracy theories—Cameroon—History—21st century. | Conspiracy
theories—Gabon—History—21st century. | Moral panics—Cameroon—History—21st century.
| Moral panics—Gabon—History—21st century. | Homophobia—Cameroon. | Homophobia—
Gabon. | Freemasonry. | Postcolonialism—Cameroon. | Postcolonialism—Gabon.
Classification: LCC HV6275.O7 2024 | DDC 001.9/8096711—dc23/eng/20240412
LC record available at https://lccn.loc.gov/2024016376

Contents

Introduction

The eruption in Cameroon around 2005 of a "moral panic" about a supposed epidemic of "homosexuality"—followed a bit later in neighboring Gabon—raises questions that are both socially urgent and analytically challenging.[1] It is too easy to see events in these countries as merely another example of the tide of homophobia that has enveloped various parts of the African continent in recent decades.[2] Clearly, in Cameroon and Gabon homophobia had—and has—special characteristics.[3] One explanation for the particular intensity of the panic in Cameroon was that accusations were directed *against* the state elite (and not from the top down, as in most other parts of the continent; Nyeck 2013). It was especially the so-called *Grands* who were denounced for sexual transgressions, ruining the nation, and perverting its youth: in Cameroon (as in Gabon) "the homosexual" about whom people were indignant is not a marginal figure but *un Grand* using his (or her) position and wealth to humiliate less fortunate people sexually.

Equally striking is the popular presumption that obviously such transgressions can be explained by the elite's associations with secret societies of Western provenance—first Freemasonry, then Rosicrucianism, and now even the Illuminati. We touch here upon a topic that is as important for postcolonial Africa as it is understudied: these brotherhoods are ubiquitous, but they receive surprisingly little attention in African studies. A major challenge for this book is to understand why for many people associations with same-sex practices have become so obvious in Cameroon, Gabon, and elsewhere in francophone Africa. It is certainly not as self-evident in other parts of the world. Tracing the genealogy of this particular trait led us to explore historical specificities in the countries concerned and also Freemasonry's history in France, where the association of same-sex intercourse with these brotherhoods has a particular and much longer genealogy. A major question is, of course, why this association has recently taken on new urgency in Central Africa. It is only recently that people in Cameroon have begun to refer to the political elite as *les pédés de la République* (the faggots of the Republic; Ndjio 2012b, 618). As Freemasons or Rosicrucians, elites are suspected of imposing same-sex intercourse as a ritual initiation on young men seeking employment.

In Gabon, similar complications emerged somewhat later. After the new president, Ali Bongo (succeeding his father-by-adoption in 2009) announced his new regime as *L'Émergence*, pop-singers answered by rapping "L'émergence n'aime pas les femmes" (*Émergence* does not like women; Aterianus-Owanga 2012). Only a few months after taking office, the new president was formally initiated as *grand maître* of the Grand Lodge of Gabon, and the ceremony was broadcast on YouTube, thus publicly announcing that he followed in his father's footsteps also in this regard. The message was clear: If you want to succeed, you have to join these secret orders. In the eyes of many, it is this occult background that explains the success of *les Grands*. Such success, invariably accompanied by indulgence in conspicuous consumption—a standard saying in postcolonial Cameroon is "oui, oui, un Grand n'est pas un petit" (yes, yes, a big man is not a small one)—is both envied and resented by the public at large. Associating such flamboyant enrichment with sexual transgression brings to the fore its illicit character.[4]

The challenge for this book is to unravel this powerful epistemological knot of Freemasonry, sexual transgression, and illicit enrichment. Such popular associations of ostensibly discrete elements should not be discounted as the umpteenth example of the classical Roman proverb "ex Africa aliquod novi" ("always something new from Africa"—Pliny the Elder). We need to take such visionary imaginaries seriously, not only because of their concrete impact on everyday life but also because they are not as exceptional as they may appear. Recent developments in the West—people's suspicions about the origins of the COVID-19 pandemic, and earlier growing obsessions about plots by "a deep state," pedophile rings, and other sexual scandals—have fanned similar conspiracy theories there as well, further promoted by the explosion of social media. The examples of QAnon and Pizzagate in the United States attest that moral panics can trigger similarly wild imaginaries even in societies that see themselves as truly "modern."[5] In the older sociology of conspiracy thinking as analyzed by Richard Hofstadter (1964), the emphasis may have been on *refuting* such thinking, but a growing insight has been that the first step might be to *listen* if we want to understand the mobilizing force of such "theories." It is not only in Cameroon or Gabon that presumed academic impartiality is put to a heavy test. A question for this book, then, is how we might understand this particular conspiracy theory about associations between same-sex practices, Freemasonry, and illicit enrichment. And, just as in the case of the proliferation of conspiracy theories that seem to increasingly unsettle Euro-America, this is not an easy challenge.

Moreover, this epistemological knot—the presumption that these associations are self-evident among many in Cameroon and Gabon—is not only crucial for understanding recent events in these countries; it also raises challenging analytical questions of wider relevance. If our focus is not so much on refuting such "theories" but rather on understanding how they attained such mobilizing impact, what circumstances deserve special attention? In this case, the international dimension is telling: the purported link with Freemasonry, a worldwide brotherhood, transforms homosexuality into a global issue as well. Second, the mantra of illicit enrichment suggests what the moral panic is about and might also explain its timing. Homosexuality became a contentious issue in these countries in the context of growing popular resentment of the ostentatious enrichment of a small elite, at a time when the metanarratives of the first decades following independence (nation-building, development) were losing their mobilizing force. Both this internationalization and the link with popular resentment of the elite's consumerism form the background to people's moral outrage. Another question is why this outrage focuses on sexuality. Again this seems to be a general trend: conspiracy theorizing seems to have a predilection for sexuality as a domain where hidden and amoral plotting might thrive—think of the ubiquity of rumors about satanism and child abuse in the West.[6] And, indeed, in Cameroon and Gabon, rumors about the misdeeds of the elites allude to a wide range of sexual aberrations. But why, in this case, the particular singling out of *homo*-sexuality? In this regard, it might be enlightening to follow an "intertextual" approach— that is, to further explore how this element relates to wider themes that dominate conspiratorial thinking in present-day Cameroon and Gabon.

Of course, in the context outlined above—popular disappointment about and envy of the spectacular enrichment of the happy few—there is a true proliferation of conspiracy thinking in these countries.[7] Two broad themes stand out: first, ongoing "neocolonial" dependence as a continuation of colonial exploitation that blocked the nation's progress. Second, and perhaps even more foregrounded in everyday life, *sorcellerie* ("witchcraft"—whatever people may mean by this term).[8] The triad of same-sex practices, Freemasonry, and illicit enrichment seems to be situated at the intersection of these two broad themes. The international implications of associating same-sex practices with Freemasonry (and other transnational brotherhoods) condense complaints about an ongoing neocolonial exploitation into an intimate, heavily charged image. Such associations also serve to convince people that homosexuality is yet another colonial imposition; this idea is particularly resonant in the case of Cameroon because decolonization took an exceptionally violent and painful course in this country, as France went to great lengths (and violence) to retain it within *France-Afrique*, Charles de Gaulle's solution for preserving a *pré carré* (protected space) for France in Africa. In chapter 4 we follow the tortuous heritage of how this particular struggle over decolonization shaped the contours of the present-day moral panic. The hope is that historicizing this conspiracy theory, now presented as self-evident, might help highlight its twists and turns over time.

Yet unraveling the epistemological knot of homosexuality, Freemasonry, and enrichment also suggests another path for our analysis. It might be worthwhile to signal here already that *homo*sexuality relates intrinsically to the other pole of conspiracy thinking in these countries: "witchcraft." In many parts of Cameroon and Gabon (as elsewhere in Africa), people see a basic link between same-sex intercourse and the purported nightly meetings of witches, who are supposed to indulge in wild bacchanals, with everything—and especially sex—being performed transgressively. This association does not receive much attention in LGBTQ literature on Africa—for understandable reasons—but it is crucial for understanding people's reactions to "homosexuality." The conceptual link can be so strong that people automatically see self-identifying gays, lesbians, and transsexuals as "witches" (or possibly as "witch-doctors") and the other way around. This is also a strong reminder of the dangers of reducing allusions to sexual practices to dimensions that may seem to be more substantial—such as political-economic inequality. Many people seem obsessed by the idea that secret networks—in this case, especially Freemasonry and Rosicrucianism—might explain the elite's flagrant riches. The association with sexual depravity, then, seems to be merely an adjunct for denouncing the illicit character of this enrichment. However, the very riches of the fantasies built around these associations caution against such a reductive approach.

For some time now, people in Cameroon have been saying that they live in an *anusocratie*—under "the rule of the anus." This is, of course, a play on words—a neologism shaped after *démocratie* that became a buzzword in the country since the formal end of one-party rule in 1990. Interestingly, the Gabonese public followed with their own neologism: *anustocratie*—apparently an improvisation on *aristocratie*. However, this recent wordplay should not hide the fact that the association of the anus with enrichment, in whatever form, has a long history in these societies. One of the unexpected byproducts of the recent moral panic about homosexuality in Central Africa is a renewed interest in the work of Cameroon's earliest ethnographer, Günther Tessmann, who conducted fieldwork—anticipating Bronisław Malinowski's turn to ethnographic research on the spot—among the Fang on the border between present-day Cameroon and Equatorial Guinea at the very moment of the imposition of colonial rule (around 1905). Tessmann developed his own way of doing fieldwork—at a time that most anthropologists still took an armchair approach—with a strange mixture of sincere interest and racist contempt, but it yielded valuable findings. One of these—his now classic monograph *Die Pangwe* (The Fang)—discussed the Fang's magical association of *biang akuma* (the medicine of wealth) with same-sex intercourse, a foreshadowing of present-day notions like *anusocratie*. More recent authors studying this region and other parts of Africa highlight similar growing preoccupations with the anus as a source of wealth (discussed further in chapter 5). The specific form of this association varies and seems to shift over time, but the linking of same-sex practices to enrichment, more or less illicit, is signaled so widely in the African continent—another aspect that remains understudied in recent literature on LGBTQ issues in Africa—that it is clear that sexual transgression plays a role of its own in this triangle.[9]

Unraveling this epistemological knot risks dragging us into thorny debates about notions of agency and personhood. Who exactly is the "homosexual" to whom such strong agency is attributed as the key figure in this conspiracy narrative? Of course, the very idea that someone can be identified as "a homosexual" expresses a modern, liberal notion of the person as a well-defined individual with his or her own core identity and responsible for his or her own actions.[10] But the association of same-sex intercourse with witchcraft suggests a completely different vision of the person—as inherently double or even multiple, capable of constant transformation.[11] This idea of the "plasticity of the person"—as "incomplete" and constantly crossing frontiers—has been the object of much attention in recent scholarship on Africa.[12] Most of these authors take their inspiration from Amos Tutuola and his classic *Palmwine Drinkard* (1952). And, indeed, Tutuola's account of the narrator's eventful trip to the "Dead's Town" offers a vision of "the" person that can seem a salutary alternative to the sharply outlined (neo)liberal subject produced by modernity. This doubleness of the person, as we shall see, has been invoked by some authors, notably Cameroonian anthropologist Cécile Séverin Abega (2007a, 2007b), to illuminate popular articulations of homophobia. Such special aspects of developments in present-day Africa suggest intriguing convergences with queer theory as it emerged in the West at the end of the twentieth century.

Clearly the triad of homosexuality, Freemasonry, and enrichment has to be studied as an assemblage of quite different elements with different implications. Following the historical articulation of these elements—in articulation's double sense of linking and expressing clearly[13]—can bring out the precarious character of such associations. Yet it is precisely the kaleidoscopic character of such a conspiracy narrative that is the secret to the cogency that it apparently assumes among many people. It can also help explain why the variety of conceptions that people bring together under the heading of *sorcellerie*, or witchcraft, in Africa—an open and kaleidoscopic imaginary par excellence—seems to be at the very heart of this triad. Freemasonry may appear to bring in a new, perhaps modern, element—after all, its very emphasis on "freedom" implies that Masons have to liberate their spirit from older attachments; this does give them a modern, individualistic aura. Yet to many (and not only in Africa), Freemasonry's practices—secret meetings and signs, special initiation rituals—evoke a new form of the occult. Through its association with same-sex practices, whether actual or simply rumored, Freemasonry is even more directly drawn into the world of *sorcellerie* and associated with very different notions of the person as multilayered and unbounded. This kaleidoscopic assembling forced us to cast our net ever wider, following apparently different directions. It is this assembling capacity—suggesting an overarching coherence despite differences—that makes conspiracy theories so appealing or convincing to those who follow them.

A Moral Panic in Cameroon and Its Broader Social Relevance

A brief sketch of the main events that triggered the moral panic in Cameroon and subsequently in Gabon brings out the urgency of the topic. In the case of Cameroon, Yaoundé Archbishop Tonye Bakot's 2005 Christmas sermon is generally seen as a turning point. Unexpectedly, Monseigneur Bakot used this solemn occasion in the capital's majestic cathedral to lash out against the country's elite, accusing them of sodomizing young men seeking employment. This was all the more surprising since many members of the elite, including the nation's president, Paul Biya, himself (who had earlier on been labeled "a homosexual" by his opponents), were attending the mass, seated directly in front of Monseigneur Bakot's pulpit. The bishop's attack was followed the next month by the publication in several newspapers of lists of prominent "homosexuals," including ministers and leading politicians, but also soccer players, artists, and priests—some women, but mostly men. The archbishop's attack on the elite's purported homosexual practices clearly tied in to deep popular resentment, but the breadth of people accused by the newspapers already suggested that this was not just an attack "from below"; in many respects, it was also an intra-elite affair. Since colonial days, Catholic conclaves have been seen as hotspots of "unnatural vice," and for some opposition leaders "homosexuality" had become a convenient accusation to denounce the colonial roots of the elite in power. The government reacted cautiously: at first, the president himself asked that people's privacy be respected. But eventually the government decided that it had to act in order to distance itself from such defamatory accusations. During subsequent years there followed ever more drastic police interventions, arrests, and condemnations.[14] Often "homosexuals" were denounced to the police by their neighbors. In Cameroon accusations come often from society, rather than from the state, and it is this aspect that made the country take the lead within the African continent in witch-hunts against "homosexuals."

The suppression of homosexuality, however, had a longer history in Cameroon. In 1972, Ahmadou Ahidjo, the country's first president, criminalized homosexuality by presidential decree,[15] but the decree was rarely enforced (although the threat of denunciation to the police often served as a basis for blackmail). Monseigneur Bakot's attack and the subsequent *affaire des listes* marked a changing climate in which "homosexuality"— became a public issue for various reasons: the growing impact of social media showing gay identities, but also the increasing pressure of human rights missions from the West demanding that consensual same-sex practices between adults be decriminalized. In Gabon similar complications emerged, albeit with a different outcome. Independence brought no change in the laws inherited from the French colonizer, and homosexuality was not criminalized, but in June 2019 a new penal code was abruptly introduced in a context of growing unrest, to address the ubiquity of Freemasons in government and a supposed proliferation of "homosexuality." The new code imposed heavy sanctions (imprisonment and a fine) on same-sex intercourse, even between consenting adults. The law was abruptly rescinded under international pressure a year later, and this sudden decriminalization led to bitter accusations in the press that the president had failed to defend the traditions of his own country against outside pressures.

A public debate in Cameroon, nine years after the 2005/6 crisis, shows how tenacious the issue had become. The broadcast in early 2014 of a documentary by the French television channel France 24 on the rise of homophobia in Cameroon triggered furious reactions within the country.[16] The documentary addressed the suspicious death of Roger Jean-Claude Mbede, a gay man who was arrested because he had sent a text message expressing affection to a *fonctionnaire* (civil servant). Just before this, a gay rights activist, Eric Lembembe, had been tortured and murdered in his home. The French television program noted that the government had formally denied any persecution of homosexuals in the country, but it also presented comments from notable figures in the Cameroonian media who, in contrast to the official comments, challenged the authorities to mount a more robust resistance to "homosexual lobbies all over the world" that sought to "impose" the "odious act" of same-sex intercourse. When Zacharie Biloa Ayissi, a former superintendent of police, later active as a journalist at the newspaper *Nouvelle Afrique*, one of the first to publish lists of homosexuals in 2006, was asked whether he believed that the French documentary was part of a broader conspiracy to "prepare Cameroonians' minds" toward accepting the decriminalization of homosexuality in the country, Ayissi answered: "It is not a montage but an intentional policy! You don't know what kind of ravages homosexuality has caused in our country. Initially, the devolution of power in Cameroon was arranged through the anal canal."[17]

In chapter 4 we will return to such allegations, which specifically targeted Louis-Paul Aujoulat, a leading politician in French colonial Cameroon during the 1950s, who played a key role in Cameroon's decolonization. In those years he was criticized by radical nationalists for creating a more cooperative elite willing to collaborate with the French for independence within the framework of *Françafrique*. Aujoulat—an almost forgotten figure at the end of the twentieth century—made a spectacular return after 2000, but now as a "homo-masonic figure" (Nyeck 2013), accused of sodomizing the new Cameroonian elite (including the later presidents Ahidjo and Biya), and thus perverting the country. The story was repeated not only by *radio trottoir* (sidewalk radio) but also in newspaper articles, in books, and on television. One of the persistent effects of all this uproar is that every young man with a promising career is immediately suspected of having yielded to *les Grands'* vile solicitations. It is striking that such aspects, more or less hidden, receive little attention in broader debates about homophobia and LGBTQ rights in Africa. Yet there are good reasons to take this moral panic seriously—as well as the wild stories it produces associating homosexuality with enrichment and Freemasonry—for a proper contextualization of the controversies surrounding LGBTQ issues in Africa. It may be difficult to separate rumor and reality in all of this, but whatever their truth value, these stories have powerful effects on everyday life—as is clear from the witch hunts against LGBTQ individuals in Cameroon that continue into the present day.

THEORETICAL RELEVANCE:
AFRICANIZING QUEER STUDIES?

Apart from its urgency for the countries concerned, our topic also raises questions that have wider theoretical relevance. Two general debates have been particularly important for us in analyzing the often surprising turns that the articulation of Freemasonry, homophobia, and illicit enrichment took in the contexts we studied. First of all, the debate on how to study conspiracy thinking—a challenge that acquires new relevance with its recent intensification on a global scale. The second debate is about "homosexuality" as a controversial issue in African contexts but also in relation to new analytical trends in the West often summarized as "queer studies" and the Africanization of this approach.[18]

To start with the second debate: In a subtle and original analysis of parallel homophobic trends in Nigeria, Steven Pierce (2016) signals that the burgeoning literature on this issue still leaves vital questions open. For him, a dominant insight in this literature—the idea that in Africa homophobia rather than homosexuality is a Western imposition—is certainly valuable since it rightly highlights the colonial roots of postcolonial panics about a supposed proliferation of homosexuality. Yet, Pierce (cf. also Rao 2020) insists that more nuanced research is necessary to answer questions such as why it is *now* that "homosexuality" is becoming a political issue, not only in Africa but also in other parts of the world (think of Russia, Latin America, or the Caribbean). Of course, there are obvious factors that play a role. Shifts in religious ideas and practices—whether under the influence of evangelical missionaries from the West (as in Uganda), or more local forms of orthodoxy, Muslim or Christian (as in Nigeria)—certainly matter. Pierce also refers to the spread of social media triggering mounting anxieties over the impact of global "gay" identities and human rights activism. Indeed, many self-identifying gays in Cameroon remember growing access to the internet around 2000 as a true turning point in their lives, personally, through the discovery of a global gay presence, but also because of intensifying official harassment.[19] Yet Pierce rightly emphasizes that we have to move beyond such general explanations. The "why now?" question clearly needs a more specific answer, taking into account manifest differences among these countries. And even more fundamental is the question of what people actually mean when they use words like "homosexual" or "homosexuality": who or what is targeted exactly? Again, the answers will vary in different contexts, even within the continent. Both in Cameroon and Gabon these notions seem to become floating signifiers that shift over time and thus can be used to express a wide array of grievances. The particular configuration of factors that makes the issue so urgent also shifts according to time and space. And, as we emphasized earlier, the "politicization" of homosexuality can follow quite different trajectories even within the African continent.[20]

One way to further explore Pierce's basic questions may be to focus in comparative perspective on the special link with enrichment, and the role that the anus is supposed to play in this context—think of notions like *anusocratie* in Cameroon, or *anustocratie* in Gabon. The recurrence of linking same-sex practices to enrichment in different parts of the African continent (also in earlier times) was one of the most striking findings of our research. In recent debates on Africa as a "homophobic continent"— whether confirming this stereotype or questioning it—this association with illicit enrichment receives little attention, and it is striking that it is also absent from the classical Western texts on homosexuality. Sigmund Freud in his stocktaking of *Inversion* (his term for homosexuality) in *Three Essays on the Theory of Sexuality* (1905) does not mention this aspect.[21] In Africa, the association of homosexual practices with enrichment and "access" (to what, exactly?) is an object of particular emphasis.

As early as 2009, Charles Gueboguo—one of the first academics inside Cameroon who had the courage to write about this sensitive topic— signaled a *homosexualization* of social climbing. In the same year Christophe Broqua broadened this insight: "If homosexuality is developing in sub-Saharan Africa, it is because it enables one to become wealthy" (2009, 61).[22] It is tempting to see this as a new phenomenon, linked to the propagation by television and other media of a global gay identity marked by new and ostentatious consumerist practices. And, indeed, in his pioneering study of hair-salons as gay spaces in rural South Africa, Graeme Reid (2013) documents how the common association of gays with modernity makes the flamboyant hairdressers with whom he worked particularly popular with their female clients, who are convinced that they have a special affinity with modern hair styles. For Abidjan, Vinh-Kim Nguyen (2010) provides a very subtle interpretation of *le milieu* (the emerging gay scene in the city) as a niche that offers "access." Again, access to what is often not exactly clear, but the interest of Nguyen's discussion is precisely that he captures so well people's idea of such "access" as linked to new opportunities in a vague, general sense.[23] This link has a much longer history in Africa, and this makes it all the more intriguing why the anus takes central stage in this imaginary and therefore also in the recent moral attacks on such enrichment as illicit. Gueboguo noted that "the behind [*le derrière*] . . . has become a privileged site of domination." As one of our interlocutors put it, "The anus is rising." Of course same-sex intercourse between men encompasses a broader range of activities, in Africa as elsewhere, than just anal intercourse. But the anus is central in the link people make with enrichment; hence our focus—in line with the popular obsession among Cameroonians and Gabonese with *anusocratie/anustocratie*—on same-sex practices between men.[24]

Academic literature has also recently called attention to this association. Two of the continent's most visionary thinkers, Cameroonian historian/philosopher Achille Mbembe (2010) and Gabonese anthropologist Joseph Tonda (2016), advanced more general interpretations of associations between the anus and wealth. Interestingly their interpretations of such "anusocracy" seem to have quite different implications. Mbembe (2010, 213, 219) sees it as a new variant of a scheme that haunts witchcraft fantasies in general: the image of powerful witches (mostly elders) feeding on the life force of their younger dependents (he speaks of a "regeneration of declining virility"). Thus, anal penetration of young men seems to be the ultimate phallocracy, fortifying *le Grand* and draining his victims.[25] Tonda, however, inspired by Gilles Deleuze and Félix Guattari's reflections on the "capitalist anus," seems to relate such forms of intercourse to the Fanonian nightmare of an "impotent" African bourgeoisie. In Tonda's examples (2015a, 57–58; 2016, 32), it is the *Grands* who allow themselves to be penetrated, being thus robbed of their life force. Such variations highlight the volatility of the imaginary relating to anal penetration and wealth. Clearly, this link suggests all sorts of different possibilities. All the more interesting to try and follow shifts in this imaginary and study the way these affect everyday relations.[26]

An even greater challenge is to explore whether "queer studies," as developed in the West since the end of the twentieth century, can offer any insights in understanding the special role of the anus in African discourses. Over the last decade, the notion of "queerness" has become increasingly present in Africa as well—even though there seems to be some reluctance to adopt the term.[27] In queer theory's Western variants, the anus and anal intercourse had pride of place, right from the start. However, here as well interpretations differed. Compare, for instance, the different tenor of two foundational texts: Italian philosopher, activist, and playwright Mario Mieli's *Towards a Gay Communism* (2018 [1977]), with the battle cry "I keep my treasure in my arse, but it is open to everybody";[28] and American literary theorist Leo Bersani's paper with the provocative title "Is the Rectum a Grave?" (2009 [1987]).[29]

At first glance, it is especially the struggle in both texts to arrive at a more positive interpretation of anal intercourse that seems to differ from African associations of such intercourse with illicit enrichment. Yet, there may be some ambiguity here. Bersani wrote his text in 1987 at the height of the AIDS crisis in the gay community in the United States. Unprotected anal penetration, which had become a focal point in gay bathhouse culture, suddenly turned out to have deadly consequences. But Bersani insisted that this should by no means imply a turning away from sex, nor a search for "displacement" (reconstructing sex as an expression of something else).[30] Rather, he looked for a solution by confronting the phallic implications of anal intercourse— top and bottom, active and passive, mastery and subordination—and over-coming these through a "redemptive reinvention of sex" (22). He insisted that intercourse does not have to be about overpowering; there is also "the perhaps equally strong appeal of powerlessness, of the loss of control"—of succumbing to desire and "losing sight of the self" (24). In such a vision, the rectum is no longer a grave but rather a place for new beginnings.

Ten years earlier—that is, before the outbreak of AIDS made sexual promiscuity so dangerous and stigmatizing—Mieli launched, in a some-what different way, a similar call to unleash the liberating effects of anal intercourse. For Mieli—inspired by French philosopher Guy Hocquen-hem, another European forerunner in the emergence of queer theory in the United States during the 1980s—a reevaluation of the anus and anal penetration was urgently needed for a "liberation of Eros"—helping het-erosexuals finally accept the homosexual element present in everybody. This would, he argued, bring about a truly revolutionary overturning of capitalism.[31] In striking contrast to such rigid Marxist jargon is the playful way in which Mieli conveyed the enjoyment that anal penetration can bring to both partners. To his battle cry quoted above, he adds: "If what in homosexuality especially horrifies *homo normalis*, that cop of the het-erocapitalist system, is getting fucked in the ass, then this can only mean that one of most delicious bodily pleasures, anal sex, bears in itself a re-markable revolutionary force" (Mieli 2018 [1977], 157).

Quentin Dubois's recent return (2021) to Hocquenghem's work of the 1970s is also of interest for our topic. Dubois deplores the recent loss of the revolutionary fervor of the gay/queer movement of the 1970s. For Dubois, the only solution to counter the gradual absorption of this movement in the neoliberal tide is a *désublimation* of the anus in order to use its capacity to *désinquiéter* (destabilize) to the fullest extent. And here are convergen-ces with the African imaginaries about the anus as a source of wealth, albeit in a different direction. Interestingly, some of Dubois's statements about *l'homosexuel comme ennemi de l'intérieur* (the homosexual as the enemy inside), "the anus as a political notion," and "a queer genealogy of the penetration of the body of the nation, the fatherland" could be taken directly from the discourse of African homophobes denouncing the spread of homosexuality as a corruption of the nation. It is precisely where these discourses meet that they also show their divergences.

So is there any relevance in juxtaposing our African examples with these texts from Western queer theory? At first sight, it is especially the differences that are striking. The negative connotations of African discourses on anal penetration may correspond to Bersani's equation of the anus with a grave, but they certainly do not correspond to his "redemptive sex project" for overcoming this negativity. And the lust that enlivens Mieli's book seems to be conspicuously absent from African texts (which, of course, is not surprising, since we mainly quote from attacks on such "homosexual" practices). Yet, on closer inspection, Bersani's and Mieli's passionate defense of anal penetration—and sex in general—as liberating and enriching may suggest other layers in the preoccupation within present-day Africa with the anus as a source of riches: less judgmental than the moral indignation that dominates the public debate, but also capable of further enriching queer theory's effort to overcome the ostensible binary oppositions and identities that still haunt Western (and other) discourses. The juxtaposition with queer studies' classics suggests looking for other voices in African contexts, maybe not yet loudly articulated in the public scene, but emerging. Of interest is, in this respect as well, the growing attention to the layeredness of the person in the work of Francis Nyamnjoh and others on "incompleteness" as a central strain in African conceptions of personhood.[32] A leading question in the following chapters will be to what extent such notions of the person as inherently "incomplete" or even "double" might help us understand special traits of same-sex arrangements in Africa as linked to secret networks and enrichment.

CONSPIRACY THEORIES GOING GLOBAL

The other major challenge for our study was working with rumors about hidden conspiracies. This challenge assumed considerable urgency recently with the growing concern—also among academics—about how to deal with the visceral and increasingly global power that conspiracy thinking is acquiring in our world. Especially in the United States, the sociology of conspiracy thinking has become a booming field since the 1950s, with Richard Hofstadter, professor of American history at Columbia University, as one of its protagonists, focusing on conspiracy theories from both the extreme right *and* left. A standard critique of his approach targeted his failure to justify the contrast he made between his "scientific" interpretations, which he (like many of his colleagues) presented as "objective," in contrast to the "conspiracy theories," which were thus classified as "nonscientific" and therefore false.[33]

For our topic French sociologist Luc Boltanski's approach is of particular interest, not only because he is a relative outsider to the field[34] and therefore writes with some ironical distance[35]—quite rare in this field—but even more because of his consequent focus on the ambiguous relationships between conspiracy thinking and the nation-state. Boltanski focused on the growing popular interest in the West in hidden conspiracies by relating it to the emerging nation-state of the nineteenth century and its precarious efforts to create a uniform social reality for its people and territory—precarious because the state project inevitably clashed with all manner of internationalizing tendencies (notably of a wider capitalist framework).[36] His 2012 book had a somewhat playful beginning, starting with the quite sudden emergence at the end of the nineteenth century of the detective novel and the spy story as established literary genres. He takes these new literary genres as a starting point for exploring varying patterns in people's perceptions of the nation-state and their doubts about the "reality of the reality" that these states were trying to impose. Toward the end of the book, there is a dramatic turn when Boltanski introduces Franz Kafka's haunting *Der Prozess* (published in 1925 but written in 1914/15) as the mirror of detective novels and spy stories, turning their world upside down: the hidden conspirator turns out to be the state itself, which characteristically never reveals itself to its victims. Thus, conspiracy thinking proves to be about the "monstrosities" of the nation-state that are "about to come" (p. 376). A powerful conclusion!

The conspiracy theory contained in our conceptual triangle—Freemasonry, same-sex practices, and enrichment—is also clearly centered on the state, but in somewhat different ways. In Central Africa, after independence (1960), the obstacles for the young nation-states to establish a common social reality were large and numerous—could one even speak of a nation-state here? The main difference was that the state elites hardly seemed intended to shape the common social reality that Boltanski saw as an overriding concern of the nation-state's protagonists in Europe. Cameroon's first president, Ahmadou Ahidjo, for example, started a formal program of nation-building—his emphasis on unity as *the* national goal corresponded to Boltanski's claims about a nation-state's central preoccupation—but with Ahidjo such a project was based on the idea of a "regional equilibrium," thus consolidating ethnic divisions in practice. And the regime of Paul Biya, Ahidjo's successor after 1982, increasingly neglected even the formalities of such nation-building. No wonder people speculated about outside support of these regimes as an explanation for their survival—by France as the former colonizer, but increasingly also by hidden international networks. And, even more importantly, the elites themselves increasingly alluded to Masonic or Rosicrucian networks as the true secret behind their power. So the "social reality" as a framework for everyday life is hardly shaped by a concerted state project. Moreover,

Boltanski's dramatic conclusion about the state emerging as the hidden actor in conspiracy thinking certainly corresponds to popular perceptions in Cameroon, Gabon, and other African countries. The state is seen by many not as the guarantor of order but as the main cause of disorder, disturbing the normal course of things. In this respect a great merit of Boltanski's approach for thinking about postcolonial Africa is highlighting that the problematic functioning of the postcolonial state is not that exceptional—the closed reality the nation-state strives for is apparently universally undermined by the increasing importance of transnational openings.

In his recent and monumental work *L'Énergie de l'état* (2022) French political scientist Jean-François Bayart puts this tension in a wider perspective by emphasizing *triangulation* as a highly variable dimension in the emergence of nation-states from preceding empires. Of special interest for this study and for understanding the escalation of conspiracy thinking in general is that he adds a third element—the search for cultural unity through fixing ethno-national identities—as central in efforts to reconcile the state's national space with the international concatenations produced by capitalism. And it is especially this search for a cultural identity—crucial for justifying the state's realities—that becomes the source of violent tensions. The problematic link between the nation-state and the production of identities has been a recurring theme throughout Bayart's work (see especially Bayart 2005). This triangle of a precarious national space, undermined by international ramifications and by insecurity about people's "real" identity is a hotbed for conspiracy theories in Central Africa as well. Another recurring theme in Bayart's work is the emphasis on "extraversion" as a powerful trend in African social formations, which relates directly to the internationalizing implications of Freemasonry and its role in popular conspiracy thinking in Central Africa.[37]

A quite different but very fruitful model for studying conspiracies was recently developed by Jaron Harambam (Free University, Amsterdam, and one of the founders of a European network on conspiracy theories, COST COMPACT). Harambam and his colleagues emphasize the futility of debunking people's narratives.[38] Relying on Bruno Latour's critique of science's claims to truth and exclusivity, Harambam cautions that any tendency to reason from fixed knowledge hierarchies (with academic knowledge as the self-evident apex) simply does not work in "post-truth times." He emphasizes the need to *listen* to people who believe in conspiracy narratives; this is why he chose an ethnographic approach, patiently listening to the theories of his interlocutors, what they revealed to him as their truth, and their anger at being disregarded by official science. It is precisely his ethnographic approach that is of interest for our project and for the more general challenge of how to work with slippery data like rumors and allusions. For some time now, academic authors have warned that, despite their slipperiness, rumors are proper topics for research since they can have powerful effects on everyday relations. For Africa, this insight has been developed in a persuasive way by Stephen Ellis (1989) in his insightful analysis of the working of *radio trottoir* (sidewalk radio), now complemented and further empowered by the ubiquity of new social media in Africa as well. A complicating factor in many African contexts is that rumors and conspiracy theories will inevitably lead the researcher into the marshy field of "witchcraft," which constantly insinuated itself into our research as some sort of shadow text behind the triad of Freemasonry, homosexuality, and enrichment, but also as a notorious trap for academics who long for facts and "hard" data.[39] Indeed, studying "witchcraft" offers interesting parallels with Harambam's and his colleagues' *efforts to develop* an ethnographic approach to conspiracy thinking, but it also raises some thorny challenges.

For Joseph Tonda, the Gabonese/Congolese anthropologist quoted earlier, *l'esprit sorcellaire* (the "witch mind"), inspiring a vision of the person as multidimensional, and of nature as animated, can be "blinding" in its kaleidoscopic mixing of ever new possibilities and implications. His earlier books paint everyday life in postcolonial Africa as beset by vivid but confusing realities, layered and full of unexpected linkages: healers who combine elements of local ecstatic cults like the Bwiti—around the trance brought about by the *iboga* weed—with biblical elements, often in Pentecostal garb; spirits appearing on television screens, when a plane crashed in a mangrove swamp close to the city of Libreville—the downed plane in sight of the city, yet for some time unreachable—the ghosts of the dead were supposed to disturb emissions.[40] In his 2015 book, Tonda adds that such *éblouissement* (bedazzlement) is increasingly becoming a global phenomenon. He speaks of an *impérialisme postcolonial* in which the whole world is becoming blinded by an overproduction of images that makes any distinction between "fake" and "real" relative, and in which social media are "colonizing" people's minds. Tonda's widening of this *éblouissement* as an increasingly global phenomenon—Africa as a forerunner in dealing with such an overproduction of images—highlights the broader relevance of our analysis of these particular African conspiracy theories. In many respects the correspondences between witchcraft rumors and the conspiracy theories that are recently invading the internet on a global scale—and notably in the West—are striking.[41]

One common trait of both is the rapidity with which different interpretations succeed each other. The idea of "witchcraft" as some sort of "traditional" remnant is very tenacious. But as far as we can go back in history, these imaginaries had a surprisingly dynamic character, in Africa but also in other parts of the world (including Europe). Visions of new secrets follow each other in a dazzling rush, and there seems to be a premium on evoking new possibilities—new forces that can break through existing defenses, whether to harm or to protect. A similar restlessness marks present-day conspiracy thinking. QAnon, whose adherents played such a prominent role in the attack on the US Capitol in Washington, DC, on January 6, 2021, attained a global presence far beyond the United States, with Facebook groups emerging all over the world within a few years of its origins in 2017, when a certain individual known as Q started to publish messages on web forums.[42] The name Q suggested that this person had access to secret documents around the White House, but this person never identified her/himself (QAnon stands for "Q Anonymous"). The messages were called "Q-drops," which meant that they never offered complete information—only allusions that people were exhorted to follow by themselves on the internet. QAnon took over a central idea—the Deep State as run by a ring of pedophiles—from earlier conspiracy theories (for instance Pizzagate, targeting Hilary Clinton); but this pedophile element has a much longer history, as a new variant of an older obsession with Satanists and child abuse.[43] Clearly, the slipperiness of rumors about witchcraft coloring conspiracy rumors in Africa has parallels all over the world. A common tendency is to claim an obvious truth presumption that is outside history, but a difference—to which we will return—might be that the history of QAnon's obsession with elites and pedophilia is easier to follow than references to witchcraft as a supposedly "traditional" given in African settings. Yet we hope to show that it pays to follow these "theories" in their restless succession through time.

The question for now might rather be how Harambam and his colleagues try to deal with the slipperiness of their data. Their emphasis on the need to maintain a distance from current epistemological hierarchies made them intent on listening to what people had to say—hence their preference for an ethnographic approach. Again, the parallel with witchcraft studies is striking. One of the reasons why Michael Taussig's 1987 book *Shamanism, Colonialism, and the Wild Man* book had such widespread appeal was the author's willingness "to go along" with the wisdom that his healer, Don Santiago, revealed to him during ecstatic nightly yagé sessions in the Amazonian jungle of Colombia.[44] Similarly, Peter Geschiere's interlocutors during his long-term fieldwork in Maka villages in the forest area of southeast Cameroon made it amply clear that, if he did not take their stories about the *djambe* (witchcraft) seriously, there was little reason for them to even start telling him about it. Yet Harambam's ethnography offers also many examples that "going along" with conspiracy thinkers in academic contexts is only possible up to a point. As ethnographers, anthropologists may want to avoid any semblance of introducing an idea of "false consciousness"—avoiding any suggestion that they are seeing the "real" truth behind their interlocutors' "rationalizations." But what should one do if one is cited as a witness for a slanderous accusation against, for instance, an old "witch" who seems to be turned into a scapegoat for people's diffuse anxieties? "Going along" may lead to ethical dilemmas.

Harambam looks for a solution for similar dilemmas in conspiracy studies by insisting that academics should adopt an "epistemological pluralism." He hopes for "deliberative citizen knowledge platforms," where different kinds of knowledge can be compared in a more democratic context.[45] He wrote this before the COVID-19 pandemic graphically revealed the Babel-like confusion that such an approach can yield when a wide array of citizens, each defending their own claim to knowledge, confront one another in the media. More useful might be his insistence that academics should refrain from trying to refute their interlocutors' often surprising interpretations. Indeed what could refuting mean in such contexts, and is it ever possible? Yet, here again, "going along with" creates difficulties.

A good example is a central issue of our project: the link that people make between Freemasonry and same-sex practices. For many in present-day Cameroon and Gabon, this is a self-evident association. But for others—both people on the spot and outsiders—it is pure fantasy that might have an impact on everyday life but still is a product of popular imagination. Clearly it is difficult to completely avoid the truth question here. Of course, over recent decades academics have increasingly accepted that the boundary between truth and fiction is porous and shifting, and that realities are multiple. But—as in witchcraft studies—it does matter whether certain actions have effectively taken place. Or to put it more bluntly: Is the association of Freemasonry with same-sex practices only rumor or is it in certain contexts credible because some Masons were (or are) interested in experimenting with alternative forms of sex? For our analysis, Harambam's shift from the truth question to analyzing why certain rumors are credible in certain contexts and others are not, is useful. Boltanski and Bayart also focus on the context in which such variations in credibility can be analyzed: clearly the link with power differences and more particularly the state is a crucial factor. Yet, it remains worthwhile to combine our approach of contextualizing rumors—following them in their twists and turns over time—with a keen interest in moments when rumors and acts in the everyday seem to reinforce each other.

Harambam's warning that attempts to refute conspiracy theories can easily lead to an idea of "false consciousness" and block deeper understanding is certainly relevant for our undertaking. Yet such "epistemological pluralism" does not necessarily imply that the certainty with which particular interpretations are presented must be taken for granted. Our particular case—Freemasonry, sexual transgression, and enrichment being condensed in a conspiracy that supposedly unsettles the future of Cameroon and Gabon—suggests an alternative solution. The very fact that we can follow these rumors and suspicions over time, highlighting striking twists and turns, suggests a further effort to historicize them. For Cameroon, we can show, for instance, that it was only around 2000 that the association of Freemasonry and "homosexuality" became a recurrent argument in attacks on the regime. How can these shifts be related to particular contexts? People present such links as given and out-of-time. "Of course" Freemasons are faggots, and "of course" they are driven by a desire for enrichment, whether illicit or not. One of the questions for this book is whether historicizing these links and focusing on historically contextualized shifts and inconsistencies can help to break through the presumption that these links are self-evident. We hope also to show that such historicizing can help relate rumors to concrete events and settings, giving our interpretations a firmer basis.

Boltanski's version of conspiracy studies and Bayart's analysis of different patterns of triangulation suggest still another set of questions. In our research we have been mainly backward looking, following the genealogies of our triad that could explain how this articulation of quite different elements could acquire such strong coherence and such visceral power. Yet, the question is also what does this particular conspiracy knot produce for the future? First of all in relation to the state, which plays such a central role in these rumors: Does it strengthen or undermine state power? Or does it promote alternative ways of governing? And more generally: What kind of citizens does it address and produce—subjects performing the roles that rumors attribute to them, or as the kind of moral person the rumors implicitly appeal to?[46]

Chapters

In line with this search for concrete anchors, our first chapter is about "anti-Masonism" in Cameroon and Gabon, followed by a brief comparison with similar movements in France. In contrast to the veil of secrecy—or "discretion," as many brothers now call it—that partly conceals the presence and activities of the brotherhood, anti-Masonism is very loud and in the open, which for us has the advantage that it thus offers concrete starting points. Its arguments and accusations—authors often use the term "lodges" to indiscriminately associate Freemasonry, Rosicrucians, and even Illuminati—constitute the very basis for people's concern about the role of these secret associations. Striking is the continuity with a determined anti-Masonic movement in France since the eighteenth century, sponsored by the Catholic Church and encouraged by recurrent suspicions of a Masonic conspiracy behind the 1789 Revolution and later by the prominent role of the Grand Orient lodge under the Third Republic (1870s–1940), with Vichy as a dark intermezzo. This continuity marks the genealogy of similar countermovements in postcolonial francophone Africa, especially after the return of Freemasonry in France's neocolonial policies under François Mitterand's socialist presidency (1981–1995).

Chapter 2 follows the historical trajectory of Freemasonry from its constitution in Scotland and London around 1700 to other parts of Europe, and from there to Africa. This chapter offers an overview of the crystallization of Masonic rituals and common points of orientation, its global coherence but also the effects of inherent tendencies toward segmentation with a special focus on the brotherhood's dynamics in the postcolonial setting in Africa. Specific topics in this context are the increasing rivalry between the two main Grand Lodges from France in postindependence Africa: Le Grand Orient, for a long time the main French lodge, versus the more recently founded Grande Loge Nationale Française. Especially since the 1990s, this rivalry has become crucial for understanding politics throughout francophone Africa. A related topic is the increasing rivalry in at least some francophone countries between Freemasonry and AMORC, as the main representative of Rosicrucianism. A final topic is the special twist that the association of Freemasonry with same-sex practices assumes postcolonial nations through the link people make with occult forms of enrichment. This chapter is followed by a short interlude offering an overview of the elusive institutional presence of Freemasonry in Cameroon and Gabon.

The next three chapters constitute the historical-ethnographic core of the book. Chapter 3, "*Anusocratie*," follows the emergence of the "moral panic" about homosexuality in Cameroon after 2000 and the way it is linked to *les Grands*, denounced as Freemasons or Rosicrucians. This chapter also highlights the tragic contrast between, on the one hand, the profile of the persons who hesitantly identify as "homosexual"—mostly younger individuals, men and women, and all too often victims of police persecutions—and on the other, the stereotype that incites so much popular anger of "the" homosexual as *un Grand* who uses his power and riches to corrupt the nation's youth. The second half of the chapter discusses the politicization of the issue in comparative perspective, analyzing the emergence of an association with illicit enrichment in other African countries. Freemasonry is everywhere, but its linking to sexual transgression follows varying trajectories. This chapter is followed by a second short interlude briefly exploring different tendencies between men and women experimenting with same-sex relations, notably in the way they react to new forms of "connectivity."

The fourth chapter, "The Return of Dr. Aujoulat," mainly on Cameroon, analyzes the historical shifts in the rumors about this medical doctor–politician who played a central role in the country's decolonization in the 1950s, helping to orchestrate the fierce struggle by the French to maintain the country inside the *pré carré* for French interests in Africa. Aujoulat's surprising "return" after 2000 in the context of the moral panic, but now as a "homo-masonic" figure, is directly related to the exceptionally violent course decolonization took in Cameroon, but also to the special role this colony played in 1940 in the establishment of de Gaulle's *La France Libre*. In this sense there is a direct line from de Gaulle's highly personal take on African politics, to the explosion of homophobia in Cameroon after 2000.

Our last chapter, "'Witchcraft,' Wealth, and Same-Sex Intimacy," follows the linking of same-sex practices to (illicit) enrichment in a longer-term perspective. The special interest of Cameroon and Gabon is that this association turns out to have a longer and quite well-documented history. The present-day tendency in popular discourse in francophone Africa to link homosexuality to Freemasonry is often used to "prove" that it is a colonial imposition, introduced in Africa under colonial rule. In this chapter we analyze the work of Günther Tessmann, who did his research just after 1900 in areas not yet under colonial control. We follow the link that Tessmann made between "the medicine of wealth" and same-sex intercourse, also through the subsequent ethnographic literature on this area ending with Séverin Cécile Abega's work (2007a, 2007b). Interestingly Abega relates the recent moral panic in Cameroon to notions of the doubleness of the person as a point of entry for understanding the link between sexual transgression and enrichment.

We conclude by returning to the main questions of this book. First, of course, the relevance of our analysis of the moral panic in Cameroon and Gabon around this particular knot of Freemasonry, same-sex intercourse, and illicit enrichment for wider discussions on the precarious position of LGBTQ persons in Africa. A question is how neglected aspects in these wider discussions—the conceptual linking of same-sex intercourse with "witchcraft" and occult enrichment (no doubt neglected for good reasons)—should be given their place. Another question is the relevance of our findings—notably the tendency among Africans to shy away from any closed identity and from radically opposing "homo" and "hetero"— for contributing to an Africanization of queer studies, still marked by their Western starting points. An even broader issue concerns the implications of our analysis for dealing with the powerful effects that similar conspiracy theories are acquiring on a global scale. To what extent is our attempt to historicize this particular conspiracy theory relevant for understanding the impact of similar plot-thinking in the present-day world?

Finally an apology to our readers. We had not foreseen that our starting point—understanding the abrupt intensification of homophobia in Cameroon around 2005 and the way it is linked to popular perceptions of the Freemasons—would lead us to such a wide spectrum of historical and comparative factors. So we beg for patience with what may seem to be digressions in the chapters that follow. We hope to show that this wide array of aspects and factors does hang together: from homophobic fantasies in the Cameroonian courts to the dignity of arrested "homosexuals"; from old ideas about *biang akuma* (the medicine of wealth, which is same-sex), to ethnographer Tessmann's idiosyncratic ways, just after 1900, of combining fieldwork with elephant hunting; from Colonel Leclerc's nocturnal attack on Douala in 1940, making Cameroon the crux in the survival of de Gaulle's *France Libre*, to Jacques Foccart, de Gaulle's *Monsieur Afrique* from the 1960s on, with his mythical personal network of African heads of state, containing them inside *Françafrique*; from Vautrin, the suspect hero of Honoré de Balzac's comédie humaine novels who saved his young lover from the guillotine, to Mitterand's reasons for introducing Freemasonry into African politics; from Cameroon president Paul Biya's "spiritual pluralism," making him stray from his Catholic past to the kabbalah, connecting him to a fearsome Israeli-run bodyguard (the secret of his amazing longevity), to his donating huge sums of money to a suspect splinter sect of Rosicrucianism; from the anger of the first Cameroonian nationalists, robbed by the French and a "cooperative elite" of an independence that should have been theirs, to the present-day courage of LGBTQ advocates standing up against grim condemnation by at least some parts of Cameroonian society. . . .

We hope to show that all of this (and much more) will add up to understanding a seemingly self-evident conspiracy narrative as an historical assemblage that is both socially urgent and theoretically challenging.

Anti-Masonism and Homophobia

SECRECY AS CONSPIRACY

While talk about Freemasonry, same-sex practices, and illicit forms of enrichment may have become a fact of life in Cameroon and Gabon, the challenge is to relate hearsay about mostly hidden practices to visible traces in the everyday. We thus begin by focusing on actions by individuals and movements denouncing the secretive practices associated with Freemasonry; this offers a convenient starting point since the movement has become strident and ubiquitous in the everyday in Cameroon and Gabon: in pamphlets, in streams of articles in newspapers, in books, on television, and in other media. Of course, rumors also play a key role in anti-Masonism's manifestations, but at least these are out in the open. The aim of this chapter is to explore to what extent our historicizing approach can serve to relativize the presumptions that Freemasonry, homosexuality, and illicit enrichment are self-evidently linked have acquired in present-day Cameroon and Gabon. To what extent can this help negotiate the porous border between rumor and fact?

Cameroon: An Archbishop's Christmas Sermon Triggers a Moral Panic

On Christmas Day 2005 the crème de la crème of the Roman Catholic faithful congregated in the cathedral of Cameroon's capital, Yaoundé. President Paul Biya, his wife, Chantal, as well as a host of government ministers and other prominent officials, occupied the first rows. The archbishop himself, Victor Tonye Bakot, led the service, and it was broadcast live over national television. Unexpectedly, the sermon—ordinarily one of the more tepid parts of the Roman Catholic mass—became a prickly and uncomfortable moment for the Cameroonian elite seated just below the pulpit. The sermon naturally focused on the birth of Jesus Christ, but Monseigneur Bakot also used the occasion for a general discussion of the sanctity of the family and the need to protect youth. He warned that there was a vast "conspiracy against the family" and therefore against society as a whole, in present-day Cameroon and across the world. In his view, the traditional institution of family in Cameroon had come under significant ideological assault because of the promotion of homosexuality, pedophilia, and other sinister forms of violence against women and children. The archbishop dwelt on several factors menacing youth—and especially young men—in Cameroon. He warned against incest, adultery, and drugs. But he went into more detail about the threat of "homosexuality," blaming two sets of forces for this conspiracy to undermine the family. First he targeted the influence of outside agents associated with Western governments, notably the European Union's Amsterdam Treaty of 1997, which required European states to recognize equal rights for different sexual orientations. These external agents, he argued, represented the "forces of evil and monetary power" that sought to "impose homosexuality" by encouraging sexual rights activists and organizations to be "involved within circles of power." The second culprit was Cameroon's national elite, which he characterized as morally depraved. Monseigneur warned that many such individuals had expressed ideological support for homosexuality and were working to make same-sex rights a reality in Cameroon. Indeed, the Cameroonian elite, he argued, "imposed homosexuality" on young Cameroonians by promising them access to jobs, expedited promotions, and admission to the nation's prestigious *grandes ecoles*.

Several newspapers in the months following the sermon published lists of "suspected" or even "prominent" homosexuals among Cameroon's national elite, which triggered what came to be known as *l'affaire des listes*.[1] Much has been written about this affair (particularly by Charles Guegobo [2006]), often linking the newspapers' lists directly to Monseigneur Bakot's speech. More recently, Patrick Awondo (2012a; 2019) pointed out that the escalation of judicial actions against "homosexuals" in the country had in fact started earlier. In Awondo's analysis, the archbishop was exploiting the wave of rumors about homosexual practices among the national elite.[2] Bakot's sermon received wide attention. It was published soon after Christmas Day 2005 in *L'Effort camerounais*, Cameroon's leading Catholic weekly.[3] In August 2015 one of the authors (Orock) interviewed members of the editorial committee, who mentioned that the archbishop himself had subsequently written an irate letter to the journal protesting the publication of his sermon; they recalled angry reactions from some politicians as well, but the team had decided to publish the sermon expeditiously, precisely because of the importance of the archbishop's words.

Monseigneur's account of "homosexuality" has interesting implications. The passages on how young men looking for a job were subjected to anal penetration clearly alluded to popular notions of Freemasonry and its lore of secret initiations. The sermon thus offered a new variant on the Catholic Church's recurring attacks on Freemasonry, stretching back to the movement's founding in the first half of the eighteenth century (see chapter 2). In the colonial context, missionaries had their own reasons to resent Freemasonry and its appeal for *la laïcité* (separation of church and state, threatening the control the missions had over schools in the colony). Monseigneur Bakot even associated his warnings against homosexuality with people "drinking the blood of children in order to strengthen their own power"—a recurring element in popular rumors about Masons and other initiates of secret societies among the elite. Indeed, as Patrick Awondo signals (2019, 60), it is this association that makes moral indignation about a supposed proliferation of homosexuality in Cameroon quite exceptionally in Africa automatically an attack on the social and political elite.[4]

The events that followed Monseigneur Bakot's provocative Christmas sermon showed how increasingly self-evident it had become to many Cameroonians to associate "homosexuality" with Freemasonry as the secret behind the elite's power and spectacular enrichment. The next month several newspapers—first *Le Météo*, then *L'Anecdote* and *Nouvelle Afrique*[5]— began publishing their by-now well-known lists of "homosexuals," naming prominent individuals from all walks of life, but especially from politics. *L'Anecdote*'s lists drew the most attention because its editor, Jean-Pierre Amougou Belinga, appeared regularly on television.[6] His paper, moreover, published two lists: the first on January 24, 2006, "Le top 50 des homosexuals présumés du Cameroun," which was reprinted in the next issue (January 31, 2006), followed by "L'autre liste des homosexuals présumés" (which named thirty-two individuals). The first list was neatly divided into categories. Almost half of the list covered *gouvernement et haute administration*, followed by shorter lists naming *opérateurs économiques*, *hommes d'église*, and *culture et sport*. The list provided a short account of each individual's alleged misdeeds, in some cases accompanied by a small photograph. The first list stretched the net very wide. It started with three ministers, but it also included two *feymen* (swindlers operating on a global scale, for which Cameroon became notorious in the 1990s; see Ndjio 2006/2012a); under *culture et sport*, the list even named Yannick Noah (a French tennis star during the 1980s, whose father was Cameroonian) and saxophonist Manu Dibango (a leading *makossa* performer, celebrated by many Cameroonians as a national hero at his death in 2021). In an accompanying commentary, *L'Anecdote*'s editor, Amougou Belinga, signaled that some of these "agitators" used a special form of "blackmail" to "sodomize their victims," alleging that the head of state himself made it a condition that any candidate for an important appointment had to accept "to be initiated" into this practice. In the same commentary, the editor added, however, that *L'Anecdote*'s "further research" had borne out that this reference to the head of state was "de la hypocrisie pure" (roughly, "unfounded allegations"). Subsequently Amougou Belinga—together with Biloa Ayissi, the editor of *Nouvelle Afrique*, who had published a list of his own—alleged that Cameroon's first president, Ahmadou Ahidjo, had been a notorious homosexual; this was one of the first public assertions that not only Ahidjo but also his successor, Paul Biya, had been linked in a "homosexual pact" with Louis-Paul Aujoulat, the politician in charge of Cameroon's arduous decolonization (see chapter 4).[7]

L'Anecdote's lists—like the others—included a hodgepodge of allegations. A recurring element was that the individuals in question had advanced suspiciously rapidly in their careers and that this was due to their access to homosexual circles (Freemasonry as part of a "seraglio of sects") and to their willingness to "drop their trousers." Another was that, once initiated, a person would, in turn, initiate others (attributing a snowball effect to homosexuality). Particularly striking is the plasticity of this idea of "homosexuality": one person is cited as having the nickname *grand maître* because of his enormous penis; another man is ascribed a female nickname, but apparently they all first had had to accept being penetrated, and then they were supposed, in turn, to penetrate new "victims." These accusations, disparate as they were, gained much traction in public discourse and clearly upset the government, particularly because they opened up a convenient outlet for popular dissatisfaction with the regime. Moreover, the political elite did not seem to know how to defend itself. None of the papers involved was banned, and while a few of *les Grands* on the lists went to court, they had only limited success in clearing their names.[8] Most of them simply kept their heads down. Clearly these accusations had found a weak spot in the regime's armor. At first even President Biya seemed to hesitate, demanding respect for people's privacy, but the authorities soon started a witch hunt against "homosexuals"—apparently in order to distance themselves from such suspicions. From 2006 on, the authorities arrested dozens of young men and a few women, levied heavy fines, and sentenced those convicted to up to five years in jail. In these actions they were supported by the Catholic Church, which contributed significantly

FIGURE 1.1. Proof that there were also other voices in Cameroon, contradicting the conspiracy narrative, is lawyer Alice Nkom, who from 2004 on launched a vocal offensive for the decriminalization of homosexuality in Cameroon, attracting great international attention because of her courage in defending persons accused as homosexuals. Photo: Nicolas Eyidi.

to the popular indignation about homosexuality. Cardinal Christian Tumi's warning against the creeping spread of homosexuality had a particularly strong impact, since he had high moral prestige as an outspoken critic of the regime.[9]

Yet there were also powerful countervoices in this uproar. Alice Nkom, a prominent lawyer from Douala and one of the few willing to defend accused "homosexuals," succeeded in getting some of those charged acquitted. She also challenged Cardinal Tumi to a televised debate in 2009 that attracted wide attention. Fabien Eboussi Boulaga, one of the country's academic éminences grises, published a special issue of his journal *Terroirs* (2007) that offered a more analytical view of the rising moral panic in the country. And already in 2006 Achille Mbembe connected the agitation about homosexuality to what he calls *le potentat sexuel* (the sexual potentate) as the dominant figure of postcolonial politics in an article in *Le Messager*. The more established newspapers—*Le Messager, La Nouvelle Expression*—were reluctant to join in the moral panic. Patrick Awondo (2012b; 2019, 65) casts the whole *affaire des listes* in another light by emphasizing that the newspapers that started the affair were struggling at the time to survive; *L'Anecdote* and *La Nouvelle Afrique* saw a subsequent rise in their circulation. Clearly homosexuality was a topic that paid off (as it still does).

A Dictatorship of the Lodges?
Ateba Eyene and "the Magico-Anal"

A resounding follow-up to the *affaire des listes* was the publication in 2012 of a book ominously titled *Le Cameroun sous la dictature des loges, des sectes, du magico-anal et des réseaux mafieux* (Cameroon under the dictatorship of the lodges, the sects, the magico-anal, and the mafia networks) by Charles Ateba Eyene, who linked the supposed proliferation of homosexuality in the country explicitly to "the lodges."[10] The reference to "magico-anal' in the title—which Cameroonians understood as an allusion to the link between witchcraft and same-sex intercourse—confirmed people's worst suspicions. It was published by Éditions Saint-Paul (Yaoundé), one of the few remaining publishing houses in the country with a Catholic affiliation; the book's title recalls the centuries-old condemnation of Freemasonry by the Catholic Church. Ateba Eyene dedicated his book to President Biya, "who wishes to be remembered as the one who brought democracy and prosperity to his people," but his second dedication was to his "fellow Cameroonians who are not members of circles of mysticism and esotericism and who despite their talents are shut out of the management of public affairs by the ostracism of the fraters" (Ateba Eyene 2012/13, 5). The book triggered animated discussions in the media. Headlines like "Ateba Eyene: Paul Biya is responsible for ritual crimes"[11] suggested that someone who was widely acknowledged as an insider was finally telling the truth about the secrets behind national politics. Two years later— and one year after the publication of a second edition of the book—the sudden death of the author at the age of forty-two triggered widespread speculation.

Charles Ateba Eyene had already built a reputation as a maverick among the national political elite. He had been an alternate member of the Central Committee of the CPDM (Cameroon People's Democratic Movement), the former sole reigning party created by President Biya in 1984, which remained in control even after the reestablishment of a multiparty system in 1989/90; this placed Ateba Eyene at the heart of political power. He also taught at the prestigious ESSTIC (National School of Journalism and Mass Communications), part of the University of Yaoundé II. As a Bulu from southern Cameroon, he was from the same ethnic group as the

FIGURE 1.2. The title of Ateba Eyene's 2012 book sharply summarizes the popular conspiracy narrative connecting Freemasonry, homosexuality, and illicit enrichment. Note especially the link the author makes between Cameroon being under "a dictatorship of the lodges" and "the magico-anal."

president. It was therefore all the more remarkable that four years earlier, in 2008, he had published a book titled *Les paradoxes du pays organisateur: Élites productrices ou prédatrices* (The paradoxes of the organizing region: Productive or predatory elites). *Pays organisateur* was his term for the president's region of origin, and the tenor of the book was that the president had not done enough for his own people. Within the ruling party, such criticisms often have severe consequences—especially if they come from someone so close to the president. Remarkably, however, Ateba Eyene was at first left alone, perhaps because the criticisms in this earlier book were quite veiled.[12] The title of the new book—notably the references to a supposed dictatorship of the lodges—promised a more direct attack on the president and his cronies and targeted a more sensitive spot. Indeed, as its subtitle announced, Ateba Eyene's book sought to debunk the futurist slogan, launched by the regime in 2010, "Cameroon: An Emerging Economy by 2035." According to Ateba Eyene, the real reason why such an ambition would never be realized is the stranglehold that Masonic and other esoteric brotherhoods have on the country: "the logics of lodges, sects, networks, and homosexuality do not lead to emergence" (2012/13, 18).

In his introduction Ateba Eyene invoked a battery of terms to substantiate his warnings: initiates of the lodges are *pseudo-templiers* (2012/13, 20);[13] they believe in *promotion par cooptation*, through *cercles mystiques* practicing *homosexualité* (2012/13, 21). To convince his audience of the legitimacy of his research, the author noted that he had accumulated a substantial library of books and reports on the history of both Freemasonry and Rosicrucianism. When he brought the books into the house, his family began to suffer numerous ailments. A neighbor warned him that literature on the lodges was strong stuff (*ouvrages forts*). Only after Ateba Eyene had gone to the *pygmies* near Lolodorf to solicit the help of their *chef* [sic] Nkodo, who gave him some protective medicine from the bark of a special tree, were the evil spirits neutralized and did peace return in his house (2012/13, 23).[14] The subsequent chapters on Rosicrucianism and Freemasonry are followed by a chapter titled "L'Homosexualité ou la dimension satanique des loges" (Homosexuality or the satanic dimension of the lodges), which elaborates on the enigmatic term *magico-anal* in the book's title. A recurring argument is that homosexual practices have become crucial for gaining access to higher positions throughout Cameroon. Even in the army, "des militaires non-pédés [sont] marginalisés" (nonhomosexual military men are marginalized; 2012/13, 106). And the *Présidence* itself has acquired all the characteristics of a lodge.[15] Ateba Eyene notes with some satisfaction the enthusiastic reception that *L'Anecdote*'s 2006 lists of homosexuals had among Cameroonians. Still—like most Cameroonians—he expects that a law to decriminalize homosexuality will be passed by Parliament since "the Cameroon of the homosexuals is so powerful" (2012/13, 102–3; his prediction has not yet come true—on the contrary).

Ateba Eyene construes a basic contrast between lodges in the West and *pseudofraters* (fake Masons) in Cameroon. In the West, Freemasonry stands for morality and freedom, while in Cameroon—and apparently elsewhere in Africa as well—"the devil has entered the lodges" (2012/13, 73; see also p. 26); elsewhere Ateba Eyene adds that "homosexuality is the satanic dimension of the lodges" (105). Yet he also denounces the link with mother lodges in the West as one of the reasons why the *dictature des loges* has had such disastrous consequences for the development of Cameroon. Cameroonian lodges, he argues, are "neocolonial extensions" of their counterparts in Western countries. Another recurring point—although in this respect Ateba Eyene seems to be more guarded—is the role of President Biya in all of this. He signals (2012/13, 75) that President Biya was first a member of the Freemasons and later switched to Rosicrucianism. But in most passages he defends Biya, downplaying the latter's involvement in this quagmire of sects, lodges, and the "magico-anal." Instead, he targets intermediaries who supposedly abuse Biya's confidence, even mentioning a cell operating under the ominous name of Brutus, which is apparently intent on assassinating the president.

In 2013 Ateba Eyene published another book with an equally sensationalist title: *Crimes rituels, loges, sectes, pouvoirs, drogues et alcools au Cameroun—Les réponses citoyennes et les armes du combat.*[16] As a specialist in "political communication," Ateba Eyene took pride in publishing at least one book per year. In his new book—more or less a sequel to *Cameroun sous la dictature des loges*—he focused specifically on the proliferation of churches and sects in Cameroon as another threat to the nation's health. But in this book as well, Ateba Eyene fitted his fulminations against this evil into the same canvas he sketched in his 2012/13 book: the lodges decide who is promoted and who is not, with homosexuality as a more or less obligatory qualification in his list of accompanying evils. Striking is that the term "homosexual" as such seems to become a more or less empty notion—it recurs constantly but is hardly substantiated (2013, 15, 106–7, 177, 181). In the main part of the book (chapters 8, 9, and 10), Ateba Eyene contrasts the judge's confirmation of the ban on his earlier book with his own election in 2012 as *personnalité préférée* by the Cameroonian public. He clearly saw this election as a resounding answer to the judge's partiality.[17] In subsequent chapters, Ateba Eyene is more measured than in his 2012 book. The tone is now more that of an elderly observer who is genuinely worried about the dangers awaiting the nation's younger generation. He closes the book with letters addressed to Pope Francis, President Biya, and Cameroon's youth (2013, 181, 184, 189) warning them of these menacing *fléaux* (plagues). All three letters end with Ateba Eyene warning of "homosexuality" as an inherent part of the lodges' activities.

In his last book Ateba Eyene seems to be more one-sided in his praise for President Biya. For instance, in his chapter on "Le paranormal et le miracle de la conscience" (The paranormal and conscience as a miracle; chapter 7) he titles the section on Biya's role "Le Président Biya n'avait pas promis le paranormal aux Camerounais en accédant au pouvoir en 1982" (President Biya did not promise the paranormal to Cameroonians when he came to power in 1982). However, Ateba Eyene's emphasis here on how essential Biya is for the country's well-being is in striking contrast with what he said, a few months before his death (February 24, 2014), on Canal 2's Sunday television talk show, *Canal Presse*, when he indicted not only the CPDM elite but also President Biya himself as the main cause of Cameroon's ongoing crisis:

> I insist. Cameroon has no problem. Cameroon's only problem is its elite. . . . This elite enriches itself; it is not just, it involves itself with homosexuality. Look at the journal *Triévenale*—"Révélation satanique d'un prostitué de luxe: J'ai vendu du sperme au ministre" . . . Now the question is when a minister buys sperm. To do what with it? Whose sperm is it? This is the question. You have read the book by Titus Edzoa [a former government minister, secretary general at the presidency and close collaborator of Paul Biya] who says that there are sessions of drinking blood. Now, whose blood is it? . . . Is this what President Paul Biya promised us? In 1982 [the year Biya became president] he spoke of rigor, morality, and social justice. Twenty years later, we are now into the sale of sperm. People drink blood, people kill children.[18]

The esoteric societies in Cameroon responded in various ways to Ateba Eyene's allegations. The Freemasons remained characteristically silent about Ateba Eyene's accusations directed at their organization and its members. However, leaders of the Masonic organization claimed that while he had attacked them publicly, Ateba Eyene also sought membership with the Freemasons, but they did not consider him worthy of admission.[19] In contrast to the Freemasons, the national leadership of the AMORC (Rosicrucian Order) chose to respond. In mid-2013, AMORC's national leader in Cameroon, Ibéa Poincaré, debated with Ateba Eyene on live television on the STV2 channel in a show called *Entretien Avec . . .* , hosted by Thierry Ngogang. During the debate, Poincaré attacked Ateba Eyene as a liar whose sensationalism and populism led him to make outlandish claims to support his unfounded accusations against Western esoteric lodges. In response, Ateba Eyene defended himself by saying that he discerned a significant difference between the practice of esoteric institutions in the Western world and those in Cameroon, which have failed to make any positive contributions to Cameroonian society.[20]

Ateba Eyene's polemical style and his tendency to swerve from one problem to the next may sometimes baffle an outside reader. So it is all the more important to signal that the same arguments and suspicions can be heard in all corners of present-day Cameroonian society. To cite just three examples from popular culture: in 2008 the celebrated singer Ntoumba Minka admonished his many fans in his song "Sexy Mac.Kéro,"[21] "The sun shines for all; we each have a chance, so why drop your pants to be appointed to a post of director?" Similarly in 2008, Valsero, a young Cameroonian hip-hop artist who opposes Biya's regime, deplored the state of the country and the misrule of its elite: "It's so hard to be young in *Rio dos Cameroes* if you're not the child of the rich, homosexual, a cop, or a politician."[22] In 2014 singer Ndong Eric—who like Ateba Eyene was from the same region as Paul Biya—released his song "Eyi Mezui Me," which he sings in the village in the old *mvet* style with a chorus of old men and women but with very new content:[23]

> Villages are abandoned because we think our elders are witches. . . . The French brought la Rose-Croix, and the Americans brought Freemasonry. . . . you abandon our customs like our Melan rite to join foreign sects that ask you to offer your mother and father. We sell our children to the sects . . . and accuse the people of the village.[24]

Such lyrics suggest that while Ateba Eyene's sweeping accusations might seem far-fetched, he is riding a popular wave of suspicion and conspiracy thinking.

At the Interface of the Global and the Local

What might explain how this particular conspiracy theory suddenly acquired such power in Cameroon? In our introduction we signaled that it situates itself on the crossroads of two major themes in conspiracy thinking in postcolonial Cameroon (and elsewhere in Africa): (post)colonial dependency and intimate witchcraft. Ateba Eyene's fulminations against the international connections of the lodges and Cameroon's global dependency ("neocolonialism") that such connections imply, relate directly to his other major theme: "homosexuality." Indeed, it is precisely this link—the lodges imposing homosexuality as part of a global conspiracy—that was at the center of this moral panic in Cameroon. Remember that Archbishop Bakot focused on this international dimension in his 2005 Christmas sermon by insisting that homosexuality was a Western vice, imposed by a national elite corrupted by their neocolonial dependency.[25]

It was because of this link that over the last fifteen years "homosexuality" became an obsessive topic in all walks of life in Cameroon. In the 1990s and 2000s Geschiere regularly gave lectures and participated in conferences at the University of Yaoundé I and at the Catholic University of Central Africa (also in Yaoundé). It is striking that the topic of "homosexuality" became a recurring theme in discussions from 2005 on: whatever the theme of a lecture might be—politics, economics, law, witchcraft, kinship—"homosexuality" was, and remains, certain to come up in the discussions. A telling example was the question posed anonymously to Geschiere at a 2010 conference at the Catholic University after giving a paper on unrelated topics (medical pluralism and healing):

> When will you Europeans stop exporting your forms of witchcraft (*sor-cellerie*) to Africa: Freemasonry, Rose-Croix, and homosexuality?

While the question strayed from the topics of discussion, the questioner managed to condense in one phrase the conspiracy narrative that abruptly came to dominate any discussion in those days. Of special interest is the manner in which the questioner conflated Freemasonry's international aura with witchcraft's local presence into a notion of "homosexuality" as an apparently ubiquitous threat.

This explosion of "homosexuality" as a major public concern was all the more striking since before 2005 it was only rarely discussed. Rumors circulated about people—especially white expatriates, sometimes also Cameroonian elites—being blackmailed by young men who threatened to denounce them to the police (same-sex acts had officially become a criminal offense in 1972).[26] But such topics were never discussed in public. The image of Freemasonry and parallel secret societies of global allure offering hidden access to new forms of enrichment formed an explosive mixture with local ideas about same-sex practices as associated with witchcraft and hence with illicit enrichment. As Mbembe remarked in December 2006 when these explosive accusations were emerging: Cameroon is a country in which the social imaginary remains deeply embedded in materiality, inspiring a "marked taste for lecherous living" and struggles for "raw material consumption." He adds that under such circumstances, people are "profoundly attached to superstition, fetishism, and magic."[27] Again, there is a direct link here with Archbishop Bakot's accusatory Christmas sermon of December 2005. The question quoted above, which astonished Geschiere at the 2010 Yaoundé conference, graphically sums up people's anger over the elite's ostentatious consumption as a result of a demonic intertwinement of the global and the local. This seems to boil down to the following formula, apparently quite powerful:

Witchcraft + Freemasonry = Homosexuality.

Gabon: Freemasonry and "Spare Parts"

In neighboring Gabon, people have expressed similar concerns about a *dictature* of the lodges. Consider the following complaint:

> It is difficult to avoid the Freemasons in Gabon. Gabon rots with Masons. The "Brothers" in Gabon control the state's budget, all the Gabonese banks, all the investments, the rents from oil. In short, they control the whole country . . . an organization whose members are the main agents of economic crimes, systematic misappropriation of the country's wealth. . . . They do so in silence and in exclusivity.[28]

This language recalls Ateba Eyene's 2012/13 book on Cameroon, but it comes from Guilou Bitsutsu Gielessen, a Gabonese politician who wrote this in 2012, in opposition to the new president, Ali Bongo,[29] who succeeded his father, Omar Bongo, in 2009, winning a contested election the same year. One of the president's first acts—only three months after being elected—was to have himself formally initiated as *grand maître* of the Grande Loge du Gabon by François Stifani himself, *grand maître* at the time of the GLNF (Grande Loge Nationale Française).[30] Stifani visited Libreville, Gabon's capital, for an elaborate ceremony, which was—to the surprise of many, and in contrast to the secrecy normally surrounding Masonic initiation ceremonies—broadcast on YouTube. One still from the ceremony shows Ali Bongo standing proudly next to his sponsors (French and Gabonese), with his white lambskin apron, which contrasts with the aprons of his companions since his is still completely white while those of the others are covered with the insignia of the various ranks through which they had passed. Clearly this *grand maître* had made an exceptionally audacious jump in the Masonic hierarchy.[31]

Such details give particular force to Gielessen's analysis of the disastrous consequences associated with the ubiquity of Freemasons in the higher echelons of Gabonese society. In many respect his attacks resemble those of Ateba Eyene against the lodges in Cameroon. Gielessen similarly emphasizes the contrast with the role of the lodges in Europe, constructive and moral, but completely unproductive in Gabon. Striking is his emphasis on the Masons' "laziness"—the way they are constantly yawning, falling asleep, and "looking at their watches when comes time for lunch." For Gielessen, this is hardly surprising in view of the lodges' lax recruitment process: "anybody can become a Freemason," he alleges; "many of the initiates can barely read or write; they are not interested in the philosophical and literary elements of Masonic teaching, so they confuse Isis with Mammywata, or think that the compass [one of the basic Masonic symbols] is about making circles." According to Gielessen, Freemasonry is for many Gabonese only a means to get access to power and riches, and he characterizes them as

> gold diggers, looking for easy ways to get rich, ready to open and close doors, pick up papers that have fallen on the ground, clean the toilets . . . *des trouves* ("my friend, find [*trouve*] me this and that . . ."), and *des ambulants* [walkers] ("my friend, I go to another lodge, here it is too harsh and the people are bad, they do not give to others . . .").[32]

Gielessen asks the European lodges to intervene since Gabonese lodges are spoiling the reputation of Freemasonry in the world. Of course, his request is almost rhetorical, since he must be familiar with the emphatic support the *grand maître* of the GLNF gave Ali Bongo only three years earlier at his initiation.

However, on one point there seems to be a difference with Ateba Eyene: Gielessen does not show a similar obsession with homosexuality. Gielessen alludes to sexual debauchery (the Gabon Freemasonry being *corrumpue* [*et*]. . . . *scabreuse*—depraved and improper) in his 2012 article, but he does not go into more detail. Yet more recent events showed that here as well popular worries about the ubiquity of Freemasonry in the higher echelons of the state were related to moral indignation about a supposed link with homosexuality and corruption in general. Homosexuality was originally not explicitly criminalized by the postcolonial state in Gabon; in contrast to Cameroon, but like most former French colonies, postindependence Gabon followed French law, which did not criminalize same-sex intercourse. However, this changed dramatically with a new code in 2019. The direct cause was probably a lively debate triggered by a purported incident of "gay marriage" in 2013. The affair followed the same pattern as in many African countries (Morocco, Senegal, Nigeria, Kenya, Malawi) a few years earlier. In Gabon as well a newspaper, *Faits Divers*, had reported on it, and the two men had been arrested. However, Gabon's chief justice refused to prosecute the two men since in her view there was no grounds for their prosecution in present law.[33] This raised a storm of protest (joined by the Catholic Church) and may have been reason for

the new article in the 2019 law, which criminalized same-sex contacts between consenting adults. This drastic change in the law mobilized critique
from other sides—notably strong international protests. Then the president changed his mind again. Less than a year later (June 2020) a bill was
passed in the Parliament decriminalizing same-sex acts. Again this raised
a storm of protest that recalled the controversy following the *affaire des
listes* in Cameroon thirteen years earlier. Yet the decriminalization also met
with some support.[34] Moreover, a recent article by Placide Ondo, sociologist at the Omar Bongo University (Libreville), on the growing *irreverence politique* in Gabon against President Ali Bongo sketches a particular
background to the president's hesitations in relation to the legal status
of homosexuality: a torrent of rumors about the president being himself
involved in same-sex relations. Most of the rumors quoted by Ondo are
from recent years, and they recall popular accusations from neighboring
Cameroon: for his initiation into Freemasonry, Ali Bongo was willing to
be sodomized by his former chief of staff; people say that in Gabon as well,
in order to be promoted to a higher position in civil service you have to
passer par le canapé (pass by the sofa) (Ondo 2021, 118–19). It seems that
the rumors in Gabon followed the Cameroonian moral panic but with
some delay.

A second set of differences, equally relative, is linked to the quite special
performance of Omar Bongo, Gabon's second president (1967–2009): not
only to his central position in the networks of *Françafrique* and his role in
including Freemasons among those networks (see chapter 4 below), but
also his talent in combining secret associations of a global allure with more
local networks of spiritual power. Omar Bongo's special role in *Françafrique* is of course related to Gabon's prominent economic position as one
of the continent's wealthiest producers of oil and other valuable minerals.
This allowed Omar Bongo to play a key role in the neocolonial frameworks
developing between France and its former African colonies after independence. In chapter 4 we will show—following notably Antoine Glaser's
seminal analysis (Glaser 2014)—that Gabon's riches allowed Omar Bongo
to claim an independent position vis-à-vis France's policies, reversing the
arrow of dependency shaped during the colonial past. Gabon's promising
economic situation—due to its mineral riches combined with a relatively
small population[35]–was not used for national development but rather for
the enrichment of a small elite and to allow the country's president to play
a prominent role on the international stage.[36]

Omar Bongo combined this international visibility with a keen interest
in local forms of spiritual power, thus strengthening also his national position. In this he followed in the footsteps of his predecessor, Leon Mba,

the country's first president, regarded with some diffidence by the French precisely because he combined a modern profile with Gabonese marks of distinction (see Bernault 2019, 190–91). After succeeding Mba, Omar Bongo followed the same line with even more gusto. On the one hand, he became a member of several Masonic lodges—strikingly not only of lodges siding with the Grand Orient but also of one associated with the latter's great rival in France, the Grande Loge Nationale Française. Such affiliations may underlie the neocolonial background to Omar Bongo's power position, but he balanced this by his very public involvement with secret associations of a more local nature. Gabon has a particularly rich history of regional cults that fuse local traditions with external elements in creative ways (see Bernault 1996; Bernault 2019; Tonda 2003). *Bwiti* with an ever-wider network of chapels since the 1920s, both in the countryside and in the city, may be the most well-known example, perhaps because of the way it uses the root of the *eboga* tree to induce a visionary ecstasy among its followers. But Omar Bongo profited from his provenance in the distant Haut-Ogooue Province to have himself initiated as well into other local cults (Njobi, also Mademoiselle).[37] This gave his Freemasonry a special cachet. His successor, Ali Bongo, is clearly trying to follow him in this balancing act (see Ondo 2021).

The most striking difference with developments in Cameroon is the persistence, for decades now in Gabon, of the popular obsession with the horrors of *pieces détachées* (spare parts) and *crimes rituels*. In Cameroon and other neighboring countries the same imaginary plays an increasing role as well, but Gabon seems to be a forerunner in this respect, at least in Central Africa. While people in Cameroon tend to accuse their *Grands* of same-sex practices, the Gabonese denounce their elite for criminal involvement with "spare parts." However, in everyday life the two suspicions seem to blur into one another (see chapter 3 below). Over the last decades, the Gabonese developed a special terminology for outlining the horrors of this trade in "spare parts." The crucial figure is a wealthy *commanditaire* (commissioner) who hires thugs to kill a random victim—often an "innocent child"—and take its organs to a ritual expert (*nganga* or *marabout*) to produce a charm (*medicament, fétiche*) that will empower and enrich the *commanditaire*.[38]

During our visit to Libreville in June 2019 we had a somewhat unexpected confirmation of how directly people associated these sinister rumors with global secret associations, in this case the Rosicrucians. While the Masonic lodges in the city were quite hard to locate (as in Cameroon), it was easy to find the lodge of AMORC, the most active branch of the Rosicrucians. It turned out to be an impressive white building on a hill, surrounded by a well-maintained garden. However, access was difficult. From the main road we had to traverse the congested and noisy Marché Banana (PK8), cross a muddy gutter over a precarious piece of board and pass two men who were urinating in full sight. As we rang the bell and waited to be admitted into the splendid garden, we noticed some people from the market behind us staring and apparently wondering what we were doing there. Once inside, Jean-Pierre (a pseudonym), a prominent member of the lodge, and his colleagues, immediately shared their sense of isolation with us. Asked why they had chosen to erect their quiet building right on top of this noisy market he replied:

> No; *they* found us here. When we built here this was a quiet place, but now our access is blocked by this market. And it is quite uncomfortable for us to walk through it. They view us as witches and wizards. They say a lot of nonsense about us, for instance that we drink human blood during our meetings and are involved in ritual killings. Hence, they fear and avoid us. So we do our best to stay away from them.[39]

Typical is the diffuse character of such rumors. In a series of short interviews we conducted during this visit to Libreville (and an earlier one in 2017), we were struck by the ease with which people pivoted from stories about same-sex debauchery by the elite to allusions to "spare parts" crimes. In such a context of general suspicion, personal accusations against prominent persons are difficult to ignore.[40]

Anti-Masonism and Its Special History in France

Readers may find the liveliness of these rumors about conspiracies by Freemasons and other secret associations in Cameroon and Gabon surprising, but similar conspiracy theories have plagued Freemasonry all over the world since its founding. Especially in France, anti-Masonism has a long and solid history that, through the colonial relationship, directly affected the increasingly wild turns that present-day conspiracy thinking has taken in Cameroon and Gabon. One special aspect is the tenacity of the association of Freemasonry with same-sex practices. In general such suspicions seem to be almost inevitable in view of the secrecy surrounding Masonic rituals and the fact that meetings are often limited to men, followed, moreover, by equally closed banquets—the Masonic *agape*. No wonder that allusions of "unnatural vice" have accompanied the spread of the brotherhood all over the world. But in France such accusations have been particularly tenacious up to the present-day. In his detailed study *Brotherly Love* about the spread of Freemasonry in France in the eighteenth century, Kenneth Loiselle (2014, chapter 3) cites a torrent of caricatures and satires in the popular press about L'Ordre des Pédérastes and so on—beginning with its very founding in France (around 1725). This author suggests that such insinuations are mostly based on a misreading of the romantic language with which the brothers address each other— not exceptional in those days as simply an expression of friendship. But he also signals that one of the reasons for French lodges being inclined to recruit women as well—which made them suspect in the eyes of the mother lodges in England—was to defuse suspicions of "sodomy" (Loiselle 2014, p. 10 and chapter 3).

Another recurring aspect of anti-Masonism in France is the staunch opposition of the Catholic Church, which has long been firmly institutionalized in this country.[41] This opposition is linked to the preponderant political role that Freemasons acquired under the Third Republic in the decades before and after 1900—a role that was formally in contrast to the general rule of the brotherhood forbidding the lodges to discuss politics. Of course, in practice, Freemasonry has always and everywhere been deeply involved with politics and the state, yet the equally general tendency toward segmentation makes its political role diffuse and fragmented. In this sense the strong commitment of leading Masonic lodges in France in support of the Third Republic and their identification with *laïcité* (strict separation of state and church) as a cherished ideal was quite exceptional. The reactions, notably from the church, were all the fiercer. Three moments in the French history of anti-Masonism can help to briefly sketch its genealogy and relevance for present-day Africa: first, Abbé Augustin Barruel's 1797 denunciation of a Masonic conspiracy as the driving force behind the French Revolution; second, the notorious Dreyfus affair in the 1890s as a victory of the Third Republic and Masonic ideals; and third, the revenge of the Vichy regime in 1940. The present-day resistance in France against abortion and gay marriage (the *Manif pour tous* movement) continues in many respects this Catholic and deeply conservative trend.

First Abbé Barruel's legacy. With his 1797 book *Mémoires pour servir à l'histoire du Jacobinisme* (Memoirs illustrating the history of Jacobinism), Abbé Barruel launched a debate that would last until the present-day: What was the role of Freemasonry in the French Revolution?[42] For the *abbé* there was no doubt: his text (1,275 pages) seeks to prove that the revolution was the work of a secret conspiracy by an inner core of Freemasonry, which he called *des arrières-loges* (or *arrières-grades*) but also *les Illuminées de Bavière*.[43] This idea would remain an anchor for French anti-Masonism up to the present-day. In his *Petite(s) Histoire(s) de l'anti-maçonnisme(s) en France*, French journalist Alexandre Starbensky (2010) notes that since its founding in Britain and its introduction in France in the early eighteenth century Freemasonry had been the target of all sorts of insinuations, varying from drunkenness to homosexuality, but for some time these remained either playful or signals of paranoia. However for Starbensky this changed with Barruel's substantial book, which made the idea of Freemasonry as a major conspiracy take root, supposedly threatening the moral order of Christianity, the state, and the family in its very essence.[44] Indeed, this conspiracy theory would prove to have great mobilizing power.

Another milestone in the history of anti-Masonism in France was the Dreyfus affair toward the end of the nineteenth century, as a high point in the identification of the Third Republic with Masonic ideals. For the Republicans—read the Freemasons notably of the Grand Orient lodge—their final victory in this case was a triumph of Masonic principles. But the affair also showed the mobilizing force that the very idea of a Masonic conspiracy had acquired among Catholics and nationalists. The affair started in 1894, when Captain Alfred Dreyfus was accused of spying for the Germans. He was convicted and degraded—his sword was solemnly broken on the knee of an adjutant (a picture that was to become famous), and he was condemned to life imprisonment on Devil's Island in French Guiana. Over the next few years reams of evidence emerged that made Dreyfus's conviction untenable. However, the upper echelons of the French military stuck to that condemnation, protecting the real culprit and even jailing an officer who had produced countervailing evidence. The anti-Semitic prejudice of the military courts became so blatant that in 1896 Émile Zola published his famous letter *J'accuse* (I accuse), turning the affair into a national issue and dividing the nation into Dreyfusards (Republicans) and anti-Dreyfusards (mainly Catholic and conservative nationalists). Zola himself was arrested and the affair was only hushed up through a compromise in 1899, despite the military leadership stubbornly refusing to rehabilitate Dreyfus.

In many respects, the affair and especially the Dreyfusards' victory became a charter of the Third Republic and the role of Masonic ideals. Indeed, it came at a moment when the new Republic was barely twenty years old and its protagonists felt constantly menaced by monarchist and conservative plots, in which the army was supposed to play a crucial role.[45] It is against this background that also the remarkable tenacity of the military leadership in the Dreyfus affair had to be seen. Indeed, they had good reason to feel under pressure, as became clear by a related scandal, *l'affaire des fiches*—a striking historical parallel to Cameroon's *affaire des listes*, albeit with different implications[46]—which came to light during the last phase of the Dreyfus affair (Mollin 2014; Thiébot 2008; Thiébot 2021). In 1904, a nationalist *député* confronted the Minister of War with the existence of a secret network around the Grand Orient de France (at the time already the largest Masonic lodge in France) systematically providing the minister's cabinet with notes on all officers submitted for promotion. The aim of this would be to favor the careers of pro-Republican military men and to block Catholics in the army. Thus, *l'affaire des fiches* became another proof of the close intertwinement of the Third Republic and the lodges—a proof that was to have serious consequences for Freemasonry in 1940 by the Vichy intermezzo.

After France's fiasco against Hitler and his Blitzkrieg, no one less than Field Marshal Philippe Pétain decided to accept defeat, concluding an armistice and founding the Vichy regime that was to collaborate closely with Nazi Germany (Paxton 2001, Laborie 2019). Pétain's enormous prestige as France's national hero of the battle of Verdun in 1916—generally seen as the turning point in the defeat of Germany in the First World War—was a true asset for the Vichy regime. Its first act was to declare the end of the Third Republic and to replace it by *L'État français*. But almost as quickly Pétain started to dismantle what he saw as the Judeo-Masonic conspiracy that he deemed responsible for the corruption of France under the Republic and its shameful defeat (Roussignol 1981; Valade 2000). In Germany the Nazi regime had already for years unleashed a true persecution of Freemasonry. Once they had taken Paris, the Germans immediately occupied the lodge of the Grand Orient, confiscating all its belongings. Vichy followed suit in the part of central and southeastern France that was left under its control. In many respects, Vichy's attack on the Masons was the revenge by the groups that had clamored for Dreyfus to be convicted. In a more personal sense, Pétain's resentment of Freemasonry seems to have been directly related to *l'affaire des fiches*, when as a young officer a note on his staunch Catholicism seemed to have delayed his promotion (Thiébot 2008; Thiébot 2021).

Moreover, doubtful as Vichy's legitimacy may have been in the eyes of at least some part of the population, its anti-Masonic policies had popular appeal. Soon after the Vichy regime had been established, it started to prepare a film together with the Propaganda Abteilung—the Nazi department for publicity in occupied France. Bernard Faÿ, known as Vichy's *chantre de l'antimasonism* (anti-Masonism "precentor"), served as middleman.[47] Launched in 1943 and embedded in a complex anti-Masonic propaganda,[48] the movie with the alluring title *Forces occultes* bore every mark of a propaganda film exposing a Masonic conspiracy, carried out mainly by Jewish Masons, to draw France into a war with Germany in the interest of American capitalism.[49] In some respects the film was influenced by the well-known UFA style (Universal Film AG, Berlin) during its Nazi days, yet it was surprisingly popular in France. Even in occupied Paris, huge lines queued on the Champs-Élysées when the movie was launched. Indeed, the movie had an authentic allure. Both the director and the screenwriter were former Masons and could therefore claim intimate knowledge of Masonic initiation rituals. Moreover, key scenes were filmed inside the famous Grand Orient lodge on Rue Cadet and the imposing Chambre des Députés (at the time both occupied by the Nazis). Thus, the movie seemed to confirm the idea of a macabre *judéomaçonnique* conspiracy that remained widespread even after the liberation. Also after 1945, French Masons maintained a lower political profile, possibly cautioned by the vicious Vichy reaction against their political prominence under the Third Republic (see chapter 2 below).

Striking is that the association with same-sex practices seems to become more pronounced in the course of these developments. It is hardly present in Barruel's attack on Freemasonry as the secret force behind the French Revolution. It is there, but very much in the background in the Dreyfus affair.[50] But it is a powerful element in Vichy's attack uniting anti-Semitism, homophobia, and anti-Masonism into a powerful assemblage (Gervais, Peretz, and Stutin 2012).[51] By 1900, the tenacious association of Freemasonry with same-sex practices that surprises so many people outside France seems to have become a commonplace in the relevant literature.[52] An eye-opener in this respect is the fascinating study by French literary historian Laure Murat juxtaposing classics from nineteenth-century French literature—notably Honoré de Balzac's work on the underside of society—with the archives of the Parisian police. The book, aptly titled *La loi du genre—Une histoire culturelle du "troisième sexe"* (The law of the gender: A cultural history of the "third sex," 2006), shows that such a juxtaposition can, indeed, signal striking convergences. Both novels and police archives highlight an obsession with *le milieu*, as this underside of society is called in France and especially in Paris. This charged term refers to a place where criminals and high-placed persons meet, indulging in alternative forms of sexuality in joint undertakings for pleasure, but also for profit. A key term in Murat's book is *une franc-maçonnerie de vice*.[53] Indeed, *le milieu* so masterfully sketched by Honoré de Balzac (and Murat in his traces), seems to color French perceptions of the underside of the brotherhood.

Murat indicates also the historical background to all this. During the French Revolution the attack on Catholic interdictions led to the already mentioned decriminalization of all nonreproductive forms of sexuality (the new penal code of 1792; see also Pastorello 2010). The 1810 Napoleonic Code confirmed this. Moreover, the restoration of the monarchy after 1815 did not bring a recriminalization, so that France was one of the first countries in Europe in which same-sex intercourse was not criminalized. However, the new regime remained strongly disapproving of it, and the police used other laws to continue harassing these *Jésus* and *tantes* (early nineteenth-century terms for gay sex workers and transvestites), who seemed to live in a world of their own, with secret codes and networks that ramified through society.[54] Such a vision of *le milieu* as a place where criminals and wealthy people meet, transgressing the codes of the conventional world with its own secrets, was a fertile breeding ground for associating Freemasonry and same-sex practices.[55] The homoerotic subtext that Murat and others[56] detect in Honoré de Balzac's *La comédie humaine*—especially around the enigmatic figure of Vautrin, alias Colin, alias Abbé Herrera, who returns in different guises in various novels— recalls in some respect the role attributed to the *Grands* in conspiracy theories from present-day Central Africa, notably in the way that "homosexuality" is supposed to play a role in their relations with young men as victims. Of course, such associations raise all sort of questions. Is it only to be ascribed to rumors circulated by detractors of Freemasonry? Or is this too easy?

An intriguing example that directly relates to the historical background sketched above is mentioned by Sophie Coignard (2009), who is a journalist with some expertise on French Freemasonry's public presence in France, and refers to a recent network of *fraternelles* (cross-cutting associations where Masons from different lodges can meet) that was named *les enfants de Cambacérès* (the children of Cambacérès). Founded in 1999, the choice of its name was a historical statement. Jean-Jacques Régis de Cambacérès was a close collaborator of Napoléon Bonaparte around 1800, who became famous as the man behind the *code Napoléon*. He was also a prominent Freemason—playing a crucial role as broker between *L'Empéreur* and the brotherhood—and very open about his homosexual orientation (apparently Napoleon loved to joke about this). His claim to fame (probably unjust; see Sibalis 1996) was that he contributed to the decriminalization of same-sex practices. So the name these 1999 *fraternelles* opted for is a clear statement.

The role of figures like Cambacérès as some sort of historical role model—and we shall see in the next chapter that in the course of the nineteenth century Jacques de Molay, the grand master of the Templars in fourteenth-century France, was attributed a similar role—suggests that at least some Masons were interested in alternative forms of sexuality. Of course, this does not mean that Freemasonry in France ever supported sodomy/homosexuality; even the Grand Orient de France, reputed to be the most progressive lodge, remains up until today very careful to avoid such a stance. Still one can wonder whether—just as in present-day Cameroon or Gabon—such anti-Masonic rumors are not reinforced by actions and initiatives by at least some brothers themselves.

It may be clear by now that anti-Masonism had (and has) particularly strong institutional backing in France from the Catholic Church—accusations of "unnatural vice" becoming an obvious argument in the church's campaigning. A telling example of the continuing interest in this supposed link among French Catholics is the particular form a recent anti-Masonic demonstration took. In 2013 a series of demonstrations organized by Manif pour tous (against a new law finally allowing gay/lesbian marriage in France) had an anti-Masonic follow-up when the organizers sent a group of half-naked demonstrators (all male) to post in front of the lodge of the Grand Orient, France's oldest Freemason lodge, in Paris, singing "La Marseillaise" and unfolding a banner that read "no to gay marriage, we will not give up" as a quite physical protest against the lodge's public support for alternative forms of marriage.[57] An additional element of this anti-Masonic association of Freemasonry and homosexuality occurred in the wake of the death of Richard Descoings, *directeur* (president) of the Institut d'Etudes Politiques (Sciences Po) in Paris, on April 3, 2012. Descoings had been found naked and dead in his room in a New York luxury hotel. Descoings was married but was widely known as a gay partner of Guillaume Pépy, the CEO of the SNCF, France's national railway carrier.[58] Raphaëlle Bacqué, leading reporter for *Le Monde*, published *Richie*, an account of Descoings's Parisian life of wealth, power, and privilege. In discussing his connections to many of the leading members of French society within the Parisian milieu, Bacqué's *Richie* shows that Descoings's influence and success were greatly aided by his networks in Freemasonry as well as what the French considered "gay power." Emmanuel Goldstein, then a well-known banker at Morgan Stanley France (now its CEO and chairman), is one of those mentioned in Bacqué's *Richie* as an associate of Descoings's.

In response, in August 2015, Goldstein sued Bacqué and her publisher (Grasset) for breach of his privacy, alleging that her book "outed" him as a homosexual and a Freemason. Only a month later, the Court of

First Instance in Paris dismissed the lawsuit and asked Goldstein to pay Bacqué's and Grasset's legal fees (€2,500 each). One of the court's arguments in finding in favor of the author was that Goldstein's identity as a gay person was, after all, not such a secret given his past role as a leader of the Association of Gay Students in France. But another, and perhaps the most compelling reason for the court's ruling on the association with Freemasonry was that any public figure or political authority could not claim privacy protections for their Masonic membership and activities given the possible public interest at stake. The trial had revealed that Goldstein's friendship with Descoings was in the public interest: Goldstein helped Descoings to be invited into a couple of Masonic lodges to make the case for his plans to undertake a set of reforms at his university institution.[59]

Clearly, the association of Freemasonry with homosexuality has a long and resilient history in France. One more thing should be noted here already. In one respect opposition to Freemasonry in Europe had a general effect there: it enforced a relative opening up of the lodges since the end of the last century. In a collection that came out in 1993 on "anti-Masonic currents, yesterday and today," Jean Dierickx signals that even in Britain, Freemasonry came increasingly under attack.[60] While public opinion there—in contrast to France—had mostly been quite respectful about the brotherhood, Dierickx signals since the 1980s an increasing shift from "amused indulgence to questioning and even a somber hostility."[61] Indeed, the new and quite spectacular museum of the Grand United Lodge of London, which opened in 1986, contains a panel explaining that the London grand master himself started worrying about this increasing antipathy against the lodges in society (probably also about dwindling membership), and began to plead for opening up to a wider audience. Toward the end of his recent book *The Craft*, historian John Dickie (2020, 409) notes that the London lodge blamed these problems on people's distrust of Masonic secrecy, and therefore decided that it was time for a "glasnost." By the end of the 1980s the lodge on Great Queen Street was opened up to the public, and there are now regularly tours that allow people to visit even the inside of the temple; researchers—also non-Masons—are encouraged to work in the rich library of the lodge; and Masons (for instance, the guide during the tour of the London temple) emphasize that the brotherhood is not "secret" but "discreet."[62] Lodges on the continent followed suit, certainly the main Parisian lodges, the Grand Orient de France and the Grande Loge Nationale Française, each of which now has its own museum. The prestigious exhibition *La Franc-Maçonnerie,* which was organized by the Bibliothèque nationale in Paris in 2016—with the support of notably the Grand Orient—is another sign of this increasing wish to open up. It remains to be seen to what extent such opening up has also affected the lodges in Francophone Africa. Will they follow in this respect as well the example of their French mother lodge?

From London via Paris to Africa

FREEMASONRY, ROSICRUCIANISM, AND POSTCOLONIAL DYNAMICS

How to place the agitation about *les loges* in present-day Cameroon and Gabon? Striking in the preceding chapter was the indignation of Charles Ateba Eyene, Guilou Bitsutsu Gielessen, and other opponents of Freemasonry contrasting the destructive—or even "diabolical"—functioning of the lodges in Africa with what they presumed to be their more positive role in the West. In this chapter we propose to give an overview of the history of these lodges and then to focus on their specific dynamics in postcolonial Africa. The chapter will be followed by a brief interlude describing the lodges' institutional presence in present-day Cameroon and Gabon.

The role of Freemasonry in postcolonial Africa is as understudied as it is important. This is a real lacuna in view of the ubiquity throughout the continent of this and similar global networks in the heart of society. For francophone Africa, a few general overviews and personal testimonies can help chart the main lines of the lodges' postcolonial dynamics, but in many respects these dynamics remain cloaked in mystery.[1] We propose to focus specifically on three aspects of special interest to the major theme of this book: the conspiracy narrative linking the lodges to "homosexuality" and therefore to "witchcraft" and illicit enrichment:

First, the growing competition in Africa between the two main
French lodges, the Grand Orient de France (GOF) and the
Grande Loge Nationale Française (GLNF), and their role in
maintaining *Françafrique*—that is, in continuing the hold of French
politicoeconomic interests over the former colonies in Africa.

Second, the relationship between Freemasons and Rosicrucians (now
   mainly represented by AMORC), which particularly in Cameroon
   turned into a fierce rivalry.
And, most importantly, the public's association of the lodges with same-
   sex initiation rituals and, in the postcolonial context, with occult
   enrichment.

A brief overview of the history of Freemasonry and its implantation in
Africa sets the stage for these three key elements.

Freemasonry and Its Tortuous History

Ever since Freemasonry's formal emergence during the long seventeenth
century, first in Scotland and then in England, Freemasons have claimed
that their origins date back much further. Their most direct ancestors,
they argue, are the masons who built the majestic cathedrals in medieval
Europe. Masonic symbols, however, allude to more distant ancestors, to
the secrets of the Egyptian pyramids, to Babylonian, Indian, and Greek
secret knowledge as well as, of course, to the secrets of the building of
Solomon's temple, signaling an original sin: the murder of the temple's
architect, Hiram Abiff, which haunts Masonic mythology. Another lineage
that is a source of pride for many Freemasons, notably in France, is the
link to the order of the Knights Templars, created in 1119 to protect the
Holy Tomb in Jerusalem, but brutally suppressed in 1307 by French king
Philippe IV le Bel, in collusion with the pope.

Yet among these baffling historical panoramas, some points offer more
stable footholds. Academic historians evoke two versions of Freemasonry's emergence in the British Isles that are in various degrees supported by
the Masons themselves. David Stevenson (1988)—at the time professor
at the University of St. Andrews and an authority on Scottish history—
emphasizes the gradual emergence during the seventeenth century of
Freemasonry from Scotland's old masonic guilds. On the basis of the archives of early Scottish lodges, Stevenson maps out a chronology in which
the guilds of "operative" masons, faced with dwindling membership and
diminishing revenues, invited "gentlemen non-operative fellows"—to join
their guilds. When these "speculative masons" gradually took over, the old
guilds transformed into "Freemason" lodges, meeting in a fixed location
(in contrast to the earlier situation in which masons moved from one
building project to another).[2] In a later study Margaret Jacob (2006), now
professor of history at University of California, Los Angeles, emphasized

the fusion of four smaller lodges into the Grand Lodge of London and Westminster in 1717 as a decisive point in the history of Freemasonry. And, indeed, most lodges in the world, despite their internal differences, see this London lodge as a mother lodge. Even the many lodges that are not recognized by this lodge as "true" Freemasons do not dispute the special status of the London lodge. In the same year the Grand London Lodge—until

FIGURE 2.1. Freemason's Hall in London. The splendor of the United Grand Lodge's Hall in London testifies to the central role this lodge played (and still plays) after its founding in 1717, in the global expansion of Freemasonry. In 1929 a big fire destroyed the building, which was magnificently rebuilt in art deco style.
Photo: Eluveitie/Wikimedia Commons, CC BY-SA 3.0.

then still meeting in the The Goose and Gridiron, a pub at Grand Queen Street—acquired land on the opposite side of the street to erect its own hall, a pivotal moment in the emergence of Freemasonry as a worldwide movement. And indeed the splendor of the building—completely rebuilt in a stunning art deco style following a fire in 1929, and since the end of the twentieth century increasingly open to the public—confirms the prominence of the London lodge.

This lodge played also a crucial role in the composition of the *Constitutions of Free Masons* by James Anderson, published in 1723. "Anderson's Charges"—a second, much more extensive version followed in 1738—became a guideline for lodges all over the world. Anderson's insistence on an open attitude toward religious differences and the repudiation of political commitments—novel principles in the historical context in Europe at the time—have remained a hallmark of the Brotherhood to the present day (even if practices differ). The initial popular enthusiasm for Freemasonry was to a large extent inspired by its aspirations to transcend the endless religious wars that haunted Europe for centuries after the Reformation. Anderson's rules made respect for God—as the "Great Architect of the Universe"—a premise but without any fixed link to a specific religion. The brothers were (and are) admonished to avoid any debate in the lodges on religion and politics.

The two accounts of the Freemasons' historical emergence are not mutually exclusive, but they have different implications. The Scottish origin narrative emphasizes the continuity with the old "stonemasons," their technical expertise, and their regional networks cemented by secret passwords and handshakes. This is reflected by the central role of "the apron" in Masonic rituals: at the first initiation, "the apprentice" receives a white lamb's leather apron; at subsequent initiations into further "degrees"— and the number of degrees has multiplied over time; some lodges now count several dozen degrees on top of the original three "craft" degrees— symbols are added on the apron, reflecting the acquisition of new forms of knowledge and insight. On the other hand, authors emphasizing the Grand Lodge of London as the origin see Freemasonry as born from Enlightenment ideas, inspiring a missionary zeal to spread the modern forms of government that had emerged in England in the seventeenth century. Indeed, a common attribute of Freemasonry has been its globalizing tendencies, which made it participate actively in the broadening of people's horizons in early modern times. Within a few decades after 1717, Freemasonry had expanded all over the European continent, and from its very beginnings it had global aspirations. Already in the second half of the eighteenth century, lodges were founded throughout the colonies.[3] In

Africa, a lodge was founded in 1772 in Cape Town, then another on Île de Bourbon in 1778, and in 1781 another in St. Louis (Senegal).

The institution of the "warrant" (*patent* in French) played a crucial role in this global expansion. A new lodge could only be founded with a warrant from an existing lodge, and this warrant implied a formal dependence. The mother lodge—initially the Grand (United) Lodge of England in London—had to verify whether the new lodge respected "the charges," notably meeting regularly and maintaining its membership. A minimum of seven members was (and is) required to constitute a lodge. Especially in the colonies, where until far into the twentieth century, members were mostly colonials who resided only temporarily in a given locality, this led to constant flux—lodges merging or disappearing altogether, sometimes to be revived at a later stage.

This expansionist drive was balanced by equally constant processes of fission—again a recurring element in the history of Freemasonry. The first split, generally seen as a key tension during Freemasonry's founding moment, was the struggle between the "Ancients" and what they mockingly called the "Moderns"—that is, the London Lodge. After the founding of this lodge in 1717, the existing Scottish and Irish lodges felt excluded and founded the Grand Lodges of Scotland and of Ireland, claiming to adhere closer to the Masonic traditions. The London lodge was built on the ritual arrangements developed by lodges in Scotland during the seventeenth century—for instance, in the initiation degrees—but added new categories. They took over the Scottish two-degree system—first apprentice, then craft-fellow—but added a third degree of master-mason. Another innovation was the institution of a Grand Lodge overseeing the lodges it had warranted.[4] Throughout the eighteenth century the three Grand Lodges—two "Ancients" and one "Modern"—existed side by side, in more or less open competition. It was only under heavy threat of the British 1799 Anti-Unlawful Societies Act—directed against associations suspected of being tainted by ideas from the French Revolution—that in 1813 the three Grand Lodges finally agreed to establish a united front. The London lodge was renamed the Grand United Lodge of England but accepted some input from the other Grand Lodges. Since then, British Freemasonry has offered a more or less united front, also in its relations with the colonies—notably with the rapidly proliferating lodges in the emerging United States.

It was not only the coherence of the constituting networks that made for a sense of collectivity, however. During the eighteenth and nineteenth centuries a shared historical imaginary developed—although the elements were subject to a staggering variety of interpretations and adaptations—creating the kaleidoscopic coherence that might be the main secret of Freemasonry's resilience for more than three centuries, despite constant change. Anderson's Constitutions and Charges lent themselves to highly varying interpretations, but they demanded general respect and provided common points of orientation. A common core is provided by the initiation rites—again, despite all variations—with their macabre threats to the candidate should he ever betray Freemasonry's secrets, his being blindfolded, the special handshakes he has to learn (different for different degrees), the undressing of legs and shoulders (again varying according to degree), the position he has to take to make first his feet and then his legs form a square (the right-angled tool that is a central symbol of Freemasonry), and so on.[5] Many of the founding myths, moreover, offer several points of agreement, despite widely varying interpretations. This applies in the first instance to the story of Hiram Abiff, the Phoenician mason who was the main architect of the Solomonic Temple, and his gruesome assassination—the original sin mentioned before, and the purported grounds for the Masonic obsession with secrecy. The story is all the more important since it became attached to the initiation for the third master-mason degree, added by the London lodge. Typical of the profoundly Christian character of British Freemasonry is that the story comes straight from the Bible.

The relevant biblical verses recount that Hiram, the king of Tyrus (one of the Phoenicians' two main trading cities) sent Israel's King Solomon building materials and builders for the construction of the Temple, among them, an expert mason. The Bible adds that this master-mason, also called Hiram, was the son of a widow from the Israelian tribe of Naphtali. Anderson in his Constitutions calls this mason Hiram Abiff ("Abiff" is his transformation of a suffix in Hebrew that might be translated as "master"). Anderson adds the story of Hiram Abiff's murder by three fellow masons, who tried to make him betray the secret of the Temple's construction. Thus, the Masonic version stresses the master's perseverance in keeping his secrets. Typically Masonic tools play a central role in the story: the first attacker struck Hiram Abiff across the throat with a builder's square, and the second one on the breast with a gauge; but he still refused to give up his secret; then the third killed him by hitting him with a hammer on the forehead. The story's central theme is that the holy secret (the *arcanum*) seemed to have been lost. However, King Solomon himself replaced it with another secret word, and this is what makes the initiation to the master degree so heavily charged with meaning.

The story lent itself to a wide array of symbolic interpretations. The emphasis on protecting the secret builds on the traditions of the old Masonic networks, when traveling stone masons recognized one another through secret codes and handshakes. But in Masonic mythology, such secrets became related to the Temple and thus sanctified. The story also sanctifies the struggle of the brothers against evil in all forms. Out of disrespect, the ruffian masons caused the loss of the secret, but King Solomon, as some sort of super-masonic master, saved the situation. Thus, in Hiram Abiff's story, Solomon's Temple stands for the Masonic obsession with secrets, which triggered (as we saw in the preceding chapter) a wild proliferation of conspiracy theories among outsiders. Another element of the story, Hiram Abiff being a widow's child, is often invoked by the brothers to identify collectively as "sons of the widow"—which similarly seems to express an anxiety about being under threat from all sides, yet at the same time opening up the possibility of redemption. But over time this element also lent itself to constant reinterpretation and embellishments. Often the "widow" concerned is equated with another biblical figure: Ruth, the Moabite who, when her husband died, remained loyal to her desperate mother-in-law and followed her in poverty back to Judea, where Ruth's plight and faithfulness moved the wealthy farmer Boaz to marry her.[6] Being associated with a Moabite—despised as the descendants of Lot's incest with his daughters—might be humbling, but is expiated by Ruth's glorious position in the line of Jesus' ancestry.[7]

The main common element in this kaleidoscopic panorama of historical and symbolical elements remains, of course, the word "Free": the idea that only persons who had liberated their spirit from older attachments could be initiated.[8] What this meant in practice remained to be seen—for many Masons (mostly white males), women were not free in this sense nor were people of other races—but "Free" remained and remains a key word, giving Freemasonry, in whatever form, a liberal aura. The brotherhood's emphasis on brotherly "love" and on a spirituality implying tolerance attracted many followers throughout Europe, which had been haunted for centuries by wars of religion. But these elevated ideals—notably the potential tensions between freedom and belief in a Supreme Being, and between brotherly love and truth—were amplified in different ways with the spread of Freemasonry to different parts of Europe and subsequently the whole world.

French Freemasonry Going Its Own Way

French Freemasonry is as rhizomatic as the British brotherhood—again as some sort of public secret, both in France and internationally. All French branches, despite their considerable differences, agree on the historical precedence of British Freemasonry: it was implanted in France from Britain. But Freemasonry's subsequent trajectory in France was quite different.[9] The first lodges in France, after the Scottish model, may have been founded in Paris at the end of the seventeenth century by the Scottish entourage of James II, the Stuart king in England, exiled to Paris in 1688 and almost overtaken by William of Orange's "Glorious Revolution." These Scottish origins continue to play a special role in French Freemasonry. Yet the first well-established lodge in Paris dated from 1725 and followed the London model (in its addition of a third degree). Lodges were subsequently founded all over France. At first the brotherhood was viewed with suspicion by the monarchy, but after 1745 the government left the new lodges alone, and a rapidly increasing number of well-placed persons, including members of the court, had themselves initiated. There was strong opposition from other quarters. In chapter 1 we signaled that from the beginning the Catholic Church repeatedly warned members of the new brotherhood that they would be excommunicated, following successive papal encyclicals condemning the new brotherhood as incompatible with faith.[10] Freemasons' references to an ancestral tie to the Knights Templar, moreover, made the church deeply suspicious. Indeed, the ongoing association with these Templars in francophone contexts has implications that are particularly relevant to our theme. So it is worthwhile to dwell a moment on what exactly made this memory so fraught.

In the centuries after its foundation (1119), the Templar order failed in its main charge to defend Jerusalem against the Saracens, but this did not stop it from becoming very wealthy, through banking and other activities. The French king Philippe IV ran up substantial debts with them. But the Templars had also become the target of rumors about their indulgence in a variety of transgressive practices. In 1307 King Philippe had their Grand Master Jacques de Molay and many other Templars arrested. The king had just emerged victorious from a conflict with the pope: in 1305 he forced the cardinals in Rome to elect a French candidate as Pope Clement V (who in 1309 agreed to transfer the papal seat to Avignon). King Philippe's hold on the new pope soon paid off when Clement V accused the Templars of heresy so that all their riches could be confiscated. The main accusation against them was disrespect for the Cross, but the second was indulging in "unnatural intercourse," especially during their initiation rites. Grand Master de Molay initially confessed to these terrible crimes, but then dramatically withdrew his "confession" in 1314 in front of the ecclesiastical court, complaining he had confessed under heavy torture. Whereupon King Philippe—invoking a rule that a heretic who withdrew his confession had to be summarily executed—had de Molay burned at the stake on a small island in the Seine at the very heart of the city. De Molay uttered a terrible curse before his death. And, indeed, Pope Clement V died only a month later, while King Philippe followed him toward the end of the year.

No wonder, then, that when Freemasonry entered France in the first half of the eighteenth century, the association with the memory of the Templars continued to evoke deep suspicion among Catholics. Indeed, for the church, de Molay with his terrible curse was (and still is) a satanic figure. But with the rise of anticlericalism in France in the eighteenth century, the figure of de Molay acquired new associations, strongly promoted by Masonic lodges, which integrated Templar rituals and symbolism in their initiation rites for various higher degrees. In 1797 Charles-Louis Cadet

FIGURE 2.2. In 1314 Jacques de Molay, Grand Master of the Templars, was burned at the stake in Paris. His furious curse that both the pope and the French king would die before the end of the year became a source of deep hostility among Catholics in France against Freemasonry. Alamy Stock Photo.

de Gassicourt published a book titled *Le Tombeau de Jacques Molay* in which he claimed that before being burned at the stake, the Templar grand master had created a secret order of which some of the higher grades of the eighteenth-century Masonic lodges were the continuation. Thus Freemasons were depicted as the avengers of the unjust fate of Jacques de Molay—vowing to kill all kings and destroy the pope.[11] In 1806, French painter Fleury Richard painted a moving picture of De Molay in a heroic pose, apparently harassed by a dark priestlike figure. Empress Joséphine de Beauharnais (then still Napoléon's spouse) bought it for her private collection.[12] However, such links with the French Revolution and de Gassicourt's versions of the Masonic vows—to kill the king and the pope—not only worried the Catholic Church but also the mother lodge in London, ever more concerned by increasingly antiroyal and antireligious tendencies in the French lodges.

Indeed, as noted already in our preceding chapter, the role of the French lodges in preparing or even realizing the revolution of 1789 has been a subject of debate among historians, even to the present day,[13] and it still haunts the relation to the British mother lodge, causing a split in the French brotherhood that has had global consequences (certainly in francophone Africa). It is clear that the Masons' relation with the French Revolution was complex and subject to abrupt changes. Freemasons were among the earliest leading figures of the revolution (notably among the Girondins), but when the Jacobins imposed their terror (1792–1794), most lodges had to close. Napoleon's Brumaire coup of 1799 brought about a glorious comeback. It is a moot point whether Napoleon himself was ever initiated; certain is that he immediately realized the usefulness of the Masonic network for building his empire. The period until his defeat in 1813 at the Battle of Leipzig is known in Masonic historiography as "the fifteen golden years."

In 1799 the Grand Orient de France (GOF) emerged as the major Grand Lodge in the French orbit. The GOF had been founded a quarter-century earlier, but it was only after the unification with other lodges under direct pressure from Napoleon that it came to assume a leading role, further reinforced when in 1804 Napoleon's brother, Joseph, became the GOF's grand master.[14] In the years following, the emperor continued to encourage the founding of new lodges in France and its colonies. Most of his generals were initiated, confirming the strong presence of Freemasonry among the higher ranks of the army.[15] Yet these golden years under Napoleon made French Freemasonry—and notably the GOF—suspect during the Restauration and the White Terror after 1815. Nonetheless, with the establishment of the Third Republic after 1871, French Freemasonry increasingly became the backbone to the new political arrangement.

FIGURE 2.3. The building of the Grand Orient de France in Paris, the oldest and biggest lodge in France and still the one that is best represented in francophone Africa. Photo: Declic/Wikimedia Commons, CC BY-SA 3.0.

As was to be expected, these political vicissitudes were followed with increasing suspicion on the other side of the channel. Anderson's "Charges" formally prohibited political debate inside the lodges as antithetical to the ideal of brotherly love. Of course, British Freemasons were also deeply involved in politics as well, but openly supporting the politics of Napoleon and even more those of the Third Republic was anathema. However, the main apple of discord was the growing secularization of the French lodges as a consequence of their increasingly open support for the Third Republic's politics of *laïcité* (strict separation of church and state).[16] In 1877 the Grand Orient voted to replace the first articles of the Freemasons' constitutions on the belief in God and the immortality of the soul with a more general reference to a *principe créateur* and the absolute freedom of conscience. The Grand United Lodge of London responded almost immediately by breaking its ties with the Grand Orient (Combes 2016, 215, 229). Advocates of the Grand Orient answered by emphasizing the difference between the situation in France, where Freemasonry was increasingly under attack by the Catholic Church, and in England, where the lodges were not confronted by a powerful religious adversary. Countering British accusations, they emphasized that the changes in the

Grand Orient's constitution did not mean a weakening of its commitment to the spiritual. These debates are still ongoing, even within French Freemasonry. The 1877 split nonetheless had global consequences. It led to a basic split between lodges—on the one hand, those that emphasize their status as "regular" (that is, recognized by the London mother lodge) and, on the other, the "a-dogmatic ones." This split became crucial for the vicissitudes of Freemasonry within present-day francophone Africa.

In chapter 1 we dwelt on the dramatic consequences for French Freemasonry of France's 1940 defeat by the Nazis, leading to the collapse of the Third Republic and the persecution of the brotherhood by Maréchal Pétain's Vichy regime, becoming a high point in French anti-Masonism. But even after 1945, relations between French Freemasonry and the regime in power remained precarious, and French Freemasonry had difficulty in recovering from the damage inflicted by the Vichy government. Due to the influence of Charles de Gaulle, the Fourth Republic opened its ranks emphatically to Catholics. Most lodges, certainly the Grand Orient, opposed the presidentialism advocated by de Gaulle (and realized after 1958), and de Gaulle himself was equally distrustful of Freemasonry. Leftist parties—notably the Parti communiste—were even less hospitable to Freemasons. Moreover, after the Vichy debacle, many Masons were reluctant to assume such an overtly political stance as they did under the Third Republic. Of course Masons continued to be present in the higher echelons of the republic's bureaucracy,[17] but they seemed to prefer a lower profile. This changed in 1981, when a number of leftist Masons—especially from the Grand Orient—threw their support behind François Mitterand as their candidate for the presidency. They formed a lobby inside the socialist party—ironically called *le club des Jacobins*[18]—to support his candidacy. Mitterand's victory in the 1981 elections—to a certain degree due to the Grand Orient's support—brought Freemasonry back again in the center of power. This development had direct consequences for its role in Africa.[19]

Into Africa: The Colonial Stalemate

In colonial times, Freemasonry was present throughout the French empire. In almost all the colonies, lodges were founded soon after the start of colonial rule. In Cameroon, the first lodge was founded in 1924—that is, only a few years after the French had taken over the colony from the Germans. This impressive presence, however, must be qualified in the sense that until independence (around 1960), membership remained mostly restricted to whites—all the more striking since this contradicted the religious and racial inclusivity that the brotherhood had always championed. Exclusion of African "subjects" seems to have become even stricter toward the end of the nineteenth century. For instance, the St. Louis lodge, often mentioned as the oldest in francophone Africa,[20] included several *métis* (a mixed group with a strong position in colonial St. Louis) among its membership in the eighteenth and early nineteenth centuries. But after 1900 this became quite exceptional (White 2005).

In his study of Masonic lodges in French West Africa before 1914, Owen White (2005, 98) notes that the oldest lodges had *métis* and even Black members until 1890, but that subsequently "the ideal of color-blind fraternity appears to have evaporated . . . and the lodges in West Africa became the preserve of white males." An obvious way for the colonial lodges in Africa to justify this conflict between the Freemasons' sacred principle of inclusivity and the practice of exclusion was to claim that the natives were not "free" and therefore did not qualify for initiation as "Freemasons." Such arguments helped colonial lodges resist pressure from mother lodges in France to take the Masonic principle of inclusivity more seriously. White notes that in 1905 the Grand Orient, at the time the mother lodge of most lodges in francophone Africa, sought clarification from the Senegalese lodges about an allegation that they excluded Blacks and *métis*.[21] The Dakar lodge, L'Étoile Occidentale, simply answered that there was no exclusion but that no Black or *métis* had ever shown interest. The St. Louis lodge, L'Avenir du Sénégal, went further in its answers, pointing out that it had one *métis* member and that another regularly attended their meetings, but that most *métis* only sought membership in order to enhance their social status and advancement. Moreover, this lodge insisted that it would be disastrous to encourage Black membership because the latter's education was inadequate—they were still like "irresponsible, big children"—and lacked the means to fully participate.[22]

In other respects as well, White's article on these lodges sketches a quite insular picture. Higher-ranking civil servants, although affiliated with lodges in France, were often reluctant to join a local lodge since being known as a Freemason was not always advantageous to one's career, and it was difficult to conceal one's membership within the colonies' closely knit white community. Hence the lodges' membership was limited mostly to members of the petite bourgeoisie: traders, clerks, and junior administrators. The lodges, moreover, were more interested in issues in French politics—notably the struggle to impose the principles of *laïcité* against the Catholic missionaries—than in local issues like the abolition of slavery (despite this being a long-standing Masonic ideal). Whether Africans were "free" enough to be admitted as "Free-masons" remained a sensitive question throughout the colonial period. An additional argument when more educated persons were emerging among the Black population was that they were mostly trained by Catholic missionaries and therefore strongly indoctrinated against Freemasonry.

Indeed, another constant in the history of Freemasonry in the French colonies is the fierce opposition of the Catholic clergy. Missionaries all over the world—both Protestant and Catholic—were suspicious of the global spread of Freemasonry with its emphasis on secrecy. In his fascinating work on the crystallization of the idea of leopard-men associations on the Cameroonian coast as a nodal point in the interaction between Africans and Europeans, Franck Beuvier notes that Baptist missionaries (who were active on the Cameroonian coast as early as 1843) had a tendency to label such secret associations as an alternative form of Freemasonry, suggesting a true preoccupation with the role of the brotherhood at home.[23] In the French colonies Catholic missionaries became even more suspicious of Freemasons because of the 1905 law on *laïcité*, which—by imposing a strict separation between church and state—threatened to directly affect the Catholic Church's control over education throughout France's colonial empire. Rightly or wrongly, these missionaries blamed Freemasonry, generally seen as the backbone of the Third Republic, as the main instigator of this hated law. They tended to take for granted that most civil servants were Freemasons, and therefore continued up till the present day to warn their flock in no uncertain terms against the sinister designs of this hidden association.[24]

The tendency to exclude Africans from the colonial lodges began to change only in the 1950s with the increasing presence of African students in France. At first it was only the lodges there that were opening up, since the presence of African students aspiring toward scholarly credentials made it difficult for European Masons to oppose Freemasonry's heralded ideals of openness and inclusivity. The moving novel by Olympe Bhély-Quenum (Benin), *L'Initié* (1979), suggests why many young Africans studying in France were attracted to Freemasonry. Apart from their feelings of loneliness and isolation far away from home, they were also tempted by the fact that these lodges seemed to welcome Africans. Many in Cameroon and Gabon are now convinced that during these years the entire future national elite, then studying in France, was initiated more or less openly into Freemason lodges. Toward 1960, things began to change inside Africa as well. Independence was followed in almost all former colonies, both francophone and anglophone, by the creation of national lodges replacing the older colonial lodges, but also by a process of segmenting and fusing—in the true spirit of balkanization that marks Freemasonry all over the globe.[25]

Different Postcolonial Trajectories

To what extent did the decolonization of the continent also trigger shifts in the role of Freemasonry? The fact that the lodges were taken over by Africans certainly inspired new elements in discourses by others about the Masons. Remember the dark associations that anti-Masonists like Ateba Eyene and Gielessen (chapter 1) summoned up in their attacks on the lodges. For them, there was a sharp contrast between the lodges in Africa, mired in witchcraft, depravity, and destructive greed, and the role that Freemasonry had played in Europe. But the official discourse of the African lodges about themselves rather emphasizes their fidelity toward the customs—especially the rituals—of global Freemasonry. Indeed, the close supervision that the French mother lodges continue to exercise over their African brothers did not allow for much formal innovation. Yet, despite this apparent uniformity, the history of Freemasonry in postcolonial Africa has been full of unexpected turns. A brief exploration indicates that it followed different trajectories in each country, depending on the vicissitudes of postcolonial politics.

In his short but seminal overview of Freemasonry as "le joker de la Françafrique" Ghislain Youdji Tchuisseu (2021) notes that after interdependence most new heads of states were weary of the brotherhood—not only the more radical ones, like Sekou Touré (Guinea) or Modibo Keita (Mali), but also those who opted for collaboration with France. This applied, for instance, to Ahmadou Ahidjo (Cameroon) but even more so to Félix Houphouët-Boigny, for some time the personification of *Françafrique*, who unleashed a true persecution of Freemasons in Ivory Coast immediately after independence (1960)—accusing them of fomenting a coup d'état and using a formal ban to eliminate his opponents. Tchuisseu nonetheless notes that most leaders eventually came to some sort of accommodation with the presence of the brotherhood. In the case of Ivory Coast, this required the intervention of French president Georges Pompidou himself. In 1971 Houphouët-Boigny lifted the ban abruptly, blaming an underling for misinformation. The case of Mathieu Kérékou in Benin highlights the volatility of such bans even more. Coming to power through a military coup in 1972, Kérékou abruptly veered toward Marxism (mixing it with a keen interest in Vodun practices and occult rituals) and imposed a ban on Freemasonry. However, in 1980 he lifted the ban on the lodges after he converted to Islam, returning to Christianity only a little later. In 1990, during the continental wave of democratization, he agreed to convene a national conference and sponsor open elections. He lost the first election in 1992 but won the subsequent election, returning as president in 1996. In the meantime he had converted to a more radical, evangelical form of Christianity that made him strongly oppose any secret association, the Freemasons included.[26] However, this time he did not impose a formal ban.

The same volatility characterized relations in Congo Brazzaville, but here the course of events highlighted how the brotherhood's transnational networks could be of decisive influence. In 1968 the Marxist regime of Marien Ngouabi imposed an absolute ban on Freemasonry. However, in 1977 Ngouabi was murdered, and after some further skirmishes Sassou Nguesso, then a colonel (and according to some, the instigator of Ngouabi's assassination) succeeded him. He officially continued the Marxist line but gradually opened up to the West. In this country as well, a national conference in 1990 reinstated free elections, and Sassou Nguesso lost by a wide margin, but he staged a spectacular comeback in 1997, starting a bloody civil war against the elected president Pascal Lissouba, and deposing him with the help of French president Jacques Chirac and Angolan president José dos Santos.

What makes Congo Brazzaville especially interesting is that Freemasonry played a crucial role in Sassou Ngouesso's comeback.[27] After his electoral defeat, he had gone into exile in France, organizing his own militia—called *les Cobras* (Combattants de Brazzaville)—and his own Masonic lodge, the Grande Loge du Congo, affiliated to the Grande Loge Nationale Française (see Carter 2014 and below). After Sassou Nguesso's military victory in the subsequent civil war, the former Marxist leader organized his lodge as a true bastion of power—"il faut s'initier pour avoir accès," as Brett Carter's respondents repeated. Indeed, Carter maintains that it was especially the power of Sassou Nguesso's Grande Lodge *and* the strict control he had over its members, that allowed him to win three successive elections without opposition.

In the other Congo (Zaire/RDC), Freemasonry had a quite different trajectory. After he came to power in 1965, Mobutu Sese Seko refused to join (according to some rumors because his wish to be initiated in a single day was not granted), and he even imposed a ban on Freemasonry. This ban was lifted in 1972, but Mobutu was never initiated and Freemasonry's presence among politicians remained more diffuse. Tchuisseu (2021, 510) mentions that Mobutu created in 1985 his own lodge—*une loge sorcière*—that was Masonically inspired (as was his famous *politique d'authenticité*). Mobutu's successors, Laurent and Joseph Kabila, seemed to have been similarly inclined to keep the brotherhood at bay. In Congo popular rumors focus rather on business tycoons and Congolese music or soccer stars being deeply involved in Freemasonry or parallel global associations.[28]

Yet, even though trajectories vary, Freemasonry seems to be emphatically present in national politics in most francophone countries. A 2016 overview by *Jeune Afrique* of membership among presidents of the various countries added up to an impressive score: six certainly initiated, six implying that they had been initiated, and only five explicitly denying it.[29] Particular to Freemasonry's role in the postcolonial politics of francophone Africa is the continuing and often quite direct involvement of the main French lodges with their African counterparts.[30] Striking was, for instance, the presence of white representatives of the French mother lodge (in both cases the Grande Loge Nationale Française) at the initiation ceremonies not only of Gabon's president, Ali Bongo, but also of President Sassou Nguesso of Congo Brazza (2014), both broadcast on YouTube. And a rich literature emphasizes the personal involvement of French Freemasons in the maintenance of *Françafrique*, irrespective of the political affiliations of the regime in Paris. This role became even more enhanced after Mitterand's 1981 electoral victory finally brought the socialists back into power in Paris. Since then Freemasonry seems to have become both more visible in various parts of francophone Africa, and at the same time the topic of endless speculation about secret conspiracies.[31]

The lodges themselves hardly seek publicity. Only the annual REH-FRAM meetings (Rencontres humanistes et fraternelles africaines et malgaches), mainly organized by lodges related to the Grand Orient, are reported by journals like *Jeune Afrique*. Individual Masons sometimes refer to the brotherhood's successes in mediating ongoing African conflicts (examples would be the success of national conferences in various African countries, at the onset of the democratization tide throughout the continent around 1990; also the purported intervention by Freemasons in bringing about the end of apartheid in South Africa). But the discreet character of such interventions makes it difficult to ascertain the actual role of Freemason networks. And there are clear counterexamples of failure. A notorious case was the fruitless attempt by a Freemason mission to reconcile the "brothers" Denis Sassou Ngouesso and Pascal Lissouba during the horrors of the civil war in Brazzaville in the late 1990s. The same is said about supposed Freemasons' attempts to bring an end to fraternal conflicts in Ivory Coast in the early 2000s. Reports on the RE-HFRAM meetings show that members are forced to also discuss darker issues (Wauthier 2003, 289). In 1996, for instance, during the REHFRAM meeting in Libreville, a local newspaper (*L'Union*) circulated a declaration by the grand master of the Grand Rite Equatorial (Malabo), François Owono Nguéma, against accusations of "satanisme" inside the lodges. The next year at Cotonou, another local newspaper, *Le Citoyen*, summarized a press conference under the headline "La franc-maçonnerie n'est pas un groupe de sorciers"; we will return to such accusations and associations.

The implantation of Freemasonry in anglophone Africa goes back further—even to the first half of the eighteenth century in the British enclaves on the West African coast (Sierra Leone, Gold Coast, Lagos). Moreover, the strong position of the coastal trading elites in these areas— already thoroughly anglicized—gave them access to lodges, during colonial times as well. Thus the postcolonial profile of Freemasonry in these areas became quite different from that in the francophone countries: the involvement of local elites gave it much more the profile of a network of businessmen and higher-level civil servants, not directly involved in politics.[32] In both Ghana and Nigeria, there are certainly rumors about politicians and even presidents who had been initiated. Indeed, in recent years Ghana's former president (2001–2009), John Kufuor, has openly talked about his membership in Freemasonry in interviews with the local media in Ghana, including his prominent recognition within the United Grand Lodge of England as a senior grand warden since 2017.[33] Yet in these countries Freemasonry is mainly seen as a businessmen's lobby. The idea of the brotherhood as the public secret behind the vicissitudes of national politics is less present in popular perceptions, and neither is such an idea fed by allusions by the politicians themselves.[34] A similar image emerges from the sole monograph on Freemasonry in Africa, Abner Cohen's 1981 book on the Sierra Leonese "Creole" elite—descendants of liberated slaves settled in the nineteenth century by the English in Sierra Leone— joining Freemasonry after World War II, creating their own lodges in an attempt to protect their monopoly over education and access to higher positions in the civil service. For these "Creoles," joining Freemasonry was a way to balance the influence of the secret associations that played such a powerful role among the people of the interior (the Mende and others with their *poro*).

Yet, there are also very different trajectories in anglophone Africa. It is striking that Cohen completely neglects the impact of Freemasonry's long-standing presence in neighboring Liberia; there the brotherhood's role was more ambiguous than in Cohen's neat analysis for Sierra Leone. In Liberia—created in 1822 by US interest groups in order to settle freed slaves in Africa who claimed independence as early as 1847 (recognized by the US government only in 1862)—Freemasonry played an important political role from the start. Much earlier than in Sierra Leone, it served to cement the unity of the "Americo-Liberians"—the descendants of these liberated slaves—in their tenuous relations with the more numerous peoples from the interior. Among the first settlers, there had already been several members of a Prince Hall lodge.[35] In 1867 the Grand Lodge of Liberia was constituted, which built an impressive temple, highly visible in the heart of Monrovia, the country's capital. Throughout the nineteenth and twentieth centuries, Liberia was ruled by these Americo-Liberians, united in the True Whig Party (also the name of the predecessor to the Republican Party in the United States), who were generally deemed to belong to one of the Masonic lodges. But in 1980 there was a violent coup d'état; "Sergeant" Samuel Doe toppled the regime of President William Tolbert and assassinated him and other Americo-Liberian notables (the pictures of their bodies hanging on poles on the beach created widespread shock in Western countries). One of Doe's first official acts was to ban Freemasonry and close all the lodges— since the brotherhood was seen as the mystic secret behind the power of the Americo-Liberian elite. The cruel irony was that in 1989, when Doe felt his hold on power slipping away, and just before he was toppled and executed by another warlord, he had himself initiated into an improvised Masonic lodge, in a last attempt to hold onto power.[36] During the following civil

FIGURE 2.4. In contrast to elsewhere in Africa, the Masonic Temple in Monrovia is a towering landmark. This reflects the long history of the brotherhood in Liberia as an identity marker for the liberated Afro-Americans who have ruled the country since the 1860s. Completely ruined during the civil war around 2000, recent renovations highlight the return of Freemasonry in the country.
Photo: Sublime Prince/Wikimedia Commons, CC BY-SA 4.0.

war, Freemasonry had little opportunity to reconstitute itself; the splendid hall, a landmark in Monrovia and a proud symbol of Masonic power, fell into ruin. But after the peace agreement of 2003, the lodges reconstituted themselves. The hall was emptied of squatters and its renovation—finally completed in 2018—marked the return of Freemasonry in Liberia. On the website of the Grand Lodge the picture of the temple, again in full splendor, seems to celebrate this renaissance.

Freemasonry in *France-Afrique*: Three Aspects

This condensed overview of various trajectories of Freemasonry in post-colonial Africa presents a dazzling variety, But three recurring aspects are crucial for our analysis of this enigmatic triangle of Freemasonry, homo-sexuality, and illicit enrichment:

the tension between two French *grandes loges* in Africa;
the rivalry between the brotherhood and various branches of the
    Rosicrucians;
and the link with same-sex practices and illicit enrichment.

All three aspects need to be analyzed against a wider, international back-ground in view of the global ramification of Freemasonry and parallel associations.

A NEWCOMER IN POSTCOLONIAL AFRICA: LA GRANDE LOGE NATIONALE FRANÇAISE

Especially over the last decades, the increasing rivalry between the two main French lodges—Le Grand Orient de France (GOF) and La Grande Loge Nationale Française (GLNF)—intensified the role of Freemasonry in the politics of *Françafrique*. But this rivalry can only be understood against the background of the nineteenth-century rupture of the Grand United Lodge of London with the GOF and other French lodges. The GOF had been the dominant obedience in French Africa, ever since the introduction of Freemasonry on the continent in the eighteenth century. But when in 1877 the London mother lodge withdrew its warrant from the GOF because it suppressed the reference to God and its increasingly public identification with the Third Republic, several French brethren expressed similar dissatisfaction with such secularizing and republican tendencies. In 1913 they formed a new Grand Lodge, reinstating God in its rules and obtaining almost immediately recognition from the London

FIGURE 2.5. Meeting room in the Masonic temple of the Grande Loge National Française, which has lately become a rival of the Grand Orient in francophone Africa. Photo: Lpele/Wikimedia Commons, CC BY-SA 4.0.

lodge (thus the new Grand Lodge became "regular," while most other French lodges remained "irregular" or "a-dogmatic"). After several name changes, this "regular" French Grand Lodge took the name of Grande Loge Nationale Française.

In France relations with the other lodges remained quite tense. Several French GLNF initiates we interviewed referred to the brothers from the Grand Orient as "those socialists." The latter tend to refer to the GLNF as conservative, a refuge for royalists and still afraid to break with the Catholic Church. Until the 1960s the GLNF numbered only a few thousand initiates. But from the 1970s on, its membership began to grow rapidly, the GLNF becoming the second-largest French lodge (after the GOF).[37] However, this rapid growth fed accusations from other lodges that the GLNF had a predilection for *affairisme* (opportunism) and lacked strict standards for initiation especially in southern France and the former French colonies in Africa. Moreover, the GLNF was plagued by several financial scandals in the 1990s. A crisis ensued after François Stifani became grand master

(2007). In 2011 several other European Grand Lodges broke ties with the GLNF, and in 2012 the Grand United Lodge of England followed suit, withdrawing its recognition of the GLNF. After an acrimonious internal struggle, Stifani was forced to step down, and the new grand master succeeded in carrying through a reorganization that convinced the London mother lodge. In 2014 it renewed its recognition of the GLNF, which made all its dependent lodges (also those in Africa) "regular" again.[38]

Omar Bongo, president of Gabon for more than forty years (1967–2009) and a staunch ally of France, played a key role in the GLNF's spread into Africa. Originally a member of GOF-affiliated lodges, Bongo combined this with supporting GLNF lodges in Paris and Gabon (Glaser and Smith 1997, 192; Glaser 2014, chapter 10). After the socialist intermezzo in France under François Mitterand (1981–1995), who leaned heavily on the GOF network in Africa, Jacques Foccart (who had served as *Monsieur Afrique* under de Gaulle) made in 1995 a spectacular comeback as the Africa specialist of Jacques Chirac, Mitterand's successor. Supposedly it was Bongo who then convinced the conservatives, back in power in Paris, that it was possible to work with Freemason networks in Africa, of course not with the "socialist" Grand Orient but with its conservative rival, the GLNF (see below, chapter 4). Yet its successes in Africa have also a reverse side for the GLNF. Especially its ongoing collaboration with Sassou Nguesso, the militant president of Congo-Brazzaville, is becoming an uneasy secret. Indeed, the particularities of Sassou Ngouesso's dealings with Freemasons Lodge can further clarify the story of his surprising comeback.

As we saw, Sassou Nguesso's turn to Freemasonry was quite surprising in itself. After twelve years in power as president of a formally Marxist regime, ruling the country through his Parti congolais du travail, it was only in exile in France, recovering from his humiliating defeat in the elections of 1992, that he created his Grande Loge du Congo. The fact that he linked his new lodge to the conservative GLNF was to prove crucial for his unexpected success when he returned to Congo in 1997. His main opponent in the ensuing civil war was Pascal Lissouba, who had been elected president in 1992. Lissouba was also initiated, but into a GOF lodge (*socialiste*). According to Antoine Glaser (2014, chapter 3; see also Smith and Glaser 1997, 192), Lissouba realized that this had been the wrong choice, so he tried to switch to the GLNF, but apparently too late.[39] The much-heralded Freemason effort in the late 1990s to reconcile the "brothers" and stop the war that was destroying Brazzaville—an initiative in which brothers from both the GOF and GLNF from France collaborated—failed because Sassou Nguesso felt assured of the continuing support from the Chirac regime through his GLNF links.

This example may be a stark illustration of how directly the rivalry between French lodges can affect politics in Africa. However, it has also another side. With the mounting crisis in the GLNF in France, Sassou Nguesso—still in power today—became an uncomfortable ally even for the GLNF. For instance, *Franc-Maçonnerie Magazine*—a journal that aims to open up Freemasonry to a broader public—featured Sassou Nguesso's portrait on the frontispiece of its 2010 (3) issue with the text "Ces dictateurs qui ont piégé la franc-maçonnerie" (those dictators who have trapped Freemasonry).[40] And after Stifani was forced to abdicate as GLNF's grand master (2012), the same journal published several articles questioning whether circumstances had really changed, citing Sassou Nguesso's ongoing GLNF membership (and that of other dictators like Chad's Idriss Deby, or Ali Bongo in Gabon) as examples to the contrary. The same journal mentioned the fact that French GLNF dignitaries were present at these dictators' initiations and other rituals as worrying examples.[41]

Especially over the last thirty years, Freemasonry has become an ubiquitous rhizome in Africa as one of the factors explaining the remarkable longevity of *Françafrique* surviving constant regime-changes and repeated declarations by incoming French presidents about starting with a clean slate. Yet, it is also a network of constant internal strife and segmentation. Developments in Cameroon and Gabon have to be understood against this background.

LA ROSE-CROIX AS A POWERFUL ALTERNATIVE

Another trait that marked the development of Freemasonry in the African continent is the emergence of Rosicrucianism as both a related movement *and* a possible alternative, or even a competitor. The increasingly global presence of AMORC (the Ancient Mystical Order of the Rose Cross), founded in 1915 in the United States, gave Rosicrucianism in many parts of the world a profile as a separate organization. But in some African countries, notably in Cameroon, the relationship has hardened into one of increasing competition over the last three decades. Such rivalry is striking since to many Masons Rose-Croix has become a precious element of Freemasonry. One of the highest ranks in the initiations of several Freemason rites is called the Rose Cross. However, we shall see that nowadays in Cameroon the two are presumed to exist as separate networks. In the 1990s a series of murders of priests—culminating in 1995 in the killing of Le Père Mveng, widely respected as the country's leading historian—triggered a stream of rumors that their bodies had been dismembered, parts serving in black masses staged in a deadly competition between Freemason and Rosicrucian lobbies. These tensions inside the national elite were supposed to be the cause of prevailing political chaos (Geschiere 2017). An important factor in all this might be what we will call President Paul Biya's personal "spiritual pluralism"—his baffling journey from one spiritual guidance to the next—to which we will return in chapter 4.

A brief history of Rosicrucianism can help to place this development in Cameroon (and elsewhere in the continent) against a broader background. Yet this is not an easy task since over time this more or less secret association has taken on so many manifestations—most of them surrounded by a mythical halo—that its history is even harder to summarize than that of Freemasonry. The first historically well-documented appearance of Rosicrucianism was the publication of two manifestos, later followed by a third, between 1607 and 1614 by German theologians with a Lutheran background (the *Tübinger Kreis*). The three manifestos celebrated the heritage from a medieval knight, C. R. C.—subsequently also called Christian Rosencreutz—who was born in 1378 in Germany. Through his travels around the world, C. R. C. gathered profound esoteric knowledge that he passed on to a small brotherhood (only eight people). In the brutal climate of the religious wars in Europe, this valuable knowledge had to be hidden. But in the course of the seventeenth century many people started to refer to this secret knowledge since it would offer possibilities for further expanding the limits of the emerging scientific method. Indeed, Rosicrucian publications abound in references to Paracelsus or other alchemists and experimental scholars, for instance from the coterie of the German emperor Rudolf II at his court in Prague in the first decade of the seventeenth century. Rosicrucians claim also that their "brothers" were involved in the emergence of the first Masonic lodges in Scotland, and that Rosencreutz's wisdom was crucial to the further expansion of Freemasonry. A problem with all this is that no historical traces of the Rosencreutz figure or his followers can be found prior to the publications of these manifestos in the early seventeenth century.[42] Moreover, later on, Rosicrucians extended their historical claims in time far earlier than Rosencreutz. They also claim now the medieval Templars as their ancestors. Others relate the esoteric knowledge, of which Rosicrucians are so proud, to much more ancient Egyptian sources. Next to Christian Rosencreutz, figures like Thutmosis III (1479–1425 BCE), the great conqueror of ancient Egypt's Middle Empire, but also Akhenaten, who founded his own religion dedicated to the sun, have become iconic figures (see Edighofer 1998).While in some respects Rosicrucianism became integrated into Freemasonry, as part and parcel of its rituals and knowledge, there emerged over time also separate Rose Cross societies, most of which were short-lived. The most stable is, until now, the already mentioned AMORC, founded in 1915 by Hubert Spencer Lewis in America, but with a clear French pedigree.

In 1908 Lewis had a mystical experience that inspired him to go to Europe in order to look for Rosencreutz's followers. By chance he met in Toulouse a certain Clovis Lassalle—in AMORC lore described as the grand master of the Rose-Croix in France—who initiated Lewis in 1909 into Rosicrucian wisdom. On his return to the United States, Lewis organized a first AMORC meeting in New York City in 1915, in which (according to AMORC traditions) he surprised the audience by his wide knowledge of the natural sciences—knowledge that accorded with the scientific claims of Rosicrucianism.[43] Subsequently AMORC developed a worldwide network, with its headquarters in San José (California). Its French wing has more recently become quite active in Africa. The present grand master, Serge Toussaint, regularly tours the continent. In a 2014 interview with a Cameroonian news agency, he categorically stated that "AMORC has no link with Freemasonry, of which I hardly know how it functions."[44]

In several countries in Africa, AMORC temples function separately from Freemason lodges. Ateba Eyene in his attack on *la dictature des loges, des sectes et du magico-anal* in Cameroon (discussed in chapter 1) may put Rosicrucians and Freemasons in one basket—as do many rumors of *radio trottoir*—but they manifest themselves as clearly separate institutions with their own buildings and their own meetings. Yet relations between the two vary. An officer of the AMORC temple in Libreville (Gabon), for instance, explained to us when we visited him in his temple in 2019 that some of his followers were also initiated as Masons, and that he had no problem with this.[45] This raises the question as to why the relationship seems to be particularly fraught in Cameroon. One of the reasons for the widespread panic about a "dictatorship of the lodges" in this country might be precisely that their mutual conflicts, fought out with occult means, are believed to pose a risk to society and harm "innocent" people. We will see that for understanding developments in Cameroon and Gabon it is important to stress that terms like "Freemasonry" or "the" Rosicrucians should not give the impression of unified movements. The field of these associations is marked by deep divisions, rivalry, and constant segmentation. This internal divisiveness feeds into popular "anti-Masonic" discourses evoking a vision of the elite indulging in fierce forms of rivalry and transgressive behavior in an unscrupulous quest for riches and power.

FREEMASONRY, SAME-SEX PRACTICES, AND ILLICIT ENRICHMENT

The easy association of Freemasonry with same-sex practices—remember the controversy at the Catholic University of Central Africa that was our starting point—may not be special to its postcolonial dynamics in francophone Africa. In chapter 1 we saw that it has a long and tenacious history in France itself. But it is important to emphasize that in the African context this association gets a special tenor by being linked to secret forms of enrichment or, more generally, to special "access." In the course of our research, we became ever more struck by the emphasis in African contexts on same-sex intercourse as a pathway to riches. In itself, this is again not new to postcolonial Africa. Remember that for Cameroon and Gabon, this idea was highlighted in one of the very first ethnographies, Günther Tessmann's monograph on the Fang before colonial conquest. Indeed his monograph, long almost forgotten, is making a comeback in the present-day panic about a supposed proliferation of homosexuality precisely because of his challenging way of linking same-sex practices to magical enrichment. It is this aspect that gets special emphasis in the postcolonial perception of Freemasonry, at least in francophone contexts: linking the brotherhood with same-sex rituals automatically makes it suspect of dabbling in occult forms of enrichment.

Of course such a link is not at all articulated in the lodges' formal discourse. But it is all the more highlighted in attacks on the lodges. Yet, there are important variations. In Cameroon the popular association of Freemasonry with same-sex practices became more intense toward the end of the last century; in this sense neither its presence in the 2005 Christmas sermon of the archbishop of Yaounde nor the subsequent *affaire des listes* should have come as a surprise. Elsewhere in francophone Africa the association is there but retains a lower profile. In Gabon people do talk about it but it has not yet become a major popular concern. In Senegal and Ivory Coast, it only became an issue more recently and with a different tenor (see below).

In our introduction we quoted Patrick Awondo's notion of "the politicization of homosexuality"—which he launched for his analysis of the rising "moral panic" in Cameroon (Awondo 2012a, 2019). His notion is also helpful in exploring variations in the urgency of the association of

Freemasonry with homosexuality as a mystic path toward enrichment in different francophone countries. Clearly the challenge for our next chapters is to understand which special factors made the issue particularly virulent in Cameroon and to follow in a wider comparative perspective how the vicissitudes of postcolonial politics affected other trajectories in the politicization of homosexuality. The reader must be warned: conspiracy narratives excel in what can be called kaleidoscopic condensation. As said, this is the very secret of their power.

Freemasonry in Present-Day Cameroon and Gabon

What is the outcome of this global trajectory of the brotherhood for present-day Cameroon and Gabon? How did postcolonial developments affect its presence in these countries until now? There is a striking contrast between the brotherhood's apparent ubiquity in present-day Africa, as suggested by anti-Masonic discourses, and the lodges' invisibility in everyday life. As noted in the preceding chapter, at the end of the last century, British and French lodges, concerned that the emphasis on secrecy was the cause of the brotherhoods' growing unpopularity, made some openings to the general public. But, at least until now, this tendency seems to have bypassed most African lodges, certainly those in Cameroon and Gabon.[1] Compare, for instance, the intellectual gymnastics that Denis Bouallo, grand master of the Grande Loge Unie du Cameroun (GLUC), was performing in his closing speech of this lodge's 2012 annual meeting, trying somewhat desperately to reconcile *extériorisation* and secrecy.[2] Apparently the *Sérinissime Grand Maître* saw such exteriorization as a necessity in order to open the brotherhood to the wider world—in line with the reorientation of Freemasonry in Europe. But he hastened to emphasize that this required at the same time a variety of precautions to safeguard Masonic secrets: first of all, absolute protection of the secrets surrounding the initiations, but also that under no circumstances can a brother divulge who is member. *Le secret d'appartenance* (belonging) still has to be respected.[3]

Indeed, both in Cameroon and Gabon, Freemasons are often reluctant to identify themselves as such—apart from certain allusions—and neither are they willing to talk to outsiders about the brotherhood; even the lodges' buildings are difficult to situate. There is a striking difference in this respect with Rosicrucian lodges, notably for AMORC, which are easy to locate and eager to welcome visitors. Indeed, African Masons are quick to repeat that "Freemasonry does not recruit"[4]—this is in contrast to Rosicrucian groups, which regularly organize open meetings to attract followers.[5] Occasions when Freemasonry manifests itself in public are rare. For the lodges belonging to the network of the Grand Orient de France (GOF) this happens with the annual REHFRAM meetings (Rencontres humanistes et fraternelles africaines et malgaches), which were held in Douala in 2016. These meetings are not open to the public, but they are announced via public media. For the lodges that belong to the rival network of the Grande Loge Nationale Française (GLNF), which became quite active in Africa since the end of the last century through its initiations "from above,"[6] these REHFRAM meetings are forbidden ground. But some of the GLNF lodges dabble in other forms of publicity by having films of prestigious initiations circulate on the internet, turning them into a public show. The idea is clearly to impress people by putting crowds of national and European dignitaries on the screen, all wearing their richly decorated Masonic aprons, and following impressive rituals, executed by Europeans and Africans in close collaboration.[7] Needless to say, these events are certainly not accessible to the public.

Due to this tendency to remain under the radar, it is difficult to get a clear overview of the lodges' presence on the ground. Estimates of the number of Freemasons vary greatly. For Cameroon, *Jeune Afrique* estimated in 2016 that the total number of initiated Masons was below 1,000—the majority (800) in Douala and the rest mainly in Yaoundé. But an estimate of *La lettre du Continent* of the same year arrived at only 500 members for the whole of Cameroon.[8] For Gabon, the American ambassador in Libreville arrived in a brief memo on "Bongo and Freemasonry in Gabon" at a somewhat higher figure: 800 Masons—out of a total population of 1.4 million.[9] Moreover, the ambassador added that the large majority of cabinet ministers, members of parliament and influential businessmen (both Gabonese and French) are supposed to be in the brotherhood.

The Masonic presence in Cameroon is further qualified by the fairly strict separation between lodges affiliated with the Grand Orient de France (GOF)—thus "a-dogmatic" (not recognized by the Grand United Lodge from London)—and the Grande Loge Nationale du Cameroun (CL-CAMC), affiliated with the Grande Loge Nationale Française (GLNF) and therefore "regular" (recognized by the London lodge). As elsewhere on the African continent, the GOF presence is much older—colonial lodges have existed since the 1920s. The first lodge in independent Cameroon, originated from this current. In 1962, two Cameroonian Masons, Henri Ned Collins and Theodore Koule Njanga (both previously initiated in a GOF lodge), founded the GOLUC (Les Grand Orient et Loge Unies de Cameroun—later GLUC).[10] In his interesting historical overview, the present Grand Orateur of the GLUC, G. Solle, notes incidents of police harassment in 1965—that is, during Ahidjo's regime with its overriding emphasis on unity and a strict ban on any form of organization outside the one-party. At the time, the mother lodges in France offered their protection to the new lodge in Cameroon. However, Koule Njanga, as GLUC's grand master, insisted on maintaining the lodge's independence and apparently managed to claim some sort of monopoly for his lodge: all lodges coming in from outside had to work under the *couvert* of the GLUC.[11] Yet, this changed apparently when in the 1990s the GLNF sought to create a lodge that could compete in Cameroon with the existing network of its great rival, the GOF. In 2001 the Grande Loge Nationale du Cameroun (GLCAM) was founded, which in accordance with the rules imposed by its warrant holder, the Grande Loge Nationale Française, refuses—at least formally—to collaborate with other lodges inside Cameroon.

In other respects as well, the presence of Freemasonry in Cameroon is somewhat fragmented. A great difference with Gabon is that the Cameroonian president himself does not have a central place in the brotherhood. In 2012 the GLUC asked President Biya as a *frère de lumière* (illuminated brother) to close the celebration of its fifty-year jubilee, and he accepted.[12] People suppose in general that he was initiated in France as a student during the 1950s. But when he came to power in 1982, he presented himself as a Catholic, and when he subsequently sought out various esoteric forms of protection, he became affiliated with Rosicrucian groups rather than with a specific Masonic lodge (see chapter 4). In ethnic respects as well, there is some imbalance. According to Georges Dougueli (*Jeune Afrique* 2016), Douala and Bassa far outnumber other ethnic groups in Cameroonian Freemasonry; the Bamiléké, generally seen as the main economic power in the national context, are not as highly represented, and neither are the anglophones. The GLUC unites twelve lodges, mainly in Douala. This seems to correspond to the strong presence of business people in these lodges (historically the Douala and Bassa dominated the city's economy). The GLCAM would be more present in Yaoundé and, in line with the general profile of GLNF lodges in Africa would mainly include high-level civil servants, politicians, and army people.[13] However, as far as we know, these are only trends. The GLUC has also at least one lodge in Yaoundé, named after an important military man (Paul Yakana).[14]

In Gabon, the Masonic presence seems to be more unified.[15] One reason is the practice, already mentioned, of former president Omar Bongo to freely cross the boundaries between the different Grand Lodges. He was apparently first initiated in the GOF (in 1965 on an occasional visit to Angoulême), but then he moved to the GLNF, creating also his own lodge, the Grand Rite Equatorial.[16] It is likely that Bongo could easily transgress such boundaries because of his prominent position—as a kind of regional pivot for the spread of Freemason networks in Central Africa and elsewhere in the continent, fortified by his control over Gabon's oil.[17] His successor, Ali Bongo, made a public effort to follow in his father's footsteps by broadcasting his spectacular initiation as grand master on YouTube. Such condensation makes Freemasonry in Gabon seem to be at the very center of power. The American ambassador to Gabon, Barrie Walker, concludes his 2007 memo by stressing that the ubiquity of Masons "created among Gabonese the belief that the best way to get ahead is to become a Mason." Similar ideas prevail in Cameroon, but the more fragmented presence of these global associations in this country makes the idea that initiation provides "access" even more diffuse. Again the question becomes: Access to what exactly?

✳ 3 ✳

Anusocratie

THE ANUS AS SOURCE OF
ILLICIT ENRICHMENT

Recently Cameroonians, ever inventive in devising neologisms, surprised the world with a new word: *anusocratie*. This became a key term in the moral panic about a supposed proliferation of homosexuality haunting the country since 2005. The term seems to originate in Yaoundé—probably no accident since as Cameroon's capital it is the seat of the country's political-administrative elite. The first mention of the term that we could trace is from the text that accompanied one of the lists published in 2006 by *L'Anecdote*, the Yaoundé-based newspaper, denouncing supposed homosexuals among the national elite, which triggered a wave of homophobia in the country.[1] Subsequently the term found its way into academic publications and popular songs.[2] *Anusocratie* powerfully condenses an idea that has become common in many parts of Africa today: the purported link between anal penetration and illicit enrichment. Cameroon and Gabon offer a particular variant on this theme because many people explicitly relate these conspiracies to the involvement of the two countries' elite in secret societies of Western provenance: Freemasonry, Rosicrucianism, and the Illuminati. The current association in francophone contexts of Freemasonry with same-sex practices has given rise to a characterization of the governing regime as *les pédés de la République* (Ndjio 2012b, 2013). The message is clear: just as Freemasonry was a colonial imposition, homosexuality has also been introduced from the outside; it is a colonial byproduct.

The *anusocratie* notion condenses the central questions raised in our introduction: Why did the association of Freemasonry with homosexuality and illicit enrichment create such a strong moral panic in Cameroon and (to a lesser degree) in Gabon? And why at this particular

moment? As Steven Pierce argued in 2016, there is value in going beyond general explanations for recent outbursts of homophobia in the
African continent, all the more so since these outbursts follow differ-
ing trajectories. Of course, one can mention general factors that apply
to the continent in its entirety: the legacy of colonial laws, increasing
popular anger about social and economic inequality, and the impact of
the internet. But why have these unique conspiracy narratives arisen in
Cameroon and Gabon?

Two approaches may be helpful in identifying specific factors that
can clarify why this particularly explosive form has arisen here and now:
a historical and a comparative one. In the present chapter we will follow
a comparative approach to outline factors that play a special role in
Cameroon and Gabon. We will start by exploring what *anus(t)ocratie*
means in everyday life in these countries, with a focus on the varying
avatars that the figure of "the" homosexual can assume in present-day
contexts. Then we will briefly compare these with other trajectories in
present-day Africa, trying to discern key factors behind these variations.
Chapters 4 and 5 take a historical approach, following how colonial
developments and even precolonial dynamics have affected present-day
relations.

But first a note of caution: both approaches—the historical and the
comparative—have their dangers. Historical precedents risk suggesting
"traditional" continuities. So it may be prudent to emphasize here that
the link to "witchcraft"—central in the reflections on enrichment not
only in present-day conspiracy thinking about *les pédés de la République*
but also in ethnographic data from 120 years ago (recall the German
ethnographer Günther Tessmann on the Fang)—does not introduce
a stable baseline. On the contrary, a common trend in recent "witchcraft" studies is an increasing emphasis on the need to historicize these
ideas—to see them not as a more or less fixed system, but rather as
an assemblage of notions, borrowed and reinterpreted, that travel in
time and space.[3] On the other hand, a comparative perspective poses
the risk of reductive explanations, certainly when politicoeconomic
backgrounds are emphasized. Popular anger at the political elite about
the sorry state of the nation and its economy is widespread in many
parts of Africa, but the question remains why in certain contexts anal
intercourse occupies such central position in moral attacks on illicit
enrichment as a particularly amoral conspiracy. This makes it all the
more important to emphasize that sexuality plays a role of its own in
such concatenations. Clearly we need to gain deeper insight into *anusocratie*'s imaginaries.

The Rise of an *Anusocratie*:
"The" Homosexual as a Predatory *Grand*

The attack by Ateba Eyene on the role of Freemasons and Rosicrucians in present-day Cameroon, discussed in chapter 1, gave some indication of the context in which the notion of *anusocratie* emerged (Ateba Eyene 2012/13). Note especially the *magico-anal* in the book's subtitle. Recall also the reverberation of such ideas in popular songs like Ntoumba Minka's "Sexy Mac.Kéro" with the graphic warning: "The sun shines for all; we each have a chance, so why bring down your pants to be appointed to a post of director?" In the 2006 newspapers' lists of homosexuals, it was politicians in particular who were accused of such transgressions. Ateba Eyene added graphic sketches of his own—such as reporting on two higher civil servants surprised in a public toilet "deeply into each other" in an act of sexual misconduct. But it is difficult to find traces of this in everyday life. In a heterosexual sense, the "phallocracy," seen by Achille Mbembe as a hallmark of postcolonial Africa, is notable in everyday office life in major urban centers like Yaoundé and Douala. *Le droit de cuissage* (claim to thighs) is a standard joke about the behavior of bosses toward their female underlings (or of professors toward their female students). And secretaries will jokingly explain their boss's absence as "Monsieur est dans son deuxième bureau" (his second office; that is, with his concubine). But people are less open about homosexual relations. There are rumors about sophisticated brothels where civil servants go to meet young men, but like the "gay bars" that are alleged to exist in Cameroon's cities, they had reportedly just closed when we tried to visit them. And there are the standard allusions that someone who has achieved success—landing a good job, acquiring expensive clothes—has engaged in anal intercourse, but of course the people concerned will strenuously deny it.

One place where one finds the image of the homosexual as a predatory *Grand* described in detail are the petitions of gay asylum seekers to European or American countries. Recurring themes in these petitions are the victim being drugged, raped by a so-called *Grand*, promised money, and then put under surveillance. Special elements are the emphasis on bleeding (apparently the victim's anus was heavily damaged by the predator) and the predator's extraordinary potency since he is alleged to do this regularly to many young men. Yet the main point in common is the asylum seeker identifying a leading Cameroonian politician as the sexual predator in his story.[4] Of course, the question arises as to what extent the petitioners' stories are based on "facts." They indicate in any case that the image of the homosexual *Grand* as a predator is very much alive in Cameroon.

This was confirmed by the most recent scandal that roiled Cameroonian politics just before we completed this manuscript. On February 6, 2023, Jean-Pierre Amougou Belinga was arrested at his sumptuous home in Yaoundé by no fewer than fifty gendarmes, accused of involvement in the murder of journalist Martinez Zogo two weeks earlier. We met Amougou Belinga at the start of our story, as the editor of the journal *L'Anecdote*, which in 2006 published a list of Cameroon's "prominent homosexuals." Since then Amougou Belinga had become the head of an important media empire and a central figure in Yaoundé's political life. His arrest came as a surprise since he seemed unassailable due to his political connections. Only the link with the drawn-out struggle over the succession of President Biya (soon to turn ninety) might explain Amougou Belinga's sudden vulnerability. Also striking were accompanying rumors about Amougou Belinga having a sexual affair with the minister of justice, Laurent Esso, his alleged partner in journalist Zogo's horrific murder. Amougou Belinga's downfall illustrates the ironic twists and turns in the ever-surprising whirlwind of accusations and counteraccusations regarding same-sex practices among the country's elite. He was one of the first proponents of the homophobic panic, but is now widely denounced as a homosexual himself. One might wonder, indeed, what "homosexuality" means in such a context.[5]

Who Are These "Homosexuals"? The Other Side

This image of the homosexual as a predatory *Grand*, abruptly put in the limelight by Monseigneur Bakot's 2005 Christmas sermon and the 2006 *affaire des listes*, was balanced by a quite different development: the gradual emergence of self-identifying gay men of a very different allure since the turn of the century. Cameroon may have been an innovator in Africa in a new, public style of homophobic actions (the Cameroonian newspapers' lists from 2006 were later copied in other African countries).[6] But it was also a forerunner in ethnographic research on emerging homosexual meeting places and gay/lesbian lifestyles. Charles Gueboguo began interviewing "homosexuals" in Yaoundé and Douala during his sociology studies at the University of Yaoundé I in the early 2000s, reporting on it in his doctoral *mémoire*, his dissertation, and in a monograph published with L'Harmattan in 2006. Patrick Awondo started his research in 2007. For both researchers, this was a courageous undertaking, especially after the escalation of homophobia throughout Cameroonian society after 2005. All the more since both Gueboguo and Awondo, as good ethnographers, clearly sided with their research subjects, whose position became increasingly endangered.[7] Their ethnographies sketch a profile of Cameroonian homosexuals that is strikingly different from the image of important men (and some women) as sexual predators in Monseigneur Bakot's Christmas sermon, or Ateba Eyene's satanic image of the "lodges" and the "magico-anal" supposedly dominating Cameroon.

Both Gueboguo and Awondo—and our own interlocutors in the field, when describing their fearful "coming out"—see a hesitant emergence of a gay and lesbian lifestyle in the 1990s, complete with its own meeting places (although these were constantly shifting) and its own secret codes and terminology (equally shifting and unsure). Others—for instance, S. N. Nyeck, who started to publish in the late 2000s about issues of homophobia in Cameroon—emphasized that in the 1990s homosexuality was not yet a public issue.[8] Similarly, in the 1970s and 1980s, when one of us (Geschiere) spent longer periods of time in Yaoundé, homosexuality was certainly discussed, but mostly as something secret and hardly talked about—as a cause for blackmail.[9] There were the inevitable rumors about illicit sexual activities at boarding schools, especially at Catholic seminaries.[10] In everyday life there were *travestis* (transvestites), biologically male but identifying as women; most of them had considerable difficulty finding acceptance in their own society. Another niche, more widely respected, was that of the *nganga* (healers) who—as elsewhere in Africa (and beyond)—included all sorts of gender-bending in their performances, mixing warriors' attributes with skirts and female jewelry.

The late 1990s may even have brought a certain liberalization. Gueboguo (2006, 95) refers to a bar in the Yaoundé suburb of Essos—called by the initiated "the mass of twenty-two hours"—where homosexuals could meet on Sunday evenings, more or less undisturbed, provided they did not draw too much attention.[11] Gueboguo also mentions *le carrefour de la joie*—"the crossroads of joy"—in Mvog-Ada, another Yaoundé neighborhood, as a favorite gathering spot for his respondents.[12] People would follow all sort of strategies and gestures—special handshakes and such—to recognize each other. Most often, people meeting at such a spot would have been introduced by someone who already belonged to the network. Awondo gives a similar account of such *lieux du nkoandengué* (gay places): constantly shifting, since they depended on the goodwill of the *patron*. Clearly, in this context, the homosexual is not a *Grand* (as Ateba Eyene alleged), but a potential victim.

Proof of the increasing visibility of this group is also that both Gueboguo (2006) and Awondo (2012a; 2019, 94) describe an emerging terminology used both by outsiders to label this group and by the people themselves as identification. In the 1990s the most common notion was *nkoandengué*. It could refer to a person, but also be used as an adjective (as in *lieu nkoandengué*—gay place).[13] Its female equivalent was *mvoë* (lesbian). The etymology of *nkoandengué* is unclear. Gueboguo sees it as a fusion of two words, one from a Beti language (the Beti claim to be the autochthons of Yaoundé) and another one from a Bamiléké language (a group from the west, but as immigrants increasingly outnumbering the original groups in Douala and Yaoundé). For Awondo, it is a fusion of two male names: Nkoa and Ndengue. But for him, writing a bit later, these expressions are already a bit passé. He cites various French words that had become more fashionable: *bilingue* (a pun on Cameroon priding itself on having two official languages, French and English); or *être dans l'affaire* (to be in the business). He notes also that more educated people often feel that *nkoandengué* is an outdated, old-fashioned term; they tend to prefer "more modern" notions like "gay" or "lesbian," because they relate to an international community. Awondo (2019, 195) notes, moreover, more gendered terms: for instance, *coujé* for a man playing the top role and *fille* for the bottom. But he adds that the difference is not fixed, since people also refer to *poissons braisés* (grilled fish—that is, grilled on both sides, hence "versatile"). Gueboguo (2006, 82) notes that homosexuality is "bisexualized" since many *nkoandengué* also have affairs with women and even raise children. Awondo (2019, 196) adds that only the more passive partners see their homosexuality as "exclusive." Striking also is the multiethnic composition of the networks. Nor was there a dominant class position. Gueboguo's and Awondo's respondents came from all walks of life (see also Corey-Boulet 2019). In many respects, the homosexual "community" remained an emergent one, with classifications and boundaries as shifting as its locations.

The 2005 Arrest of the "Yaoundé Eleven": Internationalization of the Gay Issue

A dramatic turning point for this emerging gay subculture in Cameroon was the police raid of May 15, 2005, on a bar in Essos (a Yaoundé neighborhood) that had acquired the reputation of serving as a meeting place for gay men. About thirty men were arrested; some succeeded in escaping, others bought their way out, but eleven people were taken into custody. These "Yaoundé Eleven" would acquire iconic status in further developments around homosexuality in Cameroon. In his moving account based on interviews with most of them ten years later, Robbie Corey-Boulet (2019, 15ff.) highlights the novelty of this case in several respects: on the one hand, the brutality of the police raid and the clear intention of the authorities to turn the arrests into a public statement; on the other, the international attention that the plight of these Yaoundé Eleven received—a surprise both for themselves and for the authorities. Yet in other respects Corey-Boulet's picture of these Yaoundé Eleven accords with Gueboguo and Awondo's account of gay life in Yaoundé around 2000. Corey-Boulet's interlocutors were part of a growing crowd that would meet every Sunday evening in this bar because they had learned that the owner tolerated their presence (as long as they did not bother other customers). Most knew one another, but every Sunday "there were new people . . . you had never seen"; people would come also from outside Yaoundé (Corey-Boulet 2019, 16). All sorts of people from varying ethnic backgrounds would meet there: students, fashion designers, waiters, IT technicians. Among those detained, three worked in the hospitality business, two were students, three were designers or tailors, and one was an IT consultant.[14] Most of them had severed relations with their families, or maintained contact only because they kept their visits to the bar a secret from their relatives.[15]

But the ferociousness of the police raid did have new elements. Rather than a "normal" control as a way to get a bribe, the policemen told everybody to lie on the floor and then loaded them into two vans to take them to jail. The next morning, they were paraded before the assembled reporters as persons charged with homosexual acts. In subsequent years many explanations circulated as to why the police specifically targeted this bar. Corey-Boulet quotes lawyer Alice Nkom (who soon after the arrests stepped in to defend the accused); she referred to a report by a

FIGURE 3.1. The bar in Essos (Yaoundé) where on May 15, 2005, a dramatic police raid took place, resulting in the arrest of the Yaoundé Eleven. Their subsequent trial directed international attention to the plight of gays in Cameroon. Photo: Rogers Orock.

local official about a certain house where "homosexuals and lesbians do not hesitate to indulge in their activities at night, in the open air, in front of. . . . children younger than 15" (2019, 17); others suggested that the police were looking for a gay man who had threatened to reveal his affair with an important judge (such a link with *un Grand* who risked being "outed" was a recurring pattern in many cases to come). The display of the detainees to the press the next day suggested that the authorities intended the arrest of these "homosexuals" to serve as a public statement. In line with this was also the way the prosecutors addressed the eleven detainees in subsequent hearings, amplifying their moral indignation and thus giving the homosexuality issue a new moral profile (Corey-Boulet 2019, 20; see also Awondo 2019).

However, another novelty—not intended by the authorities—was to be of greater consequence for this particular case and also for the issue of homosexuality in Cameroon in general. This was the international attention that descended on the Yaoundé Eleven. A letter that Lambert Lamba—who was to become the spokesman for the "Eleven"—managed to smuggle out of the prison began to circulate and finally reached the New York–based International Gay and Lesbian Human Rights Commission (IGLHRC). Its leader, Cary Alan Johnson, described to Corey-Boulet (2019, 18) a feeling of purposefulness when he learned of the arrest: "Now we are talking. I know how to deal with a case like this." And, indeed, Johnson succeeded in rapidly mounting an international campaign, gaining support from Amnesty International and other global organizations but also involving the local help of lawyer Alice Nkom.[16] The sheer scope of the international support seemed to baffle the Cameroonian authorities. Lamba told Corey-Boulet that two prosecutors came to visit him in jail asking why this case had created such a global uproar: "They even asked me, 'Do you work in a secret service?'" (p. 39). However, Corey-Boulet is also of two minds about the results of this international campaign. It was in some respects effective—after further judicial antics by the authorities (which were unusual even for Cameroon), the accused were set free in June 2006. But, once liberated, the Eleven felt abandoned after the publicity around their case died down. One of them, Alim Mongoche, came out of prison suffering from AIDS complications and died a few days later, when support from abroad abruptly stopped. As Lamba concluded, "Human rights feeds on horror" (Corey-Boulet 2019, 38, 73).[17]

The international indignation that so surprised the Cameroonian authorities is crucial to understanding the 2005/6 turn of events inside Cameroon—not only the concern about the Yaoundé Eleven, but also the wider impact of Monseigneur Bakot's Christmas sermon and the subsequent *affaire des listes*.[18] These events fostered a sentiment of being under siege: the West continuing to implant its vices in its former colonies and thus corrupting Africa. Two months before the arrest of the Yaoundé Eleven, one of us (Geschiere) attended a conference at the Catholic University of Central Africa about *Justice et sorcellerie* (Justice and witchcraft). The evening before the conference's opening (March 17, 2005) the keynote speakers were invited with Père Éric de Rosny, the conference organizer, for a dinner at the home of an important official of the ministry of justice who attended the conference as well (ever since colonial days judicial authorities have been under heavy popular pressure to do something about "witchcraft"). To Geschiere's surprise, the host and his colleagues could not stop talking over dinner about the issue of homosexuality (at the time a delicate topic, not to be talked about so openly). But they were still fuming with rage about the visit of a Canadian human rights mission, which had insisted that Cameroon had to decriminalize homosexuality. Our host and his friends complained of the shamelessness of the whites trying to impose their depravity on Cameroon. The mounting international pressure to decriminalize homosexuality was certainly a powerful vector for 2005/6 becoming a turning point in Cameroon, but not in the direction that outside interventions had intended.

The Internet: A New Way for Getting "Access"

The coincidence of apparently unrelated developments is striking: the Yaoundé Eleven were still in prison, with the international campaign to liberate them just starting, when Monseigneur Bakot delivered his Christmas sermon followed by the newspaper lists and all the excitement these created—all within six months during the second half of 2005 and the first months of 2006. Corey-Boulet (2019, 69) also wonders about this coincidence and concludes that "the initial catalysts for all [these events] remain obscure." Yet his own story points to the crucial role of the internet—becoming available to ever more people in Cameroonian cities since the end of the 1990s—as a driving force in raising the public profile of homosexuality. For instance, the internet played a key role in the life story of Lambert Lamba (the Yaoundé Eleven's leader). Corey-Boulet (2019, 53) describes how, as a colporteur for *The Watchtower* (when he had a brief fling with the Jehovah's Witnesses), Lambert stumbled upon one of the first internet cafes in Yaoundé. Its owner took an interest in the youth and trained him to become his assistant. After that the internet became Lamba's main occupation, all the more so when he was asked to type messages for several male clients looking for "a husband" in Europe.

Indeed, the internet cafes that sprung up in several parts of the city during those years quickly became informal meeting places for gays and lesbians. Awondo (2019, 198) describes how for his interlocutors the internet was a true discovery. It opened the world to them, helped them discover that their sexual preferences were not exceptional, and helped them get replies to all the questions they had not dared to pose to people in their surroundings. From the interviews we conducted in 2010 and 2014 with members of gay/lesbian organizations like ADEFHO and Alternatives Cameroun (see below) access to the internet was a watershed in their lives. In the first years it was only young people from a more prosperous background who had access. But with the opening up of more and more internet cafes, people with less money could put a small sum together to have at least some time on the screen. The internet seemed to provide also a safer environment for dating than meeting in bars and other public places, where, even before 2005, there was always a danger of harassment—if not from the police then from the date. However, soon the internet turned out to be pervaded by dangers too: people who visit websites to arrange a date might turn up at the agreed place in a group and threaten to drag their prey to the police unless the latter pays up (see also Awondo 2019, 200).

In our introduction we quoted the pioneering work by anthropologists Katrien Pype (2016; 2017) and Sasha Newell (2021) about the notion of "connectivity" to grasp the deep impact of access to the internet on people's everyday life in Kinshasa and Abidjan. Their studies of how internet technology offered young urbanites challenging opportunities for exploring new forms of access to new *reseaux* (networks) is also relevant for understanding various aspects of the 2005/6 moral panic in Cameroon about homosexuality.[19] Of course the internationalization of the Yaoundé Eleven's sufferings was only possible through the internet. But also Monseigneur Bakot's warnings and the newspapers' denunciations of homosexuality among the national elite related directly to people's feeling that the country was besieged by international pressure to decriminalize homosexuality, a global "gay culture" pouring in through the internet. Yet, as Lambert Lamba's life story shows—and Awondo's and our own interlocutors confirm—the internet and internet cafes also played a key role in the emergence of self-identifying gay and lesbian communities inside the country.

In 2000, Lamba used his network with people he met through internet cafes to create an Association for Gays and Lesbians and Supporters (AGALES)—probably the first of its kind in Cameroon.[20] But at the time he did not even try to have his association officially registered (even after the 1990 law on freedom of association, an incisive change formally ending Cameroon's one-party regime, such freedom did not apply to criminal activities like homosexuality). However, in 2003, Alice Nkom—the lawyer who increasingly became a protagonist of gay rights in Cameroon—succeeded in getting official recognition for her organization ADEFHO (Association de défense pour les droits des homosexuels). How exactly she managed to get this official approval is not clear. Her main aim was—and still is—to have the 1972 presidential decree criminalizing homosexuality abolished, since she believes it is unconstitutional. But ADEFHO came to function also as an orientation point for self-identifying gays and lesbians, all the more so in light of Nkom's tireless struggles to get people who had been arrested under this decree freed (for quite some time she was the only lawyer in the country prepared to defend people arrested on these grounds).[21] In 2006 a Cameroonian medical doctor named Steave Nemande, together with sociologist Charles Gueboguo (quoted above), founded Alternatives Cameroun, which mainly addressed the plight of men who have sex with men (MSM) who had become HIV positive and who risked being ignored in the battle against AIDS (seen by many as mainly a heterosexual pandemic in Africa).

For both associations, and the many that followed,[22] internet visibility was vital—also because they quickly became involved in a fierce rivalry for international support. All this certainly contributed to making homosexuality more visible inside the country. One effect was to make it the target for further violent attacks.[23] Yet these organizations also served as a

FIGURE 3.2. In 2003 lawyer Alice Nkom succeeded in getting her Association de défense pour les droits des homosexuels (ADEFHO) officially registered. Since then its office has served as a meeting place for people identifying as homosexual. Photo: Nicolas Eyidi.

rallying point for people who felt persecuted. Moreover, they did encourage the spread of more moderate views throughout society. The image they created of Cameroonian homosexuals as victims of intolerance was, indeed, the opposite of the predatory figure evoked by the homophobic chorus that drew so much attention in the country after 2005.[24] In more recent years further technological change brought new forms of "connectivity" that further promoted the visibility of homosexuality, both for self-identifying LGBTQ people and for their opponents in society. The spread of cellphones (notably the "smart" variety)—in Cameroon mostly after 2005—opened up new possibilities. For instance in 2019, "Shakiro," a trans person from Douala, suddenly attracted a lot of attention on the internet. Putting her own videos on YouTube and other media—mostly provocative trans performances but also addressing President Biya in a mock-serious speech—she surprised many not only by staging fights with a few "sisters" (of course duly recorded on Facebook), but even more with the following she rapidly built up (see Ndjio 2022). However, when she threatened to "out" one of her more prominent "clients" the general mood seemed to change abruptly. Later that year, Shakiro was almost lynched by an angry crowd at one of Douala's markets and her family spirited her away.[25] Interestingly she and her "sisters" refuse labels like "homosexual," "gay," or "trans" (and even more "LGBTQ" or "queer"), calling themselves *les branchés* (the "tuned-ins"?)—a term already common for some time in Abidjan in *le milieu* where people equally had a tendency to shun clearcut Western identifications.[26] But whatever label they use, it is clear that she and her "sisters" had a very different profile from the image of "the homosexual" as a predatory *Grand*.

Are we then to conclude that the debates on homosexuality in Cameroon turn around two completely different figures? On the one hand, we have the *Grand* who uses his/her prominent position to indulge in sexual predation and who is easily associated with esoteric societies of a global nature;[27] and, on the other, there are the harassed young people whom we met in 2012 and 2014 in the safe place ADEFHO had created under the wings of Maître Nkom in Douala. Awondo (2012b, 84) notes a similar discrepancy "at one side the *cadets sociaux* (social juniors) whose homosexual practices expose [them] to strong stigmatization and recurrent persecutions; and on the other, public persons criticized for their doubtful morality." Yet, there is one element in the discourse about homosexuality that recurs in relation to both *les Grands* and the "social juniors": the link with special opportunities for enrichment. As mentioned earlier, the link with *ascension sociale* is a recurrent theme throughout Gueboguo's work on homosexuals in Yaoundé and Douala. He spoke also of *une homosexualité de luxe* that links people from the *haute bourgeoisie* and social inferiors. Gueboguo supposed also that the unexpected police raid in 2005 on La Victoire leading to the arrest of the Yaoundé Eleven was triggered by a link with the *haute bourgeoisie* (one of the arrested young men had worked as a cook for a *Grand* and threatened to "out" his boss; Gueboguo 2006, 92, 97, 141, 171). In 1995, in one of the first publications by a Cameroonian academic sociologist paying attention to homosexuality, Séverin Abéga emphasized the link with Freemasonry and the view among the young men he interviewed of homosexuality as a path to riches.[28] Several of the neologisms mentioned by Awondo (2019, 94, 198) to label a homosexual, like *être de l'affaire* or even *dans l'affaire*, signal also the idea of same-sex practices as providing "access."[29] Here we are back to the idea of *anusocratie*. This idea pops up not only from the homophobic discourse that dominated public debate in Cameroon after 2005 that targeted the national elite's depravity, but also from the ethnographies "from below" on an emerging gay/lesbian scene in Yaoundé and Douala. Apparently the association of same-sex practices with enrichment and "access" is a powerful theme. We shall see that it marks both the horror and the fascination same-sex practices evoke also elsewhere in Africa.

Gabon: Criminalization and Decriminalization

In Gabon, similar patterns unfolded, albeit with different accents. Popular anger about the consumerism of the elite focused here first of all on the *Grands'* supposed involvement in the "spare parts" trade (body parts of innocent victims "harvested" for producing fetishes to protect the elite's enrichment). Yet homosexuality is also there as a closely related theme—remember the public outcry when the new 2019 law article criminalizing homosexuality was suppressed only a year later (introduction), and the torrent of recent rumors about President Ali Bongo's involvement in same-sex practices mentioned by Ondo (2021) in his text on "irreverence" as a popular weapon against Bongo. We visited Gabon in 2017 and 2019[30]—so, just before the brief criminalization intermezzo—and homosexuality was then a widespread topic of discussion. Yet the fact that it was not criminalized clearly made a big difference. People were quite eager to discuss it, either positively or negatively, and—for us even more striking—also in personal terms. During both trips we were besieged after our presentations by journalists bombarding us with questions: "Aren't you against gay marriage? What about a gay person betraying his family? Isn't it proof of Freemasons' depravity?" and so on. The excitement of the journalists showed in any case that our lectures had touched upon a topic that stirred people's feelings in Gabon as well. Even more interesting was that in the next few days people came to talk to us about personal things. One student started to explain that he wanted to write his master's thesis in literature on traces of homosexuality in Gabonese novels. He added, moreover, that out of curiosity—since this concerned his thesis topic—he had decided to have sex with a good friend (male) who always showed special interest in him. He had rather enjoyed the experience—it was something new—but he was not certain that he would try to repeat this "experiment." Another student wanted to talk about the experiences of his "friend" (originally it seemed like he was talking about himself, but further details of his story made this improbable). The friend, a gifted singer, regularly performed for elite audiences and thus had fallen into the habit of having sex with rich men who propositioned him. The consequences had been terrible. After a string of sexual encounters he could not control his anus anymore; in the end his intestines came popping out. He had finally been saved by a priest who told him that sleeping with a man was not wrong in itself as long as you loved your partner but he had chosen the wrong men to sleep with. The "friend" was getting slowly better, but he did not sing anymore.

Not all stories ended with such a tolerant message. Prior to the 2019 conference, two Gabonese colleagues at the University talked at length to Orock about a rumor concerning a leading male politician. According to their story, this man (they did not mention his name) had been caught and filmed in a toilet in the city center having sex with a young Gabonese man. To buttress the story, the colleagues showed Orock a blurred video of two men having intimate contact. The colleagues did not see it as a problem that the images were not clear enough to establish the real identities of the people in it; their point was rather, as they expressed it, that "such a video, like the newspapers or radio gossip, animates a perpetual sense of hostility in the country to the elite for supporting same-sex rights."

Such stories are similar to ones we quoted from Cameroon. Yet, the difference is that people in Gabon talked more easily about the subject, and not always in a negative sense. Another effect of homosexuality not being criminalized (apart from this one-year intermezzo) is that one pole of the homosexual binary in Cameroon, the *cadets sociaux* (the victimized homosexuals), are less visible in Gabon, simply because the police will not arrest and jail them. However, the stories above show that the other pole, the *Grand* as a homosexual predator, is as visible in Gabon as in Cameroon, at least in popular attacks on the elite.

African Comparisons

Can a comparative perspective help to understand why this predatory *Grand* figure of "the" homosexual became so prominent in Cameroon and Gabon? Are notions like *anus(t)ocratie* special to these countries? A brief comparison with developments elsewhere in the continent may highlight special factors that made the triad of Freemasonry, same-sex behavior, and illicit enrichment particularly powerful in these Central African countries.

IVORY COAST

A comparison with Ivory Coast is of particular interest in this respect. Here, the same elements are present in public debate, but this has not (yet) lead to a similar moral panic and intensification of homophobia as in Cameroon. The story of a scandal that rocked this country in 1998 and its aftermath can serve as a starter for exploring correspondences and striking differences in the politicization of these issues.[31]

In August 1998, four years after Félix Houphouët-Boigny, the grand old man of Ivorian politics, died, an Abidjan tabloid named *Soir-Info*—known for reporting on homosexual incidents to boost its sales figures—published a short article entitled "Un Libanais appréhendé pour pédophilie" (Lebanese arrested for pedophilia).[32] A fourteen-year-old boy, who called himself UAA, accused the owner of a nightclub in the small port city of Dabou—60 kilometers outside Abidjan—of having drugged and sodomized him (this was confirmed by a medical doctor). Later on, he involved other persons—notably an Ivorian minister, as well as other prominent Ivorians—in his accusations. Around the same time, President Bédié, Houphouët-Boigny's successor, announced a cabinet reshuffle in which this minister was sidelined. Only several weeks later did UAA's story get wider attention. On October 5 a more respectable newspaper, *Le Jour*, known as a leading opposition paper, put the news on its front page. Then the Abidjan District Attorney decided to follow up on the case. Six persons—several Lebanese but also a few prominent Ivorians—were arrested. The ex-minister sued the paper for libel, but in letters to the editor, several people emphasized being shocked, noting that such practices were contrary to African traditions and blaming foreigners for importing such vices. Such expressions of indignation further kindled the fire. After initial hesitation, even the state-run newspaper *Fraternité Matin* began to pay regular attention to further developments.

However, in this case, the ruling party, President Bédié included, closed ranks round the ex-minister, who won his court case. In the beginning, the boy had attracted considerable sympathy as a victim of child abuse, but he soon lost his credibility—not only because of his blatantly feminine behavior but also because his denunciations became ever more inconsistent. A few months later he disappeared altogether, his relatives hiding him in a township in order to avoid further shame to the family. The excitement gradually died down. Yet UAA clearly had opened a quite effective vent for popular anger. In his book on Ivorian citizenship Nguyen concluded that *l'affaire pédophilie* showed that "sexual deviance was a powerful metaphor. . . . for expressing widespread dissatisfaction, even disgust, with the Bédié regime" (Nguyen 2010, 166).

All the excitement about UAA's sordid stories had to be understood against the background of growing feelings of crisis, even panic. The "Ivoirian miracle," which during the first decades after independence had made Ivory Coast under Houphouët-Boigny's leadership the continent's showcase of capitalist development, had collapsed in the 1980s, and Houphouët-Boigny's death in 1994 seemed to seal the country's demise. It was in this context that—to quote again Nguyen (2010, 161)—"rumors about predatory sexual practices by powerful men worked to extend the metaphor of illicit consumption into the more charged realm of sexuality."

Many aspects of this story resonate with the Cameroonian examples above: the crucial role of a newspaper eager to raise its sales though reporting on rumors about homosexual debauchery, the attack on prominent people, and the growing public indignation. However, there are also cardinal differences, the main one being that UAA's scandal—some seven years before the moral panic in Cameroon—did not lead to a similar intensification of homophobia. In both cases, the socioeconomic context may have been marked by a general feeling of intensifying crisis and a concomitant resentment of the government, and there was a similar tendency to relate the elite's shocking enrichment to illicit sexual practices. People's moral indignation in Ivory Coast did also serve as a gauge of their anger about the ineffectiveness of the Bédié regime and the corruption of his "barons." But this did not lead to an outing of prominent homosexuals as in Cameroon or to making homosexuality a major public issue. Indeed, as Corey-Boulet (2019, 126) concludes in his chapters on Ivory Coast, it is not even clear that the affair created an antigay climate there, its main actor UAA being depicted instead as a victim of a pedophile.

Several factors can explain such differences. First is that homosexuality was never explicitly criminalized in Ivory Coast, since Houphouët-Boigny did not take the step Ahidjo took with his 1972 decree. Another difference, possibly related, was that after independence (in 1960) there was more space for alternative sexualities than in Cameroon. The short-lived Ivorian "miracle" is also of importance. Especially in the 1960s, Ivory Coast—earlier more or less a backwater of French West Africa—experienced a spectacular boom through the rapid expansion of cacao cultivation throughout the southern forest zone (which was until then quite sparsely populated). In only a few years Abidjan grew from a relatively small town to one of the continent's most booming cities. In 1977, Claudine Vidal characterized this rapid modernization process as a *guerre des sexes* (war of the sexes). The booming economy allowed for a fairly abrupt emergence of new consumption patterns. Vidal showed that people adapted quickly, leading to a celebration of new forms of consumerism. It is during this period that Ivorians' reputation—for both women and men—for being well dressed and "modern" was established.[33] Over the course of the 1980s, the emergent crisis due to the collapse of cash-crop prices and the drama of structural adjustment added an increasing nervousness, but the admiration for showy performances remained.

In such a climate a hairstylist from Mali could, for instance, organize in 1978 a drag show in Abidjan that became such a hit that he could open a small cabaret where he and his costars regularly performed (Nguyen 2010). At the time the main concern was not whether they were homosexual (or not); it was the glitter that counted. Still, in 1994, when the same tabloid that started the *affaire pédophilie* by publishing UAA's complaints wrote a nasty article about a "transvestite meeting," these transvestites assaulted the newspaper's office and manhandled several of its journalists, without being bothered by the police. The contrast with Cameroon should certainly not suggest an image of a free-for-all space. The reactions to the *affaire pédophilie*, quoted above, showed that in Ivory Coast the tide was also turning. If the reception of Oswald's cross-dressing cabaret after 1978 was already mixed—appreciation of the glittery performance, but unease about the gender confusion—then reactions to UAA and his shocking denunciations became increasingly stern. Initially UAA may have been seen as an innocent child victim, but increasingly he was resented as a lascivious gay. When Corey-Boulet asked people in Abidjan in 2014 about the 1994 event several of them said that things had changed since then; now UAA would have evoked more homophobic reactions (2019, 128). Still, in 2019 the fifth annual "Miss Woubi" pageant—*Woubi* is the local term for effeminate gays—was once again a success, this time again "supervised by the police to make sure everyone would be safe" (Corey-Boulet 2019, 133). People's pride in Abidjan as one of Africa's most modern cities still created at least some space for experimental forms of sexuality.

Another element missing in the story above—and one that is central for our analysis—is Freemasonry. UAA's wild accusations confirmed a general suspicion that predatory sexual behavior by big men was part of a general drive toward illicit enrichment. But people did not make an explicit link with Freemasonry or other secret associations. This is striking since Freemasonry has a long history and a strong presence in Ivory Coast—at least as long as in Cameroon.[34] Yet, until recently, the association with same-sex practices—so central to the moral panic about homosexuality in Cameroon and Gabon—did not play a major role in Ivory Coast. A common element is the staunch opposition of the Catholic Church to Freemasonry. In 2015, for instance, Monseigneur Jean-Pierre Kutwa, the archbishop of Abidjan, created a shock by announcing that Clotaire Magloire Coffie, a well-known representative of Freemasonry in the country who had just died, could not get a Christian burial; henceforth the Church would refuse the last sacrament to any Freemason. But Monseigneur did not evoke the kind of sexual initiation rituals perverting the nation's youth that made the Christmas sermon ten years earlier of Monseigneur Bakot, the Yaoundé archbishop, create such a stir in Cameroon.[35]

Another important factor is the difference in years. The *affaire pédophilie* in Ivory Coast emerged in 1998; Monseigneur Bakot's Christmas speech and the consecutive *affaire des listes* in Cameroon followed only seven years later. But access to the internet became quite abruptly available in the meantime, and we have seen already in the comments of the *nkoandengué* of Yaoundé how important the internet had been for the discovery of "homosexuality"—for themselves but also for their opponents. As several of Corey-Boulet's spokesmen in Ivory Coast emphasized in 2014 when they were reflecting on events from the end of the last century: "In those days we didn't see many homosexuals. . . . like we do today" (Corey-Boulet 2019, 129). And indeed, in a more recent scandal in Ivory Coast all the elements that gave events in Cameroon such an explosive charge did come together. But the outcry it created still had a different charge.

On August 11, 2019, Ivorian pop-star DJ Arafat had a motorcycle accident in Abidjan; he died the next day in hospital. His many, many fans, both in Ivory Coast and all over the world, were overcome with grief. DJ Arafat—he loved that nickname, given to him by some Lebanese friends in Ivory Coast—had grown into an international star. After his death he was hailed by the *Guardian* as "the king of *coupé-décalé*," the latest musical craze in Ivory Coast and West Africa. Many *Chinois*—as he called his Ivorian fans—refused to believe he was dead. There was a huge farewell concert, but his family chose to bury him in private. Then his fans rushed the entrance to the cemetery, opened the coffin, and even tried to undress the corpse. Several of them were arrested by the police.[36]

Afterward the unrest did not die down, and this time many people did make a link to Freemasonry. For many the link was obvious since DJ Arafat had become quite close to one of the *Grands* of the Ouattara regime, Hamed Bakayoko, at the time minister of defense, who was known to hint in public about his important role in Freemasonry. Bakayoko played a prominent role at DJ Arafat's funeral, priding himself on being the deceased's mentor. This further aggravated the suspicions of the *Chinois*. One of the reasons that they insisted on opening the coffin was that many believed it to be empty since Bakayoko would have "sacrificed" his mentee.

A few days later, a woman who called herself *la servante de Dieu* attracted a lot of interest on the internet by declaring that she had spoken to DJ Arafat in her dreams and that he had killed himself. The reason was that his mentor (she did not mention a name but referred to *l'affection* and *l'amour* between the two men) had obliged him to join the Freemasons and offer a relative for his initiation.[37] A long lecture (almost two hours) by Professor Franklin Nyamsi—philosopher at the University of Rouen (France), originally from Cameroon but considers Ivory Coast his second country—also circulated on the internet in which he let loose a whole spectrum of mystical allusions about a Masonic conspiracy, well known in Cameroon since the 1990s, but now in relation to the Arafat affair in Ivory Coast: black masses in which body parts of innocent victims were used to "armor" politicians in their insatiable thirst for power, deviant sexual practices, and so on. Nyamsi especially focused on Arafat's intimate link with Minister Hamed Bakayoko, seen as an icon of Ivorian Freemasonry who had also served as the grand master of the Grande Loge de Côte d'Ivoire (GLCI) at the time of Arafat's death.[38] In this case all the elements are there: popular discontent about illicit enrichment by the elite, Freemasonry, and (though rather weakly) rumors about deviant sexuality. Cameroon seems to serve here as some sort of regional model. Yet, until now, this mixture has not triggered a moral panic in Ivory Coast comparable to the 2005/6 events in Cameroon.

So, the question remains: Why did this link become so powerful in Cameroon? The Ivory Coast case suggests that contingencies of time and coevality play an important role in this. We will return to this, but first some further comparisons may help to outline different trajectories in this linking of transgressive sexualities to illicit enrichment through secret societies that seems to be an emerging theme on the African continent.

SENEGAL

Another obvious country for comparison is Senegal. As in Cameroon homosexuality became explicitly criminalized here after independence (in 1966), but this had few concrete effects. Freemasonry had a much longer history compared to in Cameroon (the first Senegalese lodge was founded in Saint Louis in 1781), yet popular concern about Freemasonry being active in national politics manifested itself only recently. When Abdoulaye Wade became president in 2000 (after long years in opposition) his supposed adherence to Freemasonry did become a political issue. In 2009, Wade chose to formally deny such rumors, declaring that he had been initiated in 1959 when studying in Besançon but soon after chose to leave the Masonic brotherhood.[39] This public denial showed how detrimental any association with the Masons had become since then. Indeed, in the next elections in 2012 when Wade was beaten by Macky Sall rumors circulated about both candidates being affiliated with the brotherhood. Equally typical was that for both of them such rumors linked this affiliation to their supposed tolerance of homosexuality, but there were no rumors about them being involved in same-sex practices themselves.[40]

In those same years homosexuality did become a highly politicized issue in Senegal as well. This came as a surprise to many observers since, ever since colonial times, the country—and especially the two main cities Dakar and Saint Louis—had acquired a reputation of license for same-sex practices that was exceptional for West Africa (see Gorer 1935). A focal figure in this respect was the *goorjigeen* (literally, "man-woman") who played a conspicuous role in the culture of the Wolof (the largest group in Senegal) through their more or less refined behavior during rituals and other meetings—often mentioned as proof of a "traditional" tolerance for homosexuality in Senegalese society.[41] In Senegal the turning point in this respect came a few years later than in Cameroon. The well-known urban ethnographer Tshikala Keyembe Biaya, a Congolese who came to live in Dakar in the 1990s, noted that around that time homosexual lifestyles became much more visible in everyday life (Biaya 2001). But it was only in 2008 that this became an issue when newspaper *Icône* published a picture of a party that was supposed to be a gay wedding. People identifying as gay began to complain of increasing police harassment, but the police has not yet proceeded to a prosecution, as in Cameroon. The initiative in Senegal came instead from Muslim spokesmen, both from the Sufi brotherhoods that play such a dominant role in Senegalese politics and society and from the more orthodox Salafists who have been on the rise since the beginning of the twenty-first century. The great difference with Cameroon is that neither the politicians nor these religious leaders are themselves targeted by popular anger about a supposed proliferation of homosexuality undermining the nation.[42]

For Senegal we have an excellent thesis by Ndeye Ndiagna Gning (2013), who through a very sensitive ethnography shows the other side of the coin: the views of those who practice same-sex intercourse. The great merit of her thesis is that she refuses fixed categories by consequently referring to *hommes aux identités sexuelles multiples* (men with multiple sexual identities). She uses Western terms like "homosexual" when her spokesmen use them but also highlights the subtle ways in which they mix local categories and such "modern" notions. This helps her to come very close to people's everyday experiences. Her ethnography vividly conveys the strong attractions that the emerging gay scene has even for men living in more or less stable heterosexual relationships—not just the desire for a same-sex partner but also the pleasure of getting dressed in a tantalizing way, the *soirées sénégalaises* in the night clubs, dancing and singing with their friends. Yet Gning's ethnography similarly highlights all the hesitations and dangers of joining such an alternative scene.

Relevant for our topic are in particular the special ways in which she relates this lively scene to promises of access to power and riches—in Senegal as well (Gning 2013, 135, 163–85). A direct link is through profiting from possibilities for prostitution with expatriate tourists as well as with Senegalese clients. Gning's main explanation for the growing visibility of homosexuality is, indeed, the ever-sharpening economic crisis that forces people to make money in all sorts of ways. But she notes wider material considerations as well, such as the idea that the gay scene provides access to modern ways of life and to contacts in the outside world. Gning notes also enticements that have a local background. Several of her informants tell her that as visibly gay men they have been occasionally approached by men who are completely outside their circle but turn out to be looking for another man to have sex with. Asked why, these men will explain that their *marabout* (Islamic saint) has told them they must have intercourse with another man to magically protect their riches.[43] Gning shows also that this "mystical" belief has a long history, quoting a manual from a Damascus *ulema* from the 18th century (Abd-al-Ghani al-Nabulsi) who gave similar prescriptions for those who want to have their success in life guaranteed.[44]

The broader relevance of such more or less hidden transgressions is that they show that Islam also has ambiguities in relation to same-sex arrangements. It is not superfluous to emphasize this in the Senegalese context because of the all-overriding role Muslim spokesmen came to play in the intensification of homophobia around 2008. Jamra, an Islamic NGO founded in 1982 and initially mainly active in the battle against AIDS, has been very vocal in its warnings against a proliferation of homosexuality, seeing this as an increasing danger for the Senegalese nation and its culture.[45] Other Islamic leaders joined the chorus, criticizing the government for not taking the threat seriously enough. However, in all three key events in the rise of homophobia in the country—the just mentioned 2008 publication of a picture of a gay wedding by *Icône*; the 2009 arrest of nine AIDS activists accused to be gay; and the 2008/9 digging up of the bodies of several *goorjigeen* who had been buried in Islamic graveyards and were supposed to "desecrate" the place—the Muslim activists did not implicate leading politicians in person in their attacks. And there was no mention whatsoever of Freemasonry playing a special role. Gning—who did field work in 2013—does not even mention the Masons.

However, times are changing. In 2018, Cheikh Oumar Diagne publicly summoned the government to block a visit of popstar Rihanna to Senegal. According to him "everybody" knew that she was a member of the Illuminati, who according to the cheikh are "a branch of Freemasonry," and "therefore" Rihanna was sure to use her visit for propagating homosexuality.[46] In the same year, Islamic leaders—notably the new vice president of Jamra, Mama Moctar Guèye—started a vociferous protest against a proposed REHFRAM meeting in Dakar. As mentioned in chapter 2, these REHFRAM meetings are one of the high points for Freemasonry in Africa. Interestingly the protests against the Dakar meeting—notably by the Jamra spokesmen—targeted not Freemasonry in general but explicitly the Grand Orient de France, the mother lodge of most African lodges and the patron of the REHFRAM network. Islamic spokesmen denounced the Grand Orient for its atheism, associating it with homosexuality in the same breath.[47] The protests became so loud that the *préfet* of Dakar forbade the meeting. When the *grand maître* of the Grand Orient in France together with the local lodges protested that this had never happened before, the government intervened and cancelled the interdiction by the Dakar *préfet*. But the meeting did not take place, for fear of repercussions.[48]

So the circle is closing itself in Senegal as well. Freemasonry and homosexuality are ever more associated, but, strikingly, not in terms of a criticism about elite consumerism as in Cameroon. In Senegal the attack is mainly in terms of religion—as can only be expected in view of the increasing Islamization of Senegalese society and politics. The association of same-sex practices and enrichment is certainly present but does not focus on the political elite. The ambiguity of Islam in both respects is also striking. The radical condemnation of sexual transgression is balanced by mystical beliefs encouraging alternative forms of intercourse as magical protection. And long-time peaceful coexistence of Islam with Freemasonry could suddenly switch to an outright attack.

SIMILAR ISSUES ELSEWHERE

Further comparison would be most interesting for tracing factors that lead to different trajectories. We previously referred to the Democratic Republic of the Congo, where the triangle of Freemasonry, transgressive sexualities, and success comes starkly to the fore in the wild world of popular music. Inside francophone Africa the case of Congo-Brazzaville is also of particular interest since Freemasonry there has developed into a major force since the spectacular return of Sassou Ngouesso as president (see chapter 2). Unfortunately very little has been published about same-sex practices or homosexuality in this country.[49]

In chapter 2 we also addressed differences with most anglophone countries, where Freemasonry seemed to be less directly involved in political battles, having more the profile of a business network. Neither was it directly associated with same-sex practices. This is striking since there is certainly a tendency in anglophone countries to link same-sex practices to illicit enrichment and empowerment. Many examples from Nigeria can be cited. In 1988 *Quality*, a Nigerian magazine, warned its readers in these terms:

> They [the homosexuals] are getting more and more aggressive and courageous by the day and are made up of the top brass in the society— successful lawyers, doctors, swanky businessmen, military men, ex-politicians, diplomats, and university graduates—all with a passion for men. . . . One bizarre yet interesting feature of homosexuality in the country is that it is cult-oriented and is making millionaires out of those who belong. . . . After every love session, *Quality* learnt, the big shots who normally play the aggressor role rush home keeping mum. At home they wash with some charms in a bowl and perform a ceremony. . . . its success is said to bring about a windfall of money.[50]

During the same years, the brutal military dictatorship of Ibrahim Badamosi Babaginda between 1985 and 1993 was described as "a homosexual circle." When on April 22, 1990, a group of young officers from middle and southern Nigeria attempted a coup against Babangida (a Fulani from the Muslim North), the leader of these young officers, Major Gideon Orkar, justified their action by complaining that Babanginda's regime was "dictatorial, corrupt, drug baronish, inhuman, sadistic, deceitful, *homosexual-centred*" (Omoigui, n.d., our emphasis).[51] In these Nigerian examples people seem to take it for granted that these celebrities take on the "active" role in order to further empower themselves.[52]

The perceptions of same-sex practices in Liberia are also most intriguing in this respect. In his chapters on this country, Corey-Boulet (2019, 203) gives a subtle overview of the oral history on the long-time existence of a gay scene under the old regime of the Americano-Liberian elite, also with the by-now-familiar emphasis on it providing special access to circuits of power and money. The civil war brought a cruel end to this, most of the warlords having "homosexuals" beaten up or killed on the spot. But peace and a return of a formal democracy after 2003 brought new challenges, in the form of a most aggressive religious offensive against LGBTQ people—not directly supported by American missionaries as in Uganda, but hardly less aggressive (see Corey-Boulet 2019, 230ff.; Currier and Cruz 2016). Yet Corey-Boulet's interviews show that here as well people identifying as gay or queer did find their own niche in everyday life, precarious as it may be. And again, there is the emphasis on links with well-to-do people. In chapter 2 we dwelt on the long history of Freemasonry in Liberia, its dramatic eclipse after Sergeant Doe's coup in 1980, and its spectacular return in national politics after 2003. Many of the "well-to-do people" referred to by Corey-Boulet's interlocutors must be in the brotherhood. But there is no trace of his interlocutors assuming an intrinsic link between Freemasonry and same-sex practices, as in Cameroon. Similarly striking is that one of the most notorious figures in the Liberian civil war, Charles Taylor, began a determined offensive against homosexuality when he was officially installed as the country's president (1997–2003).[53] Taylor was equally negative about Freemasonry. During his later trial before the Sierra Leonean court in 2009 he made light of allowing his troops to exhibit human heads and skulls of enemies at checkpoints, saying it was no worse than the display of skulls in Western fraternal organizations, clearly referring to Freemason rituals. But there is no indication that he tried to bring his homophobia and his anti-Masonism together—a link that in subsequent years seems to have become increasingly obvious to many in francophone Africa.

Can we distinguish certain recurrent patterns in this quite motley enumeration of situations in which the association of illicit enrichment, secret associations, and anal penetration emerges?[54] The theme seems to be common in all these cases, but its impact in everyday life follows different trajectories. Apparently the timing of the internet becoming more generally available plays a role (remember the difference between developments in Ivory Coast and Cameroon, where similar scandals emerged but, respectively, before and after access to the internet became more general). Religion is another factor (think of the particularly strong role of Islamic and Pentecostal fundamentalism in Senegal and Nigeria). But there is also the varying way national leaders related to Freemasonry, directly affecting its role in politics. Remember also the different interpretations of Achille Mbembe and Joseph Tonda (see the introduction) of popular imaginaries around the anus as a focal point for enrichment. We will come back to all this in the conclusion. For now it may suffice to note that the comparison above does suggest different degrees of intensity. Clearly it is especially in Cameroon and Gabon that the link between anal penetration and illicit enrichment has visceral power to mobilize people's anger. How do we explain that in these countries in particular there occurred a "condensation"—to borrow a notion from Freud (*Verdichtung*) that is also used in the analysis of class and inequalities—of Freemasonry with people's preoccupation about alternative sexualities as a key to understanding illicit enrichment? The abruptness of this condensation is striking—it is only after 2000 that it took on the appearance of a full-fledged conspiracy theory, becoming so self-evident in both countries that it functions as an unassailable truth, confirming an idea of a conspiracy that corrupts politics and the nation. Below we will see that such an abrupt "click"—the revelation that different elements are "in reality" inherently linked—recurs in many conspiracy theories and can explain their visceral power. Can a more historical approach relativize this self-evidence and highlight special factors that explain this particular click? The question is worth exploring in view of the dramatic effects such condensation has had in recent times in Cameroon (as elsewhere). In the next two chapters we will look at historical trajectories that have given developments there a special twist. But first we want to include a brief interlude to signal interesting ways in which gender seems to affect the role of the internet in this context—notably for balancing access and secrecy.

Gender, Secrecy, and Access

In our introduction we regretted that our focus on the association of same-sex practices with Freemasonry and illicit enrichment in popular conspiracy narratives seemed to make a male-centered view inevitable. All over the world Freemasonry remains a masculine bulwark.[1] We also saw that the popular imaginary of the anus as a source of wealth in Cameroon, Gabon, and elsewhere in Africa is mainly about anal penetration between men. However, a series of recent studies focusing on everyday sexual arrangements between women in various parts of Africa offers interesting contrasts to our analysis in the preceding chapters.[2] Such contrasts can also help highlight intriguing points in our up-to-now male-centered analysis.

In the recent upsurge of studies of same-sex intimacies in Africa, female authors have had a prominent place.[3] Most of these studies focused understandably on human rights issues. But over the last few years several studies have come out based on sensitive ethnography of more hidden forms of intimate practices between women, who tend to shun the world of activism and projects. A striking difference with our analysis in the preceding chapters is the relative absence in these studies of access to the internet as a crucial moment. Remember the way spokesmen of the Yaoundé Eleven, arrested in 2005 during one of the first police raids against "homosexuals" in Cameroon, talked about their discovery of the internet as a turning point in their lives. Like our gay interlocutors, they remembered the opening of the internet for people at large—in these countries around 2000—as a revelation, making them realize that their private feelings were not that exceptional and answering questions they had never dared to pose to others (Corey-Boulet 2019, 53ff.). Internet cafes soon became gay meeting places. Such an obsession among gays with "connectivity" seemed to be related to a general idea that gay relations offer "access" (cf. chapter 3). Access to what often remains vague—wider networks? new opportunities for advancement?—yet such an expectation seemed to be a point of convergence between the widely different men that in Cameroon and elsewhere are brought together under the label "homosexual": both the so-called *Grands and* the marginal victims of the police raids are associated—by outsiders but also by themselves—with special forms of access. We concluded also that people's increasing entry to the internet created the historical context in which recent homophobic panics could acquire momentum in Africa.

Such a preoccupation with access to the internet as an opening up to wider horizons seems to be less present in the studies of everyday sexual intimacies between women quoted above. Of course this should certainly not suggest that women are less active on the internet,[4] but it might point to different accents in relating to publicity and secrecy—or at least discretion. A factor might be that public space is perceived as dominated by men.[5] The reverse, domestic space as a primarily female space, might allow for special forms of conviviality. Serena Dankwa's fascinating *Knowing Women: Same-Sex Intimacy, Gender, and Identity in Postcolonial Ghana* (2022) offers vivid examples of this. In her extraordinarily subtle monograph, building on sensitive ethnography and considerable theoretical sophistication, she sets out to explore "the oceanic fluidity of same-sex intimacy" (36) among Ghanaian women of varying backgrounds. Her book is a plea for "freeing our imagination by refusing prescribed categories" (43), and thus she focuses in her research on same-sex intimacies, "not captured by the language of sexual identity"—that is, on women staying out of the activist scene, who refuse (or at least "re-signify") the international LGBTQ language. Dankwa notes that the dominant focus in queer studies on processes of coming out and the metaphorical closet is hardly relevant for women in Ghana who have no private closets or bedrooms—indeed, throughout the book Dankwa manages to maintain an admirable balance between feelings and material circumstances. Her women manage special discretion that allows for forms of conviviality of heterosexual and homosexual intimacies (in some cases a woman lives with both her male husband and her female lover in one family house, the lover helping with running the household and looking after the children).

This does not mean that hierarchy and exploitation are absent from these relations. On the contrary, in Dankwa's chapter 4 on liaisons between "sugar mommies" (that is, rich market women) and their "little girls" (who often boast of their butch role in bed), domination and exploitation are central issues, in some respects reminiscent of the Cameroonian *Grands*. Possibilities for enrichment are most present here. But these are not directly linked to politics or the state as is implied by the association of "the homosexual" with Freemasonry in Cameroon and Gabon. Of course an important factor is that the political sphere remains dominated by men: powerful as rich market women may be in many African countries, they are not associated with secret networks of a scope that Freemasonry or other global associations are supposed to add to gay "connectivity." The Ghanaian world of "same-sex desiring women" (to follow Dankwa's careful terminology) seems to be more turned into itself.[6]

Further comparative research is needed to check whether such differences also emerge in other contexts. Directly relevant for our research is in any case the seminal view on secrecy and discretion that Rachel Spronk deduced from such special aspects of everyday intimacy between women in African contexts.[7] In line with Dankwa's doubts about what "coming out of the closet" might mean for African women, Spronk advocates another view of secrecy—not as an obstacle for openness and self-identification but as enabling and productive of protected spaces that can provide special possibilities for women for experimenting with different forms of sex.[8]

Of course such differences between the world of male and female same-sex intimacies are at most diverging tendencies, certainly not radical contrasts. The gay men figuring in the preceding chapters on Cameroon and Gabon practice their own kinds of secrecy. Similarly, there are many examples of African women proudly acting as "lesbo" or "trans," with ostentatious and often highly public displays.[9] Yet the promise of special access, as an opening to the world, that quite strongly emerged from our research on gay men in West-Central Africa seems to make for a different balancing of ostentation and secrecy. The very idea of same-sex contacts as a form of networking, linking the local to new forms of globalization, makes the supposed proliferation of male homosexuality easily associated with international configurations that can outline a promise of new openings but also of threatening conspiracies.

This quick comparison is no more than a first sketch. Yet it highlights the interest of gaining deeper insights into the different things secrecy can mean. It can also bring out the special contours of a central topic in our research: people's preoccupation—both negative and positive—with the special access anal intercourse can bring.

The Return of Dr. Aujoulat

DECOLONIZATION AND THE GENEALOGY
OF A HOMO-MASONIC COMPLEX

The present-day state of Cameroon is the product of special processes of colonization that produced a particularly tormented decolonization. Colonial rule was multiple: it was first conquered by the Germans, but after the First World War it was divided between France and England, each ruling their part as a mandated territory for the League of Nations. This mandated status inspired the UPC (Union des populations du Cameroun), an exceptionally militant nationalist movement in the African context, to claim full independence already at the end of the 1940s, appealing directly to the UN to end France's and Britain's mandates. France launched a harsh struggle to sidetrack these militant nationalists and create a more "cooperative" elite, willing to keep the colony inside the community of *France-Afrique*. Thus, the decolonization of French Cameroon became a particularly violent process. This chapter will show that the scars of this decolonization—going back to the idea, so dear to de Gaulle, that the French colonies should be retained as a *pré carré* for France's interests even when independence had become inevitable—contributed directly to the "homo- Masonic" complex that marks Cameroonian politics today. The durability of coloniality remains an important theme of current social analyses.[1] Ongoing struggles to emerge from what Achille Mbembe (2010) calls "the dark night" invest the term decolonization with variable meanings. We contribute to these discussions by examining the role of rumors about Freemasonry and homosexuality as a direct expression of these struggles.

In this chapter we focus on the enigmatic figure of Dr. Aujoulat, a medical doctor who played a key role in Cameroon's decolonization between 1945 and 1970 but who made also an unexpected return as a "homo-Masonic" figure (Nyeck 2016) in the rapidly intensifying rumormongering on elite depravedness during the moral panic haunting the country after 2005. As said the rumormongering on Aujoulat—slippery as rumors are—can be followed over a fairly long period, and of particular interest is that there is a decisive turn in it that can be precisely dated. During the heyday of one-party rule, Ahidjo, Cameroon's first president after independence (1960), did everything to erase the memory of the UPC nationalists, but then Aujoulat became the main target of UPC proponents in exile. They depicted Ahidjo as Aujoulat's lackey, created by the latter in order to retain Cameroon for *France-Afrique*. In the 1990s Aujoulat was almost forgotten. However, after 2000 he made a spectacular comeback, now as the "homo-Masonic" guru who would have "corrupted"—"sodomized"—the young men who were to become the country's political elite. Thus he became the linchpin in a historical conspiracy narrative, supposedly still corrupting the nation and, moreover, responsible for the proliferation of homosexuality in the country. These new accusations attracted great attention, placing Aujoulat again in the center of public notice. The challenge for this chapter is to follow this surprising trajectory and to understand in what context his "return" took place. Why did this new version of *anti-Aujoulatisme* have such public appeal?

The deeper importance of these rumors for understanding the present-day preoccupation with a homo-Masonic conspiracy may be clear. As said, Freemasonry is a colonial imposition, and putting the blame on Aujoulat and his more or less secret networks confirmed the idea, widespread in present-day Africa, that homosexuality is a colonial implant, unknown in "traditional" Africa. The idea of a "homosexual pact" links Aujoulat not only to Ahidjo, but also to the latter's successor Biya, the current president. This supposed "pact" is often cited as an explanation of Ahidjo's enigmatic choice of Paul Biya as his successor in 1982: it would have been Aujoulat who had earlier on forced Ahidjo to take Biya as his close collaborator.[2] Moreover, Ahidjo would have only selected Biya as his successor after concluding another "homosexual pact" that would ensure the latter's loyalty. In these images Freemasonry is added as some sort of inevitable afterthought. This idea of an occult "pact" has become a recurrent motif in Cameroonian politics, sometimes referred to as *fidelisation* (bondage) or *faire partie de la mutuelle* (literally, "belonging to the association").[3] It is also linked to the implantation of Freemasonry in Cameroon, in which Dr. Aujoulat would have played a key role. As S. N. Nyeck (2016) remarks, the popularization of rumors about him constitute "a political narrative" intended to underline not only that homosexuality is of European provenance and therefore "un-African" but also to highlight that the Cameroonian state was born through a masonic regime of neocolonial dependency that lasts to this day. It is against this background that people explain Biya's quest for spiritual empowerment from one occult source to the next one—his "spiritual pluralism" already mentioned—by relating it to his guilt about betraying Ahidjo and his morbid feelings of insecurity after the 1984 coup, staged by his former mentor. It is also since the 1980s that the omnipresence of Freemasonry and Rosicrucianism in higher circles has become ever more noted, triggering increasing rumors about same-sex practices as a ritual for empowerment and enrichment.

We will first address the role of Aujoulat in the decolonization of Cameroon. How could this medical doctor assume such a pivotal role? The painful course this process took in Cameroon can only be understood against the wider background of the particularities of the French conception of decolonization, with de Gaulle and his *Monsieur Afrique* Jacques Foccart as key figures. Then we will address the way this past still marks popular conceptions of the "homo-Masonic" complex around President Biya and his companions. Relating the strong current of homophobia throughout Cameroonian society in the present day to de Gaulle's dream of retaining the African colonies within a *France-Afrique* network may seem an audacious step. However, as we've noted, it is important to place homophobia—like homosexuality—in a longer historical perspective. Avoiding the tendency to see both as some sort of natural givens requires understanding the varying trajectories of the "politicization" of these issues with due attention to historical particularities.

Dr. Aujoulat: Rumors and Facts

The turmoil of rumors around Aujoulat might best be addressed by first trying to introduce some undisputed facts about this historical figure. Louis-Paul Aujoulat came to Cameroon in 1935, at the age of twenty-five. He had spent most of his youth in Algeria, where his father worked as a teacher. Later he studied medicine at the Catholic University of Lille, where he developed a strong missionary interest, becoming president of the Ligue missionaire des étudiants en France. Later he co-founded—together with abbot Prévost, then his spiritual mentor—AD LUCEM (Association des laics universitaires et chrétiens missionnaires), aiming to animate the mission's social work by focusing healthcare and involving laymen to complement the clergy's activities. In 1935 Aujoulat made a first trip to Cameroon, which also included a detour to visit Dr. Albert Schweitzer in the latter's hospital in Lambarene (Gabon), then already a sort of pilgrims' place for European humanitarians. In his report on this

FIGURE 4.1. After 2000, the "return" of Dr. Louis-Paul Aujoulat confirmed the popular association of the Cameroonian elite with a supposed proliferation of homosexuality. In the 1950s Aujoulat played a key role in creating a cooperative elite, keeping Cameroon inside the French *pré-carré* in Africa. Almost forgotten, he made a surprising comeback in popular pamphlets after 2000 for having allegedly submitted "his" young men, the nation's future leaders, to a "homosexual pact." Courtesy of the Bibliothèque nationale de France.

trip Aujoulat expressed alarm at the sad state of healthcare for the local population in Cameroon. In 1936, just married and this time accompanied by his wife, he left for Cameroon for a longer stay, applying AD LUCEM ideas in a hospital he founded in Efok (36 kilometers from Yaoundé). As in his later projects he closely collaborated with the Catholic Church, while he emphasized at the same time the need to give priority to local needs and, again, to have laymen play their own role next to the clergy.

After 1946 he embarked on a political career, becoming deputy for Cameroon in the French National Assembly—first in the seat representing French citizens in Cameroon, but in 1951 successfully running for the seat that was created to represent Cameroonians (that is, for the small group that was entitled to vote at the time). His spectacular success in marshalling the African vote during this election earned him—especially in Catholic circles—the nickname of *Aujoulat l'Africain*. Moreover, he held the position of secretary of state for France's *Outre-Mer* (Overseas) Territories and other ministerial positions in various French cabinets between 1949 and 1955. He combined these key positions with his seat as deputy in the consecutive representative Assemblies that were created in Cameroon after 1946.[4] However, in 1954, he was outvoted as chair of Cameroon's Assemblée and replaced by a Cameroonian politician, Soppo Priso. But the final blow to his political career came in 1956, when he was beaten in the next elections for the Cameroonian seat in the French National Assembly by his former protégé, André Mbida. Clearly the days of *Aujoulat l'Africain* were over and Cameroonian voters wanted to be represented by their own people. Aujoulat then retired from parliamentary politics, still holding various positions at the World Health Organization until his death in 1973. Yet even after his formal retirement from Cameroonian politics he remained a highly influential person through his close links among the emerging Cameroonian elite, both during their study days in France and after their return to Cameroon.[5] Indeed, the two successive presidents after independence (1960)—first Ahmadou Ahidjo and then Paul Biya— were seen as his creatures, having been closely tutored by Aujoulat during the 1950s, at crucial moments of their careers.

While there had been appreciation in Cameroon for Aujoulat's medical work, his postwar involvement with politics rapidly made him a controversial figure. He came under increasing attack because of his untiring efforts to shape what he called a "responsible" elite willing to work with the French toward increasing autonomy for the colonies, independence remaining a forbidden word for him until far into the 1950s. His views were deeply influenced by the vision General De Gaulle articulated at the 1944 Brazzaville conference, also meant as a recognition of the crucial role French Equatorial Africa in particular had played in the consolidation of de Gaulle's *France Libre* during critical moments in 1940. For the general this meant a deep and lasting attachment to France's African colonies, inspiring consequent efforts to retain a special bond also later on, when the global context made some form of decolonization inevitable. Identifying "cooperative" elites was crucial for this.[6]

Some more history might be helpful here in order to understand why these African colonies—and notably Equatorial Africa and Cameroon— played such a large role in de Gaulle's vision of the future of the French empire and France itself; this gave the French way of doing decolonization special traits. Earlier (chapter 1) we referred to the painful Vichy intermezzo in France's history: the national hero Maréchal Philippe

Pétain accepting defeat after Hitler's Blitzkrieg in May/June 1940 and opting for an armistice that allowed him to be installed as the president of a puppet regime in Vichy in the hope that collaborating with the Germans would give him scope for reconstructing France in line with his staunchly Catholic and conservative ideas. However, General Charles de Gaulle—who, like Pétain, had distinguished himself at the 1917 Verdun battle that sealed France's victory during the First World War—proudly refused the armistice and any form of collaboration with the Germans. He managed to escape to England and announced himself as leader of *La France Libre*. Hard-pressed to convince his British allies that this idea of a "Free France" was not just an illusion, he sent out envoys to all parts of the French empire to marshal support (Muracciole 1996). They found a willing ear in French Equatorial Africa (until then a relatively backward part of the French empire, certainly next to French Ouest Africa, where most governors remained staunchly pro-Vichy).

In Equatorial Africa it was especially Félix Éboué, then governor of Chad, who showed himself willing to side with de Gaulle. The fact that Éboué was the first black governor in the French empire gave his support particular meaning, and so did the fact that Chad was the only remaining part of the French empire that had a common border with an enemy country—the Italian colony of Libya. However, Chad was a land-locked territory, and this made a foothold in Cameroon crucial for giving Free France forces access to this "liberated" part of the French empire, allowing them to invade enemy territory on their own account. In early August 1940 Philippe Leclerc (who had escaped from a German prisoner camp and joined de Gaulle in London) travelled to Nigeria, where he promoted himself to colonel in order to impress the British authorities. From there he left with only a handful of soldiers for Cameroon, took a boat from Tiko (some 50 kilometers west of Douala), and landed on the foggy morning of August 27 at the port of Douala. Despite his small numbers he succeeded in winning over the French settlers in the city and took the train to Yaoundé, where he was received by the high commissioner for Cameroon, Richard Brunot, who had already been discharged by Pétain, probably because of doubts about Brunot's loyalty to Vichy. This made Brunot all the more ready to side with Leclerc. A pro-Vichy newspaper brought the news of Brunot's defection with the typical comment that the latter was both a socialist and a Freemason.[7]

In the next few days, Chad, Oubangui-Chari, and Congo also sided officially with de Gaulle, to his great relief. Indeed, it was only then that Free France could claim a territorial presence on the world map. Afterward August 27, 28, and 29, 1940, became known as *les trois glorieuses* (the

FIGURE 4.2. The memorial for General Leclerc in Douala still celebrates the crucial role Cameroon played in 1940 in the consolidation of General de Gaulle's Free France after France's disastrous defeat against Hitler in 1940.
Photo: Rogers Orock.

glorious three) in Gaullist historiography. After the French authorities in Gabon, who remained staunchly pro-Vichy, had been beaten by Leclerc (November 1940), Equatorial Africa acquired a pivotal position in the re-establishment of the French state. From Chad, Leclerc led the Free French troops in 1941 to attack Italian troops in Libya. After the conquest of the Koufra oasis in the Fezzan region he made his soldiers swear the "Koufra pledge," which became another icon in French military tradition—to never lay down their arms until the French flag was raised again over the Strasbourg cathedral.[8] By the end of 1942, from Koufra he could join the allied forces in their combat with German troops in North Africa. And with the agreement of General Eisenhower (Eisenhower was about the only American military leader who took de Gaulle seriously) Leclerq's battalion was allowed to have pride of place in the liberation of Paris. One can understand that Equatorial Africa's key role in the final apotheosis of the Free France vision made francophone Africa particularly dear to de Gaulle.

Aujoulat and the Dream of a *Françafrique*[9]

Some Africanist historians, especially those oriented toward archival study, have severe doubts about the utility of the *Françafrique* notion and its reality on the ground. Indeed, this assemblage consisted—and still consists—of nebulous networks between French and African elites that never acquired any formal existence. Moreover, it is true that these links—as is the case for most networks—were marked by deep ambiguities and surprising turns. But as fluid as they may be, these networks continue to be vital for understanding our central theme, the popular preoccupation in present-day Cameroon with the intertwinement of Freemasonry, illicit enrichment, and transgressive sexual practices. This *Françafrique* as a nebulous but resistant assemblage developed out of the paradox, noted above, that was to mark French-style decolonization: grudgingly accepting independence of its colonies as inevitable in the changing global context, yet working hard—regardless of whether the Right or the Left is in power in Paris—to maintain a *pré carré* for France in Africa. This paradox still haunts the relations between rulers and their people after independence in the continent's francophone countries.

As mentioned in chapter 2, Jacques Foccart, de Gaulle's *Monsieur Afrique*, is generally seen as the main architect of this imposing and yet elusive assemblage. The personal network he built with a motley collection of upcoming politicians and businessmen from the emerging nation-states in French Africa is still proverbial. Foccart himself simply denied that such a network existed.[10] Yet a recurrent theme in journalistic articles is the image of his crammed study—nicknamed *la case à fétiches*—in his villa in Luzarches, just outside Paris, that for most of the second half of the last century served as a political hub of Francophone Africa, where African heads of states regularly came to visit—to "confess" (to borrow Antoine Glaser's term)—and where Foccart was constantly on the phone with Africa (Smith and Glaser 1997, 10).[11]

Indeed, after de Gaulle's comeback in 1958 as the only leader who could handle the crisis about Algiers, he immediately appointed Foccart as his advisor for Africa, a formal position the latter would also keep under Pompidou, until 1974. He only lost it when Valéry Giscard d'Estaing became President, but he made a comeback as Africa advisor to Jacques Chirac when the latter became prime minister (1986) and subsequently president (1995). Foccart still had this position when he died in 1997. Even though after his discharge in 1974 the coherence of the network he had built weakened, he remained a central figure behind the scene of French-African relations. Since 1990, with archives opening up, he has become the subject of a whole series of academic and journalistic publications.[12]

After De Gaulle's forced abdication (1968), every newly installed French president felt obliged to proclaim the need to "reform" the nebulous *Françafrique* networks, lifting the veil of secrecy and cultivating greater transparency. This was, for instance, emphatically announced by the new socialist regime of President François Mitterrand when a socialist finally took over from right-wing governments in 1981. In practice, however, such brave intentions have had little effect—especially not with Mitterrand, who in line with his earlier politics clung to the tenets of *Françafrique*. Up until today, France continues to support heads of state like Paul Biya in Cameroon. This cloak of secrecy over this web of relations has the effect of fueling an all-pervasive climate of suspicion about French conspiracies everywhere in francophone Africa.[13]

Cameroon's Violent Decolonization

For Cameroon, keeping the country within a French *pré carré* soon proved to be a particularly difficult project. The vociferous claim of the UPC, beginning right after the end of the Second World War, for immediate and full independence risked undermining the French UN mandate over the territory. The French government reacted by branding the movement as "communist." Yet the charismatic UPC leader Ruben Um Nyobe succeeded in quickly mobilizing considerable support both inside the country and internationally. After increasing harassment the French officially dissolved the movement in 1955. Excluded from elections that were

FIGURE 4.3. A recent statue (2014) for Um Nyobe in Eseka, his homeland. To many Cameroonians, Um Nyobe, the secretary-general of the famous UPC (Union des populations du Cameroun), remains the true hero of independence. Photo: Brice Molo.

increasingly important for deciding on the ever more complicated French proposals for shaping a French union with limited autonomy for the colonies, Um Nyobe saw no other possibility than to start a guerrilla in the densely forested area between Douala and Yaoundé in 1956.

This determined marginalization of the UPC created a void for setting up some sort of political autonomy under French control. And it is by stepping in to fill this void that Louis-Paul Aujoulat came to play a crucial political role. In 1951 he founded his own party, the Bloc démocratique camerounais (BDC), mainly based in the region around Yaoundé where he had been active as a medical doctor (also a region marked by the strong presence of the Catholic mission). But, as said, Aujoulat spread his net wider, acting as a patron for Cameroonian students of diverse origin in France. He was ready to serve as their mentor but held them to a very strict program: they should *work* and not dabble in politics. It was in this context that Aujoulat became the patron of future leaders like Ahmadou Ahidjo and Paul Biya. Opponents, especially proponents of the UPC, saw Aujoulat, even after his departure from Cameroon (following his defeat in the 1956 elections), as the main architect behind the strenuous French effort to eliminate their movement and promote more moderate allies who were willing to work towards the idea of a *pré carré*.[14]

To understand the fierce hatred that many Cameroonians (particularly UPC supporters) nowadays still express in their attacks on Aujoulat, it is important to take into account the struggle of the colonial and postcolonial governments of the 1950s and 1960s against the UPC. Um Nyobe launched his guerilla movement only a little more than a year after Dien Bien Phu, the 1954 French debacle in Vietnam that seemed to spell the end of its colonial empire. In following years, the shocking harshness of the struggle in Algeria got ever more attention. This wider context is crucial to understand to what lengths the French military, but also French politicians (socialists as much as *Gaullistes*), were prepared to go in order to prevent another debacle. A recent study of the UPC war—the authors call it "a forgotten war at the origins of *Françafrique*"—by Thomas Deltombe, Manuel Domergue, and Jacob Tatsitsa (2011)[15] shows in full detail, through a careful analysis of the finally available relevant archives, the enormous investment French military leaders were prepared to make in order to quench this relatively small-scale conflict. This time a "revolutionary war"—a term they used to launch a mix of military and psychological violence, isolating the fighters by interning the rest of the population in camps and brainwashing them—*had* to work.[16] Um Nyobe's guerilla in the forest of Sanaga-Maritime was smothered in two years, but this required an amazing military effort in light of the relatively small group of fighters in the bush, who were moreover very badly armed.[17] On September 13, 1958, Um Nyobe was surprised by some soldiers when he was fleeing—his hiding place had been betrayed—and he was shot on the spot. A parallel UPC guerilla in the West Province among the Bamiléké resisted much longer. Their last military leader, Ernest Ouandié, was captured and executed only in 1970.

Little wonder, then, that Aujoulat became a favorite target for ideological attacks by all those who saw with increasing indignation that in Cameroon the French scenario for excluding the "real" nationalists seemed to succeed against all odds. He was and is still seen by many as the main architect— first openly, and after 1956 behind the scenes—of raising a neocolonial elite to step in to reap the fruits of the national struggle. His hospitality, often mentioned, for African students in his big house in Paris was ridiculed as the place where he held "court." Opponents were convinced that he decided scholarships for Cameroonians—who would get one and whose would be withdrawn. The despised cooperative elites were called *les Aujoulatistes* or even *les femmes des colons* (the colonials' wives), and the BDC, Aujoulat's party, was nicknamed *Bande des cons* (Band of assholes).[18]

A complicating factor was the surprising coup in 1958 by which the French catapulted Ahidjo into the seat of prime minister of the new autonomous government that was to lead the colony to independence. A lot has been written about this carnivalesque episode. The French authorities became increasingly embarrassed by the first prime minister they had installed in 1956, André Mbida (the former protégé of Aujoulat, just having beaten him in the elections for the French Assemblée), who turned out to be almost too cooperative (for instance by radically refusing any idea of independence). It took French Haut-Commissaire Jean Ramadier, specially appointed to clear this job, no more than six weeks to have Mbida demoted and Ahidjo installed in his place. Yet it may be important to note that Ramadier's musical chairs must have made Ahidjo quite insecure. Apparently the French could repeat such a maneuver any time. Indeed, Ramadier and others made it quite clear that they saw Ahidjo—who until then had played a minor role in the Assemblée—as an in-between figure (Chaffard 1965). Maybe this explains Ahidjo's passionate statement of fidelity vis-à-vis Aujoulat, his faithful patron: "he is my personal friend and my political friend. . . . I will remain attached to him until my death" (Nken 2014, 141).

Ahidjo as Symbol of *Aujoulatisme*

After independence, it took Ahidjo only two years to consolidate his one-party rule by imprisoning all opponents inside the country or forcing them into exile. In the first years after independence in particular, the stubborn UPC guerilla in the West Province constituted a serious challenge, in part because it was supported by a vociferous UPC leadership abroad and Bamiléké migrants in other parts of the country. Due to heavy military support from the French, the guerilla was gradually contained in the West Province as well. After 1962 it served Ahidjo's purposes to maintain the UPC as an omnipresent specter for constructing an authoritarian one-party state. Qualifying any form of opposition as "subversion" that had to be forcefully suppressed, the regime used the past divisiveness as a pretext to justify an obsessive celebration of the Cameroonian nation uniting behind the president.[19] Outside the country the various UPC cells in the diaspora (splitting up and reuniting in complicated patterns) kept producing vociferous critiques of the new president and his neocolonial regime. A major theme in the stream of pamphlets and more in-depth publications was, as expected, Ahidjo's close link with Aujoulat, proving that independence had only meant continuing the colonial relationship with France. Most texts discussed below excel in vitriolic and highly personal attacks on the man who in the same years was built up in the national press of Cameroon as the "Father of the Nation." It is striking that in all these attacks of the 1960s and 1970s the idea of a homosexual pact was completely missing. Below we will focus on the attacks by three proponents, Mongo Beti, Abel Eyinga, and Ngouo Woungly-Massaga. All three were leading figures in the nascent Cameroonian elite, and their attacks on Ahidjo's rule

FIGURE 4.4. Ahmadou Ahidjo, Cameroun's first president (1960–1982), now seen as a creature of the French (notably of Aujoulat), ensuring that Cameroon remained inside *Françafrique*. Courtesy of the National Archives of the Netherlands.

were very much ad hominem. But apparently they did not deem matters of sexuality to be of political importance, so they did not deploy this theme to delegitimize the political status quo.

MONGO BETI: AHIDJO BETRAYING THE NATIONALIST DREAM

One of the fiercest early attacks came from the well-known Cameroonian novelist Mongo Beti (1932–2001) in his 1972 *Main basse sur le Cameroun* (The plundering of Cameroon). Written in exile and in reaction to the execution in 1970 of Ernest Ouandié, the last guerrilla leader still active inside Cameroon, the book reads as an explosion of the author's pent-up rage about what independence under French tutorship had brought his fatherland. Its publication was initially blocked in France by Jacques Foccart himself, then still *Monsieur Afrique* under President Georges Pompidou: a clear sign of how damaging the attack was supposed to be for the Ahidjo regime. Only after a sustained effort by the publisher, François Maspero, was it released in 1972. The focus in Mongo Beti's vitriolic portrait of Ahidjo was, indeed, the latter's utter dependency on Aujoulat. The latter is introduced by Beti as "a small missionary who adorned himself with picturesque nicknames—like the guardian angel of Cameroon." Beti emphasizes that, in the 1950s, Aujoulat became almighty in Cameroonian politics due to his combined positions as deputy in Cameroon and minister in France (Beti 1972, 41). For Beti, Ahidjo's sudden rise to power was certainly not due to the latter's personal merit, but only to Aujoulat's unfailing support. Indeed, during the critical episode in 1958 when Ahidjo was suddenly pushed by the French to replace Mbida, the first prime minister, Ahidjo would have shown a remarkable lack of initiative. And this continued in subsequent years when the French (apparently with Aujoulat still in the background) deemed it absolutely necessary to surround the new prime minister with "a brain-trust . . . of veterans of Indo-China and North Africa, tainted by revolutionary wars . . . experts of the most shameless forms of psychological manipulation" (Beti 1972, 44). In Beti's view, Aujoulat—in his determination to eviscerate the UPC from the emerging political scene in Cameroon—played a key role in laying the foundations for the authoritarian state Ahidjo developed after independence, still under French guidance. Beti emphasizes the close personal link between Aujoulat and Ahidjo, the latter belonging to the "the inner core of Aujoulat's followers" (42). However, further personal details are clearly seen as politically irrelevant by the author of *Main basse sur le Cameroun.*

ABEL EYINGA: A VIEW FROM INSIDE

Twelve years later, a similar portrait of Ahidjo and his dependence on Au-joulat and the French was published by Abel Eyinga, then professor of law in Algiers (Eyinga 1984). As a politician himself, Eyinga (1923–2014), like Beti, developed similar sympathies for the UPC. However, he followed a different trajectory. In the 1950s he belonged to Aujoulat's "stable" in Paris, and after independence he was appointed to an important position in Ahidjo's government. Yet he soon exhibited "subversive" tendencies—as this was called in Ahidjo's days—and had to secretly leave the country in 1961. For the presidential elections in 1970 in Cameroon—under the one-party regime these were ritual occasions since there would be only one candidate, Ahidjo himself—Eyinga even had the audacity to declare his candidacy from Paris, which led to an international arrest warrant. Un-der the threat of being extradited from France by the Pompidou regime, Eyinga fled to Algeria, where he lived for some time under a false name with an Algerian passport. Like Beti, Eyinga dared to return to Cameroon only after 1991, where he was still closely followed by Biya's regime as a potential opponent (even though he came from the same ethnic group as Biya himself).

As a former *Aujoulatiste*, Eyinga was able to fill in Beti's portrait of Ahidjo with many more details from their life in Paris. Like Beti, he insisted that Ahidjo owed his rise to Aujoulat rather than to his own merits. But Eyinga goes into more personal details. He quotes High Commissioner Ramadier's letter that, in choosing Ahidjo as Mbida's successor, Ramadier had explicitly *not* looked for a "man of action." Ey-inga mentions also the general opinion of Ahidjo as "the youngest and the laziest parliamentarian" (Eyinga 1984, 120, 153) during the period that he spent in Paris (1953–57). Quite striking are Eyinga's detailed de-scriptions of how Ahidjo was coached by the French during the crucial sessions of the UN Assembly and its Fourth Commission (on mandated territories) in 1958 and 1959. This committee had to decide on whether elections should take place before independence (giving the UPC a chance to participate) or only afterward, under control of Ahidjo's new government (as the French wanted at all costs). In the end the French won despite the eloquent opposition of UPC representatives (and coun-tries like Egypt). But Eyinga depicts in detail how the passive role of Ahidjo, stiffly reading the texts that were clearly prepared for him by the French delegation, could only confirm the image of *un satellite indigène de l'occupant* (1984, 121, 129).

NGOUO WOUNGLY-MASSAGA: THE SWITCH
TO A "HOMO-MASONIC" FIGURE

Similar interpretations can be found in Ngouo Woungly-Massaga's writings of the same period.[20] Woungly-Massaga, alias Commander Kissamba (1936–2020), was a UPC-*iste* of the first hour who retained his formal links with the movement, through many splits and reconciliations. In 1965 he even opened a new but short-lived *maquis* (guerrilla front) against the Ahidjo regime in the very south of the country, just across the border with Congo-Brazzaville (then under a Marxist government that nonetheless offered only limited support to "Commander Kissamba"). In his earlier writings, Woungly-Massaga also depicts Ahidjo and Biya as products of Aujoulat's stable (Woungly-Massaga 1984, 14). In those writings there is no reference at all to any homosexual pact that would secretly link these three men. In Woungly-Massaga's case this is striking since in a subsequent publication in 2004 (a long series of interviews with the Cameroonian historian Daniel Abwa) he is very explicit on this point. In this long book,[21] the word homosexuality appears only twice but in both places quite bluntly and with considerable emphasis, adding a new aspect to Aujoulat's central role in creating his own following among Cameroonians in Paris:

> We recognized these *Aujoulatistes* (and they were quite numerous) as fellow Cameroonians who were ready to do anything to have money or to be promised a post or a degree, included and notably this homosexuality. We called them the colonials' wives. (Abwa 2004, 47)

On the same page Woungly-Massaga states that it was still Aujoulat who imposed Biya on Ahidjo as his closest collaborator and successor. In a later passage the author makes a link with Freemasonry to explain why he himself was always kept at bay by the regime:

> Who am I? A mystic Christian, like my father. I was never member of a philosophical, religious or whatsoever sect. And if you add that I am not homosexual, you will understand the lively hostility of the political class of this neocolonial power against Commander Kissamba. (Abwa 2004, 215)

Woungly-Massaga launched this new version of the Aujoulat rumor in a special context. It was in precisely those years that "homosexuality" was emerging as a major political issue in Cameroon with the *affaire des listes* of early 2006 and the Yaoundé archbishop's 2005 Christmas sermon.

Freemasonry Enters the Stage

In his new version of his attacks on Aujoulat, Woungly-Massaga added Freemasonry as another new element ("I was never a member of . . . whatsoever sect . . ."). This had to do with new turns in French decolonization processes. Both Verschave (1998, 290) and Smith and Glaser (1997) emphasized that after 1974, when Giscard d'Estaing became president in France and put an end to Foccart's official position as *Monsieur Afrique*, the latter's network fragmented, and the *Françafrique* assemblage entered a more disorderly period with several networks competing each other, Freemasonry being one of them. As said, an important moment in this respect was the switch in France in 1981 from a series of center-right governments to François Mitterrand and the socialists. Foccart seemed to have kept Freemasonry at bay since he was suspicious of the Grand Orient—at the time still dominating the masonic lodges in francophone Africa—and its close links to French socialists.[22] But, as noted in chapter 2, in 1981 Mitterrand's victory brought Freemasonry, and notably the Grand Orient de France, back to the heart of power. Moreover, for Africa Mitterrand had special reasons to lean on the Grand Orient. The quite abrupt return of the socialists to power meant that they lacked their own network in Africa to help them balance Foccart's ongoing influence. The main qualification of Guy Penne, Mitterrand's first *Monsieur Afrique*—himself a dentist without any previous experience of Africa—seems to have been that his dense relations as a prominent member of the Grand Orient assured him of a useful Masonic network on the continent.[23] In 1986 Penne was succeeded by Mitterrand's son, Jean-Christophe, who claimed to have constructed his own network through a busy social life during his long-term stays in Africa but who inherited much of the Grand Orient networks of his predecessor.[24]

The metamorphosis of Aujoulat in the attacks on him, from the great spoiler of "true" Cameroonian nationalism to a homo-Masonic figure perverting the new Cameroonian elite and ensnaring them in the bonds of *Françafrique*, raises all sorts of questions: What does "homosexual" mean in this context, and what about its links with Freemasonry? And why did such accusations have such mobilizing effects at this particular moment, placing Aujoulat abruptly at the center of popular attention again after 2006? We will make up the balance below, but first it might be helpful to look at the continuation of the story around the third figure in this idea of a "homosexual pact": President Paul Biya, as the junior partner in the troika with Aujoulat and Ahidjo.

The Story Continues: President Biya's Search for Spiritual Protection

For Cameroon there are special reasons why "the lodges"—Freemasonry and Rosecrucianism—were becoming more visible over the course of the 1980s. One was the ever more frantic search for spiritual protection, noted before, by the new president, Paul Biya, who had succeeded Ahidjo in 1982. At the time, the sudden withdrawal of Ahidjo and especially his choice of his successor came as a big surprise. In the course of his twenty-two years of rule Ahidjo had been surrounded by various ambitious barons who posed more or less openly as his chosen successor, but in the end he made an abrupt choice of Paul Biya. This may have been on formal grounds, since Biya was at the time prime minister and therefore the person to replace the president if need be. However, there were rumors immediately about secret dealings. Ahidjo's personal doctor would have warned him that he was seriously ill and had only a few months to live. Moreover, the doctor concerned was a Frenchman and in close contact with Mitterrand, who had just come to power in Paris and for whom Ahidjo was a somewhat compromising ally, as Ahidjo was all too clearly

FIGURE 4.5. Paul Biya, Ahidjo's successor as President of Cameroon (1984–present): also one of Aujoulat's young men? Photo: Bubakar NG/Wikimedia Commons, CC BY-SA 4.0.

a creation of the France's *Francafrique* policies.[25] But later on, after the "return" of Aujoulat in the early 2000s as a homo-Masonic figure, another explanation became more popular: since Biya was the third partner in the Aujoulat–Ahidjo pact, Ahidjo had to choose him as a successor.[26]

Biya's beginnings in his new position were quite hesitant. His uncertain performance, not helped by his limited talents as a speaker, fed the idea during most of his rule that he was only a strawman and that the real strongman of the new political constellation was hiding behind him. Yet many have been named as the power behind Paul Biya—military men like General Pierre Semengue (retired in 2011) or General Asso'o Emane Benoit (retired in 2017 and deceased in 2019), as well as politicians like Joseph Owona (all key figures in resolving the political crisis of the 1990s through half-hearted constitutional reforms). But all have faded away, and despite one crisis after another, Paul Biya is still there, now almost the longest ruling president in Africa (Teodoro Obiang Nguema Mbasogo of the neighboring Equatorial Guinea holds that record with almost forty-five years in power as of this writing in 2024). Clearly, Biya has a talent for surviving.[27] There are two explanations for this. A very material one is the Batallion d'intervention rapide (BIR), the stronghold former Israeli intelligence men created for him inside the state organization. But in Cameroon people are more fascinated by a spiritual explanation: the president's arduous quest for spiritual protection, making him step from one potential source of hidden power to the next one.

Both explanations go back to the first crisis Biya confronted, once in office. In 1984 a coup d'état, carried out by a substantial part of the presidential guard, nearly toppled the new government. In 1982 Ahidjo, after appointing Biya as President, had retained the presidency of the UNC (Union nationale cameroonaise), the *parti unifié* he had created himself in the 1960s. However, Biya rapidly showed that he intended to govern alone. In 1983 he profited from Ahidjo staying in France to take over the presidency of the UNC. In early 1984 Ahidjo was sentenced to death (for supposedly preparing a coup) but this was reprieved shortly after. Then Biya announced a reorganization of the presidential guard: all elements from the north (Ahidjo's part of the country) were to be transferred to other military units. However, these northerners—some seven hundred altogether—suddenly staged a coup trying to arrest Biya himself; Biya succeeded in escaping due to the support of other elements of the guard who remained loyal. After three days of combat the putschists were arrested. The fighting left more than five hundred people dead.[28]

Apparently, being so suddenly in mortal danger by an attack from close by had a traumatic effect on the new president. Ever since, when he is leaving the palace, the presidential cortege has a special allure: the presidential car is followed by an ambulance loaded with sufficient blood to give the president a complete blood transfusion on the spot. Moreover, on such occasions strict security measures have drastic effects on everyday life in Yaoundé (the capital) since the whole route from the palace in Etoudi to the airport—which crosses the entire city center—will be blocked for a few hours, effectively cutting the city in two. All curtains have to be drawn and nobody is allowed to be in the streets. The image that remains of such outings is that of a president who is mortally afraid of his own people.

The 1984 crisis also carried the seeds of a very effective solution to Biya's trauma, albeit from an unexpected source: Israeli support. Biya seems to have suspected that at least some elements in the French army were involved in the coup.[29] This made him look elsewhere for maintaining his own security. Apparently on advice of Mobutu, who had himself his personal guard organized by Mossad agents, Biya turned to Israeli contacts.[30] Whether by accident or not, there is an interesting parallel with the turn his quest for spiritual security took at the time into Jewish occult knowledge (see below). According to Emmanuel Freudenthal and Youri Van Der Weide, two journalists working with the prestigious series *African Arguments*,[31] an Israeli businessmen, Meir Meyuhas, former Israeli secret agent (in other sources called Meyoukhas), and his son Sami, who held an exclusive license from Israel's Ministry of Defense to negotiate arms deals, put Biya in contact with former Israeli military men.[32] In a recent report the two journalists show how from this collaboration the BIR (Bataillon d'intervention rapide) was formed, inside the Presidential Guard and under direct command of Biya himself. Thus, this BIR remains outside the formal structures of the Cameroonian army, is trained and supervised by (former) Israeli military, and is equipped with Israeli weapons. Striking also is the fact that the BIR is financed through an off-budget account of Cameroon's national oil company. The *African Arguments* article focuses on the luxurious position of the Israeli BIR leaders (mansions in the Bahamas and such) but also on their ruthless methods of training BIR recruits. It quotes also a certain Kah Walla, "an opposition politician," as saying, "It is a very bizarre setup to have an armed force [with] a foreign national as a commander . . . even if these are private Israeli consultants. . . . . most of them are former Israeli soldiers." Clearly Israeli military efficiency—all the more effective since it is organized outside the Cameroonian military hierarchy—offers a very concrete explanation for Biya's remarkable longevity through stormy years.

As said, there is an interesting overlap with the other pole of security on which the president seems to bet, and which gets a lot more attention in popular debates in Cameroon: his search for special forms of spiritual

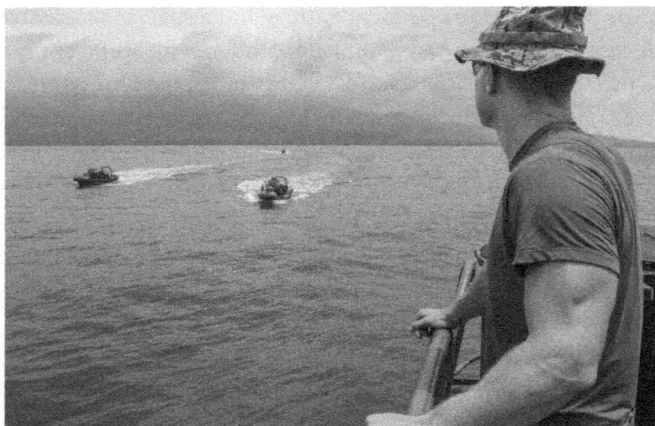

FIGURE 4.6. A naval training in the Ambas Bay—near Cameroon's oil resources, and an iconic place for the anglophone secession movement—of the Batallion d'intervention rapide (BIR), the secret of Biya's remarkable longevity as president. The continuing control of outside experts (especially Israelis) over this presidential guard proves time and again to be effective protection. Photo: US Navy/Theron J. Godbold.

protection. Observers have been struck by the president's interest in occult forms of empowerment and his tendency to single out people with whom he could talk about such topics, in any company.[33] In contrast to his predecessor Ahidjo, who was a Muslim from the north, Biya is a man from the south, a practicing Catholic and a product of Catholic schools. Indeed, at the time of his inauguration many Catholic priests enthusiastically celebrated his rise to power. Yet rumors soon had it that Biya was developing a keen interest in alternative sources of spiritual power. In the 1980s—and here is the parallel with his close collaborations with Israeli military men—he showed a keen interest in Judaism. He became a follower of Rabbi Léon Ashkenazi, son of the last rabbi of Algeria and an influential spiritual leader in the Israeli-Francophone community in the 1970s and 1980s, who had himself called "Manitou" by his followers (see Glaser 2014) and instructed Biya in the secrets of the kabbalah. A fixed corollary in sources who mention the rabbi's name is that at his death in 1996 this Manitou promised Biya that he would remain in power until his death as long as he never made his country vote against Israel in the UN—which Biya, indeed, never did (Glaser 2014, 127).

Subsequently Biya became increasingly involved with secret societies from a European background. People now take it for granted that, like Ahidjo, he joined Freemasonry during his time in France in the 1950s. However,

FIGURE 4.7. The huge skeleton of a house generally attributed to Titus Edzoa serves as a landmark in many parts of Yaoundé since it is on one of the city's highest hills. It is also a continuous reminder of the dramatic downfall of Dr. Edzoa, one of Biya's closest collaborators, after Edzoa had the audacity in 1997 to stand as a candidate for president. In his book from jail (2012) Edzoa displays his vast esoteric knowledge—a silent reminder that he has a higher rank in the Rose-Croix than has the president? Photo: Albert Bergonzo/Wikimedia Commons, CC BY-SA 4.0.

in the late 1980s, Biya seemed to have switched to Rosicrucianism. In the 1990s this inspired a series of rumors, mentioned in chapter 2, about secret conflicts inside the national elite between Freemasons and Rosicrucians. However, in 1997 a quite different event created similar consternation. Titus Edzoa, until then brother-in-arms of President Biya, announced his decision to stand candidate in the presidential elections of that year. By that time it was normal that opposition parties would put forth candidates for such elections. But the very idea that someone like Edzoa from inside Biya's own party would dare to stand against the president himself was unheard of. As was to be foreseen, Edzoa was arrested only a few days later and he was subsequently sentenced to fifteen years in jail for mismanagement of public funds. Of course, people never tired of speculating how Edzoa, a seasoned politician, could have been so foolish as to make such a suicidal step. The only explanation that seemed to make sense was that he had a higher rank than Biya in the Rose-Croix. In 2012, Edzoa was sentenced to another twenty years in jail, but under international pressure (notably from French President François Hollande) Biya finally released him in 2014.

In 2012, the year that he hoped to be liberated, Titus Edzoa had his book *Méditations de prison* smuggled out of jail and published with Karthala. Strikingly, the book does not offer a political explanation of his amazing decision to run for president, nor does it give an analysis of the political context that made this step have such dramatic consequences for him. The book instead offers—after a few short chapters containing poetic reflections on his life in jail—an ever more complicated demonstration of secret knowledge about numbers as well as secrets from various backgrounds, notably referring to ancient Egypt. A leitmotif is the contrast Edzoa makes between occultism/*sorcellerie* (witchcraft) on the one hand and *mysticisme authentique* on the other (Edzoa 2012, chapters 11 and 12). The first, as some sort of negative pole, is associated with all the evils Charles Ateba Eyene dwelled on two years later in his book on the role of the *dictature des loges* in Cameroon: satanic pacts, cannibalism, and homosexuality (see chapter 1). Edzoa adds:

> to practice homosexuality as a purification and initiation ritual is a discriminatory criterion for the honorability of such a prestigious brotherhood. . . . And why? In order to appropriate ever more power, ever more . . . wealth. (2012, 58–59)

However, in contrast to Ateba Eyene, Edzoa does not associate these horrors explicitly with the *loges* (whether Freemasonry or Rosicrucianism—names that do not figure in his chapters). He instead seems to suggest that these evils are part and parcel of the distortion that ambitious but "obscurantist" people make of mystical secrets. In the second half of his book on the true secrets—"authentic mysticism"—Edzoa seems to offer some sort of synopsis of Rosicrucian wisdom with references to the "Nile delta" and magical names. After he came out of jail Edzoa emphasized in interviews that both President Biya and he had been initiated into AMORC for quite some time.[34] His book from jail can be read as a demonstration of the powerful knowledge this initiation—maybe even to a higher grade than Biya?—still put at his disposal.

Biya's Involvement with a Special Rosicrucian Circle

Should the lodges be seen à la Edzoa as a positive counterpoint to obscurantist *sorcellerie* or, in Ateba Eyene's line, as a perversion of European ideals and thus exercising a satanic dictature over Cameroon? It remains difficult to find firm footholds in this quagmire of allusions and suggestions.

Yet there is a concrete lead: President Biya's long-term association, well documented, with Raymond Bernard, a leading but also contested figure in AMORC, the Rosicrucian organization that set the stage for the Biya–Edzoa confrontation in Cameroon. Interestingly, Biya's personal association with Bernard did leave some concrete traces. However, a caveat: even these traces are difficult to follow in the confusing process of segmentation and fusion that besets the world of the lodges. On December 24, 1999, *Le Monde* published an interesting article by Philippe Broussard, "Les millions africains d'un ancien grand maître," concerning a court case handled by Lucien Fontaine, *juge d'instruction* (investigating judge) at the Grenoble tribunal (in the southeast of France), in which Biya's name had turned up.[35]

There is a gruesome story behind this. In 1995, one month after Judge Fontaine assumed his new position in Grenoble, he was confronted with what later became known as "the Vercors drama." On the morning of December 23 the remains of thirteen adults and three children were found at a spot appropriately called "the wells of hell" (*les puits de l'enfer*). All thirteen adults turned out to be members of the Order of the Solar Temple (OTS, Ordre du temple de soleil), founded in 1984 by New Age adept Joseph Di Mambro—a former AMORC member—in collaboration with Luc Jouret, a Belgian homeopathic doctor and philosopher.[36] The judge concluded that the Vercors drama was another case of a series of mass suicides for which the OTS had become notorious. After its founding in 1984 in Geneva, the order rapidly spread to Quebec, France, other parts of Switzerland, and even Guadeloupe and Australia. Similar cases of mass suicide had already occurred in October 1994 in Quebec and Switzerland (in which both Di Mambro and Jouret died—apparently after having enjoyed a copious meal they referred to as "the Last Supper"). All these cases showed a similar pattern: bodies were dressed in the order's ceremonial robes—a loose interpretation of the ancient Templar robes—and were lying in a circle, feet together, most with plastic bags tied over their heads. Some victims were drugged and shot or smothered (in the Vercors case the judge concluded that the victims had been drugged and then shot by two people who subsequently burned themselves). Apparently, in the teaching of the order, the mass suicides were believed to enable a transfer to the planet Sirius. Farewell letters spoke of approaching ecological disasters and an escape from the hypocrisies and oppression of this world.[37]

Following Di Mambro's networks in particular took the judge on a journey along a maze of secret societies, since AMORC was certainly not the only association Di Mambro had joined. An important one was the OSTI (Ordre souverain du temple initiatique), founded in 1988 by Raymond Bernard, who describes himself as "esotericist and author," an old friend of Di

Mambro, also from southeast France. Di Mambro's association with Bernard's OSTI was reason enough for Judge Fontaine to look further into their exchanges, and it was here that President Biya's name came up. The headline of *Le Monde*'s article, "African millions of a former grand master," referred to this Raymond Bernard, who had indeed been grand master of AMORC in France and received important sums of money from African followers.

The OTS mass suicide affairs raised a lot of attention, in part because there were large sums of capital involved (the organization turned out to possess important real estate all over the world, controlling equally impressive money flows). Moreover Di Mambro (like Bernard) had a long-term association with Charles Pasqua, at the time a prominent minister for the Gaullist Rassemblement pour la république (in Prime Minister Balladur's right-wing cabinet), who was supposed to be involved in important transfers of money and weapons inside *Françafrique*.[38] It was in this charged context that Judge Fontaine interrogated Raymond Bernard about his dealings with Di Mambro, and his own finances, notably those important transfers of money from Cameroon. For instance in 1988 a sum of 3.6 million French Francs had been transferred into Bernard's account by the SNH (Société nationale des hydrocarbons, Cameroon's national oil company) even though there was no clear link between him and this company. However, Bernard declared that he was a personal adviser to President Biya, notably for cultural affairs. Asked by *Le Monde*, the president's staff replied that Mr. Bernard was only "an old friend, but certainly not an adviser," and refused to give any further information. Mr. Bernard explained other payments by Biya as "friendly gestures": the gift of a painting worth 5.3 million Francs, and in 1990 (this time once more through the SNH) a sum of 5.6 million Francs to CIRCES (Centre international de recherches culturelles et spirituelles), another organization Bernard created in 1988 as the "humanitarian branch" of his OSTI and of which he was also grand master. In 1990 President Biya also granted him a gift without interest of 40 million Francs to buy a venue in Paris for this organization. Mr. Bernard added that Biya was certainly not the only African head of state associated with CIRCES. Aside from Biya, Presidents Houphouët-Boigny of Ivory Coast, Eyadema of Togo, and Bongo of Gabon also became honorary presidents of CIRCES. Bernard was acquitted of any involvement in the Vercors affair, but the judge raised critical questions about large sums of money transferred from accounts close to President Biya.

The research by Judge Fontaine and *Le Monde* shows in any case that the world of the lodges is not only about rumors; things can become manifest in very concrete ways. However, impressive as the figures mentioned above may seem, the whole Biya/Bernard affair is also symptomatic of the difficulty in disentangling the links between African lodges and their mother organizations in Europe—vital as this may be for getting more clarity about the dynamics of these organizations. Even a "hard" fact like Biya's important payments to Bernard gets lost in a jumble of ephemeral organizations, constantly splitting up or emerging under new names. In this case, for instance, the present grand master of AMORC in France, the already mentioned Serge Toussaint, declared in a 2014 interview with Cameroon Link that Raymond Bernard had been expelled from AMORC in 1977, and that AMORC was in no way involved in Bernard's subsequent initiatives. Does this mean that Biya's membership in CIRCES would make him only a marginal Rosicrucian? To complicate things further, even if Raymond Bernard had been expelled as grand master of the French AMORC (as Toussaint maintains) it seems that at the time he was succeeded by his own son, Christian Bernard, who in 1990 even became the imperator of the global AMORC society.[39] Small wonder, in view of such inconsistencies and elusiveness, that these organizations are shrouded in mystery, in Africa maybe even more than in other parts of the world.

But what about the popular tendency to link this proliferation of secret associations and rituals to same-sex practices? It is clear that there were always such rumors about Paul Biya—as with Aujoulat, his mentor—but it is also clear that for both of them the early 2000s brought an intensification of such allusions. In 1991, one of us (Geschiere) returned to Cameroon for a PhD defense at the Yaoundé I university during the tormented days of *Opération ville morte* (the opposition shutting down all major cities in protest against Biya). These were also the days of new freedom of the press, resulting in a torrent of all sorts of newspapers, leaflets, and magazines. The first paper Geschiere bought opened with the headline "Le pays ne peut pas être gouverné par un homosexuel" (The country cannot be governed by a homosexual). In retrospect (remember Ateba Eyene's 2012 attack on "the magico-anal" and the "satanic dictature of the lodges" discussed in chapter 1) this headline, still very surprising in 1991, acquires a deeper meaning.[40] Compare also Lucien Toulou's 2007 article with the telling title "Scenes reminding of Sodom and Gomorra?" This article was published in a special issue (mentioned before) of *Terroirs* by Fabien Eboussi Boulaga which proposed to articulate a more analytical view on the growing moral panic about homosexuality. Toulou—referring to *la souillure du corps* (literally, "the defiling of the body")—also highlights the depth of popular indignation about the role homosexual practices are supposed to play in the way the elite (that is, Biya's cronies) recruits for these secret societies. Such rituals are supposed to be *an ascenseur contraignant* (an obligatory lift) to enter *la nébuleuse sectaire* (the misty world of sects; Toulou 2007, 88–89).[41]

The idea of Biya being involved as the third party in a homosexual pact with Aujoulat is what especially keeps coming back in people's comments on *les pédés de la République*. In the 2006 turmoil created by Cameroonian newspapers publishing lists of "supposed" or "prominent" homosexuals, Ahidjo was soon targeted because of his close relations to Aujoulat. But Woungly-Massaga's accusations (see earlier this chapter) clearly included Biya as well. After all, the latter had been equally close to Aujoulat during his study days in Paris. The powerful idea of such a "homosexual pact" effectively sums up how the specificities of French-style decolonization—in Cameroon the difficulty of forming a cooperative elite in the face of uncooperative nationalists—had unforeseen consequences for present-day relations between rulers and their people.

Homosexuality: A Label and Its Shifting Meanings

The historical shifts in the rumors about Aujoulat and their impact up until today are striking. He had been a contested figure ever since he entered politics in 1946 in what was then the colony of Cameroon. But it was only after 2000 that the association of his person with both homosexuality and Freemasonry really took hold. And it was also only then that the idea of a "homosexual pact," sealed by a sodomizing ritual with Ahidjo *and* Biya (both to a large extent Aujoulat's creatures), took root. Such striking turns over time show that there is good reason for our question in the introduction about the meaning of the term "homosexual." When people start denouncing Aujoulat for having "sodomized" the emerging political elite in the 1950s, what do they mean exactly? And what does it mean that since the turn of the century he is increasingly denounced for having sown the seeds of "homosexuality" that are now supposed to "ravage the country"?[42] Such twists and turns are quite relevant for the questions Steven Pierce (2016) raises in his seminal analysis of similar rumors in Nigeria. Remember his warning not to take terms like "homosexual" or even "sodomize" for granted. Apparently these ideas can take on special implications in varying contexts.

For the Aujoulat case, it may be important to note that the association with same-sex practices was, as said, not completely new. There are clear indications that at the time of his direct political involvement (1940s and 1950s) rumors were already circulating about sexual intimacies with the younger attendants at his "court."[43] But this makes the question about why it was only much later that his critics saw fit to evoke these aspects in their public attacks all the more urgent. Why did references to "homosexual" contacts and "sodomization" become more explicit and much more damaging by this time? It was certainly not the cogency of the notion as used in Cameroonian debates that gave it new impact. Elsewhere we have highlighted that, on the contrary, the term "homosexual" is becoming a floating signifier in these debates (Geschiere and Orock 2020). A wide array of sexual practices is caught under this label and often attributed to one and the same person. To stick to the Aujoulat rumor and its recent ramifications, Ahidjo is supposed to have been sodomized by Aujoulat but, in turn, Ahidjo is supposed to have assumed an extremely phallocratic role, sodomizing his courtiers, notably Biya, who subsequently imposed himself on his own allies.[44] Apparently the country's recent political history— notably the special traits of decolonization and the gradual emergence of Freemasonry as a crucial presence—has provided a context in which the notion of "homosexuality" can take on special urgency despite (or because of?) a loose and open meaning. It is against this background that one can understand why in Cameroon both "homosexuality" and "Freemasonry" serve to express people's sense of a historical conspiracy around same-sex practices as a special form of postcolonial subjection. In other African countries, for instance in Kenya, there seems to be at least some space now for LGBTQ people to claim public space (Van Klinken 2019; Nyanzi 2013). Understanding why popular anger against "homosexuals" remains so strong in Cameroon (Ndjio 2012a; 2022) clearly requires closer attention to the specific historical developments outlined above. The analysis above suggests that "the politicization" (Awondo 2012a) of homosexuality as a public issue is formatted in Cameroon, as in other countries, as a special articulation of more general and more particular historical factors that has to be patiently unpacked in order to understand the roots of homophobia and the trajectories it can assume.

This chapter shows how crucial the colonial past is for understanding present-day moral panics about homosexuality in various African countries. But it also shows that we have to go further than general statements about homosexuality or homophobia being colonial impositions. The centrality of the Aujoulat figure, the striking turn in public attacks on him, and the special impact his relations to Cameroon's subsequent presidents— both Ahidjo and Biya—have on present-day debates about sovereignty and subjection show that closer attention is needed to special historical trajectories of decolonization. The importance of the Aujoulat figure in present-day debates is directly linked to the particular *Gaulliste* vision of how to retain an African *pré carré* for France in a global context that made decolonization inevitable, a vision that was again related to the special role the French colonies in Africa played in the birth of de Gaulle's *France Libre* in 1940, as a counterpoint to fascist Vichy. As said, it may seem audacious to relate this broad historical vision to the present-day moral panic on homo-Masonic figures in Cameroon. But the ever-closer personal network with "cooperative" African elites built up by Jacques Foccart, de Gaulle's *Monsieur Afrique*, complicated by the special problems in Cameroon in applying this *Gaulliste* vision against the UPC resistance, plus the much later switch by François Mitterand after the socialist victory in 1981 to Freemasonry as an alternative network, form crucial links in this chain. The stain of being a creature of France still sticks to the memory of Ahidjo, the country's first president, and even to his present-day successor, Biya. The figure of Aujoulat, who played a major role in destroying the UPC nationalist leadership, has become a hated icon of these French manipulations, evoking a powerful image of a neocolonial conspiracy built around occult networks and transgressive forms of sexuality. By connecting Aujoulat explicitly to "homosexual pacts" and the subjection of these cooperative elites through "sodomization," the discourse of homophobia in Cameroon can be read as an expression of people's anger at such neocolonial manipulations. The consequence of these historical articulations is that Cameroonians who now identify as "gay" or "lesbian" become victims of "colonial blackmail" (Nyeck 2016): they are automatically depicted as stooges of an ongoing neocolonial plot, a most painful and dangerous position.

The crucial role of Freemasonry and Rosicrucianism in the crystallization of this imaginary highlights the weight of the colonial past. But this also raises the question of whether older elements do or do not have to be taken into account. Does the story of sexual transgression and illicit enrichment start, indeed, with colonial subjection—as proponents of the thesis of homosexuality as un-African emphasize? Or is there another story to tell?

"Witchcraft," Wealth, and Same-Sex Intercourse

TESSMANN AND HIS EPIGONES

If the challenge for academics is to historicize conspiracy narratives, our example offers special possibilities. In the preceding chapter we noted a striking turn in the (post)colonial articulation of Freemasonry, homosexuality, and illicit enrichment. In addition, there are also special possibilities to develop a longer time perspective on the articulation of these three themes by going back to the work of Günther Tessmann (1884–1969) and his ethnography of *biang akuma* (witchcraft of wealth) among the Fang before colonial conquest. By linking this *biang akuma*, and riches in general, to same-sex practices, Tessmann touched upon a theme that seems to have a long history in other parts of the continent as well. Transgressive forms of sexuality are often equated with "witchcraft," but in Africa this especially applies to what nowadays is called "homosexuality." It is this equation with witchcraft that links same-sex intercourse to enrichment—a link that is often ignored in present-day debates on homophobia and LGBTQ issues in Africa.

Tessmann's ethnography, based on fieldwork just after 1900 among groups who had not been in direct contact with Europeans, shows that same-sex arrangements have a longer history than proponents of the increasingly popular idea of homosexuality being "un-African" pretend. Yet this should not imply that Tessmann's *biang akuma* among the Fang and even more his findings of the currency of same-sex arrangements among the Bafia can be invoked as a "traditional" given. Tessmann clearly brought in viewpoints of his own. Before coming to Cameroon, he was already interested in the emerging discipline of *Sexualwissenschaft* (sexology) and the idea of *das dritte Geschlecht* (the third gender; Hirschfeld, Karsch-Haak, and others) that inspired a general interest in alternative forms of sexuality among people who were supposed to represent earlier phases of human evolution. His findings in Kamerun therefore have to be seen—like most of the themes we are dealing with—as emerging from the interface between Africa and the West. Yet they do show that such arrangements have a history of their own in African societies.

It is also in this respect that a more recent text, a reaction by Cameroonian anthropologist Cecile Séverin Abega to the panic the 2006 *affaire des listes* created in his country, is of particular interest. In Abega's view the newspapers who published lists of "homosexuals" were participating in the construction of "a myth of *une homosexualité rituelle, sorcière et criminelle* [a homosexuality that is ritual, witch-like and criminal] as a current practice at the top of the state" (Abega 2007a, 97). He adds that such homosexuality is "presented as an act of witchcraft" and thus related to "social mobility structuring the political setting" (101). But then Abega draws the circle wider by stressing that this can only be understood in relation to a vision of the person as "double." In his view, the idea that everyone has a double is crucial for understanding this complex of witchcraft, same-sex practices, and enrichment. Indeed, as Abega rightly emphasizes, "Thus, what people commonly call *sorcellerie* (witchcraft) is the world of the doubles" (103). In this respect Tessmann was also some sort of trailblazer: we will see that his 1913 *Die Pangwe* evokes so much doubleness around the person that it might make the reader dizzy.[1]

With this conceptual assemblage of the plurality of the human being and "witchcraft" as rooted in a person's doubleness, we stumble upon an epistemological complex that has wide implications and plays a central role in many African societies, in the past and up to the present day. It is the strength of both Tessmann and Abega (separated by almost one hundred years)[2] that they bring out the direct relevance of this complex for understanding people's views of transgressive sexualities. People's common equation of homosexuals with "witches" does deserve more attention, but here we enter slippery ground. It is clear that, despite a long series of studies by anthropologists in particular, the field of "witchcraft" remains haunted by ambiguities and misunderstandings, for academics as for others. Abega is very wise in taking some distance toward the term itself ("what people commonly call *sorcellerie*"—Abega 2007a, 103).[3] Indeed—as emphasized in our introduction—the term, common as it may have become among academics *and* Africans in everyday life, has severe problems (see also Geschiere 1997). The importation and appropriation of the term coincided with the missionization of African societies since 1900, and—as several anthropologists have recently highlighted—this had drastic implications for the ideas concerned (see Tonda 2005; Ceriana

Mayneri 2014). Gabonese anthropologist Joseph Tonda has even stated categorically that in Africa the "witchcraft" of today is a colonial creation.

One problem is that the translation of local notions through Western terms like "witchcraft," *sorcellerie,* or *feitiçaria* affirmed a one-sided view of these forces as basically evil. Yet the great challenge is precisely to try and understand the paradox that people simultaneously see these invisible forces as evil *and* empowering, even necessary for the functioning of the community. The doubleness of the person seems to allow for all sorts of variations in this regard, but it is clear that, even if labelling these forces as "witchcraft" has become quite widespread now, their basic ambiguity as both terrifying and promising remains omnipresent. The heavy accent in African epistemologies on the doubleness—or more generally the plurality—of the person therefore has basic implications for understanding the enigmatic link between same-sex practices, witchcraft, and enrichment.[4]

Lately, several observers have pointed out the similarities between this emphasis on a person's doubleness in African settings on the one hand and, on the other, recent Western social science theories advocating a so-called "posthuman" approach, beyond the current focus on human agency.[5] This convergence might have its limits. African witchcraft discourse seems to have, in many respects, a humanizing tendency. In their diagnosis *nganga* (healers) mostly look for a human actor who would be behind the clients' suffering; even if the attacker is hiding behind all sorts of appearances, human action has to be identified as the cause before any therapy becomes possible. Yet it is true that even if a diagnosis in terms of "witchcraft" tries to outline the figure of a human perpetrator, this "actor" remains multiple, not to say fuzzy, in many ways. In his Abiola Lecture Mbembe (2016a) shows that in a wider sense the centrality of humans' doubleness gives African epistemologies particular relevance in modern settings marked by new parameters of truth and knowledge, where the real becomes relative and the distinction with the virtual precarious.[6]

These are good reasons, therefore, to follow Tessmann in his struggles, more than one hundred years ago, with such doubleness. We will see that he combined his interest in such doubleness with a most unambiguous (Western?) view on binaries, notably the one between good and evil, leading to complicated schemes that have the unfortunate effect of draining out all the fluidity that stands out so starkly in his empirical descriptions. Indeed, the riches of his ethnography highlight all sorts of ambiguities and inconsistencies that blow life into his often quite schematic analysis of the way the Fang tried to order their world. His work is followed later in the twentieth century by a whole series of anthropological studies on the same region that add new accents in their versions of the doubleness of the person and its implications for witchcraft and empowerment. We will mention Meinrad Hebga, Marie-Paule Brochet de Thé, Louis Mallart, Jeanne-François Vincent, and Jean-Pierre Ombolo, but we will give special attention to Philippe Laburthe-Tolra's magnum opus (1977) on the Beti because of the central place in his work of the struggle with the doubleness of *evu* (witchcraft) between good and evil. Apparently not only the Beti struggled with this, but also this anthropologist himself. And it is this ambiguity that is crucial for the link people see between *evu* and enrichment. We close with Sévérin Abega (2007a) who returned, as said, to this topic in a most creative contribution, in a setting where homosexuality and Freemasonry had suddenly become major public issues.

To what extent can following consecutive anthropologists' efforts to make sense of the plurality of the person and the concomitant centrality of *evu* (witchcraft) for the Fang and related groups provide a deeper understanding of our central theme? We will see that "witchcraft"—or better, "the world of the doubles"—is in many respects the missing link in understanding the conceptual association in popular conspiracy thinking of Freemasonry and illicit enrichment on the one hand, and same-sex arrangements on the other.[7]

Tessmann: "King of the White Spot"

Günther Tessmann has become an almost mythical figure in Cameroon because the reputation of his early monographs, notably the 1913 one on *Die Pangwe* (Fang),[8] is balanced by their inaccessibility. Indeed, nothing of his work has been translated into French or English. Born in Lübeck in 1884, he left for Kamerun in 1904 to work for plantation companies on the slopes of Mount Cameroon. However, only a year later he was sacked and had to opt for the humble position of labor recruiter, mobilizing workers by whatever means necessary in order to solve the urgent shortage of labor on the plantations (Oestermann 2023). But Tessmann was quite happy with this, since it enabled him to make a long trip into the interior from which he profited by accumulating all sorts of plant and animal specimens (not yet ethnographica). This was followed by a most adventurous period in which he tried to make a living by hunting elephants in the Fang area, on the border between Kamerun and Spanish-Guinea, thus financing a long-term stay as researcher in this not yet "pacified" area. During this period he enriched his original focus on natural specimens with a growing interest in ethnographica, both people's material culture and their world order. On return to Germany, early in 1907, the Lübeck museum became so interested in his collection that it helped finance a special expedition to the Fang area so that

FIGURE 5.1. Günther Tessmann, Cameroon's first ethnographer, on his return to Lübeck in 1912 after several years of fieldwork. Recently his work was rediscovered when homosexuality became a hot issue in the country. Tessmann wrote about its variable role in precolonial societies, thus contradicting present-day claims that it is an un-African vice, imported by the colonials. © Völkerkundesammlung, Lübeck.

he could work there for two more years (1907–1909). In 1913 his magnum opus *Die Pangwe* was published. In the same year the colonial government sent him on a research mission into the newly acquired Neukamerun, a strip of dense forest on the border with French Congo.[9]

In 1916, after the combined British and French forces had beaten the German army in the south of Kamerun, Tessmann was interned with the rest of the German troops on the island of Fernando Po (present-day Bioko, at the time a Spanish colony). Returning to Germany after the war, he published several more monographs (on the Bafia in south Kamerun, the Baja in the east of the colony, and the Bubi from Fernando Po). However, he failed to get the academic recognition he felt his work entitled him. After the Nazi regime excluded him from teaching, he migrated to Brazil (1936). But after the Second World War, and despite his continuous efforts, he was still not offered any acceptable post in the German academy. He died in 1969 in Curitiba, Brazil. Nowadays, his Fang monograph in particular is a rare collector's item fetching impressive prices on the antiquarian book market, and there has been a general resurgence of interest in Tessmann's work.[10]

The 1906–7 period of elephant hunting annex research in a "white spot" was in many respects a turning point in Tessmann's tortuous career. Some more details can help to give an idea of his quite original and adventurous style of *Völkerkunde* (anthropology) that he developed during this period.

The idea of realizing in this way his dream of becoming an independent researcher took form during his trip into *Jaundeland* (the land of the *Jaunde*,
German for Ewondo) as a labor recruiter. As noted he very much enjoyed
the trip for the possibilities it offered for exploring his "beloved forest,"
but it ended in a disappointment. On his return to the coast he was again
fired (according to him because of the vengeful interventions of his first
boss). Looking somewhat desperately for another way to make a living in
the small colony, his experiences on this trip gave him an idea of how to
finally realize his dream of living independently in the forest and doing
research. One of his big feats during the *Jaunde* trip was that he shot several
elephants. So he decided that his next step should be to try and set himself
up as an elephant hunter and to use the income from the sale of their tusks
to set up his own *Forschungsstation* (research station) somewhere at an iso-
lated spot in the forest (Tessmann 1940, 70–71; Tessmann 2012, 333, 346).

In his autobiography, entitled *König im Weissen Fleck* (King in a White
Spot),[11] Tessmann describes how shocked his fellow colonials were by his
adventurous plan. His firm idea was to go into "untouched" territory—
that is, outside the area under German control—not only because he
dreamt of a "white spot" but also for very practical reasons: inside German
territory he would have to pay taxes for any elephant he shot; moreover,
elephants were already becoming scarce there. So Tessmann opted for
crossing the border into Spanish territory to the south (so-called Spanish
Guinea), where the Spanish had not yet shown themselves. However, this
area was inhabited by Fang who had a particularly threatening reputation
for *Menschenfresserei* (cannibalism) and other forms of wild behavior.
Before embarking on his adventure Tessmann tried to persuade a friend
(another German he knew from the last plantation where he worked) to
join him, since the latter was "an old hand" at colonial undertakings. The
man was tempted, but in the end refused since it was too risky. Tessmann
wrote with some pride that from then on the older man admired him, with
obvious respect for his daring and independence despite Tessmann being
much younger (Tessmann was then only twenty-two years old). Indeed,
Tessmann left with minimal means, taking great risks, yet the whole en-
terprise worked wonderfully well (Tessmann 2012, 346).

For his first independent expedition Tessmann left Kribi (the closest
town in Kamerun to the border with Spanish Guinea) in January 1906 accompanied by only two "boys," a cook, five porters, and a carabine. The
beginning, when he was still travelling in charted territory, was difficult. He
had such severe problems with porters refusing to go on, and with village
heads refusing to deliver new porters, that he considered giving up. But
once he approached the Ntem River, which more or less coincided with

the border with Spanish Guinea, villages were competing to receive him. To Tessmann's own surprise, his adventurous idea turned out to be a master stroke. What he, and others who kept warning him about Fang cannibalism, had not foreseen was that the villagers were very keen on having him since it assured them a regular supply of elephant meat. In one of the first villages where he arrived beyond the border the chief begged him to stay, offering his own son as an accomplished elephant hunter and promising to have all the houses built that Tessmann would need. On his *Jaunde* trip Tessmann still shot elephants himself, but now he let his carbine be handled by local hunters who brought him the valuable tusks that he had his assistants sell near the coast, while he dedicated his attention to making his *Forschungsstation* function. It was no problem to get porters from the local chief for a small monthly caravan to Kribi to buy provisions. Moreover, the surplus of elephant meat could be exchanged with food products with the locals.

This happy convergence (which later turned out to become soon quite precarious)[12] was typical for the ambiguities of Tessmann's style. In many respects he fitted very well in the rough colonial world of planters on Mount Cameroon and traders along the Batanga coast near Kribi (Tessmann spoke with clear admiration of the latter as "the Batanga lions"), and he clearly enjoyed using terms like *bush horse* (*Negerenglisch*) for the local men who had to carry white people on their shoulders when a stream or a moor had to be crossed. As a labor recruiter he had no qualms about using all the well-known tricks to make young men sign harsh contracts. And *die Peitsche* (the whip) always seemed to be at hand; in Tessmann's view even his trusted assistants constantly needed be disciplined with a few *Hiebe* (slaps). Yet in his diaries all this is constantly balanced by long passages on the marvels of the forest—Tessmann never tired of proclaiming his love for its rich nature and the vibrancy of the tropical night; later on he similarly celebrated the fascinating riches of the locals' customs, their rituals, and their practical common sense.

The way he describes his arrival in Kamerun offers a vivid example. He is told to set off immediately to the plantation where he was to work. Yet he and his porters are surprised by a huge thunderstorm and forced to spend the night in a village in a very shabby hut. But this humbling experience fills Tessmann with deep satisfaction: his first night in the tropics! (Tessmann 2012, 208). Even more striking is his description of what he saw as a crucial turn during his fieldwork. In his autobiography (1940, 192–200) Tessmann describes how one night he is taken by the splendor of a moonlit tropical night. He steps down from the "veranda" of his research station and goes for a short walk, enjoying the splendor of the night, the mysterious light, and the orchestra of bush sounds. However, he is overcome by sudden fear, returns in haste, and in his urgent need to talk to people enters the quarter of his "boys." He finds them telling each other stories, which enraptures him. Soon he is telling stories in his turn. The boys' stories make him realize that these *Naturmenschen* (nature people) also have a culture. Thus, as he notes himself, this night's story telling becomes a crucial moment in his trajectory from a natural scientist to a *Völkerkundige* (anthropologist).[13] In line with this experience, folktales play a crucial role in Tessmann's ethnography. Time and time again he uses them to introduce one of his more daring interpretations. Just as he deduces his spectacular view on sexuality as the crux in man's fall from grace from a Pangwe creation myth, he also develops his other insights—often equally daring—from other stories people told him, rather than engaging in debates with the theoretical viewpoints of his academic contemporaries. Unfortunately he did not feel the need to discuss his ambitious interpretations with the people around him. But

FIGURE 5.2. Tessmann with his "boys" in his field station, showing how he combined a highly colonial approach with a then-original way of doing "fieldwork." Beginning in 1906 he managed to live for longer periods in Fang villages. Despite his highly disciplinarian behavior toward the villagers, the fact of living among them and sharing their everyday life enabled him to collect precious data on Fang society and culture. Thus he became a pioneer of "participant observation."
© Völkerkundesammlung, Lübeck.

Tessmann always at least tried to present his explanations as deductions from his empirical observations and the things people told him.

The adventurous way in which he organized his first research expedition also meant that he opted for a highly original style of fieldwork. In a sense he was a Malinowski avant la lettre, living for a longer period of time on the spot amongst the Fang and thus practicing an at-the-time novel form of participant observation. Yet he also developed a special version of this, as the title of his autobiography, *König im weissen Fleck*, indicates already. The title *König* (king), at first attributed to him by his "boys" as some sort of joke, clearly pleased Tessmann. In his conception, fieldwork had to have military overtones. Indeed, his fixed adage was that

FIGURE 5.3. A young Fang warrior: opening picture from Tessmann's book *Die Pangwe* (1914). Tessmann's obsession with working in "a white spot" made him cross the border of German Kamerun into what was then Spanish Guinea. There he stayed for almost a year in villages where people had hardly ever seen a white man; this allowed him to observe rituals and dress codes that have long since disappeared.

black people only understand the language of force. At the various *For-schungsstationen* he built successively in various villages where he lived for months at a time, the day started with a military parade of "his boys." And, as said, he regularly deemed a show of physical force necessary—against querulous neighboring villages but also against the people who worked for him—in order to drive home who was the king.

Thomas Klockmann, in his insightful study of Tessmann's life and work, shows in detail how this dream took shape (Klockmann 1988, 47ff.). He attributes a central role to two of Tessmann's first assistants—Max, a Batanga man from the coast, and Mabale, a Mabea man from close to the coast—who accompanied him into the interior on his first expedition. According to Tessmann's own memories, they took everything in hand, at least initially: ordering the locals to serve as porters, arranging his lodgings, organizing food, and so on. One of them, Max, even used pictures from the violent German campaign against the Herero in southwest Africa to frighten people by explaining that these were the brothers of his boss. Again, Tessmann had no qualms about such tricks. He jokingly calls Max his "minister," or "Gross-Wezir," and emphasizes time and again that Max's verbal violence was necessary to keep people under control. Indeed, a constant presence in Tessmann's stories about his work with the Fang is that of *meine Jungen* (my boys). Their identity may change (during the 1907–9 expedition two *Jaunde* men had a key role seconded by a larger group of Fang "boys"), but Tessmann's ambivalent relation to them did not. He regularly disciplined them, but he also writes at length about all the jokes he shared with them. The striking thing is that despite this harsh regime, "his boys" were apparently quite committed to him, saving his life several times by carrying him for days through the dense forest in order to get medicine for yet another fever attack. A similar paradox is that despite his utterly colonialist behavior, Tessmann succeeded in gathering a rich amount of data—notably on Fang secret societies—that have become all the more precious for present-day people of Fang descent because these rich "traditions" have faded away without leaving much trace.

Die Pangwe: Sex and Sündenfall (Fall from Grace)

A recurring aspect of Tessmann's research is the central role he attributes to *das Geschlechtsleben* (sexual life) in people's ordering of the world. In *Die Pangwe*, for instance, is *das Geschlechtliche* (the sexual) presented as the crux in their *Weltanschauung* (worldview). For Tessmann it also indicates the "phase" a society is in. Doubleness is central in his analysis in *Die Pangwe* because Tessmann tries to make sense of their order through a concatenation of binary oppositions: between God (*Nsambe*/the Sun) and people, between men and women, between good and evil. He deduces this dualism from their creation myth, which recounts an original fall from grace: Man is seduced by the snake to have intercourse with Woman. This transgression of Nsambe's interdiction had dramatic consequences: Nsambe withdrew from his people, death is their punishment, and they have to live with a constant tension between good and evil. *Geschlechtsverkehr* (intercourse) is therefore the original sin. In practice it is only allowed at night when Nsambe (the Sun) does not see it, and only for procreation between men and women. All other forms of sex (in daylight, but also those that are not linked to procreation) are severely sanctioned. For Tessmann this basic theme—a very special form of heteronormativity, to say the least—is at the heart of the secret cults (Sso, Ngi, and several others) that have center space in his book.

Another basic opposition on which Tessmann insists is the one between religion (chapter 11) and sorcery (*Zauberglauben*; chapter 12), which coincides with the contrast between the soul (*die Seele*/*nisim*) and magic force (*Zauberkraft*/*evu*). In his view the two have to be sharply distinguished. By introducing this *evu* notion Tessmann relates to what has become a major theme in the literature on the Pangwe/Beti group as a central but enigmatic force in these societies. This notion, nowadays always translated as *sorcellerie* (witchcraft), evokes a wide range of associations, varying over time, but some basic conceptions seem to occur in all the literature to be discussed here: *evu* as a frightening little animal with sharp teeth living in people's bellies and allowing those who take the trouble of developing it to "de-double" themselves at night in particular and fly off to nocturnal meetings with their fellow conspirators. Such conceptions are certainly not special to the Pangwe/Beti, but occur in varying forms in many parts of Africa and elsewhere.[14] Indeed, in Cameroonian French *dédoubler* has become a key word that puts people on the alert in everyday conversations, just as *evu* has become a standard term throughout southern Cameroon to refer to the occult. Tessmann tries to catch this force in binary oppositions (*gute*/*schlechte Zauberkraft*), thus ending with a one-page figure— somewhat frightening in its thoroughness—in which all these oppositions are neatly ordered into one overarching genealogy (Tessmann 1913, 2:126).

This struggle to classify what is basically ambiguous also marks Tessmann's analysis of the notion of *biang akuma* (medicine of wealth) that present-day authors like Charles Gueboguo (2009) and Patrick Awondo (2019) dug up, relating it to current debates about Freemasonry, same-sex behavior, and popular anger about ever more blatant forms of illicit enrichment.[15] In *Die Pangwe* it appears in various contexts and with various implications. It is first mentioned with quite negative overtones in relation to the *Mekukmann* (Tessmann 1913, 2:149), the evil sorcerer who kills people to use their crane for mystical access to wealth.[16] Later on (p. 158) Tessmann notes with some surprise that this wealth medicine is directly related to same-sex intercourse. He suggests as a possible explanation that the medicine, passed on by intimate touching, can bring prosperity to the two *"Freunde"* (friends; quotation marks by Tessmann) because of their mutual support of each other—all the more so since they are conscious of committing a sin and having to hide it.

Much later in part 2 of the monograph, Tessmann returns to the topic in a section on *Abarten des Geschlechtslebens* (Sexual Deviations; pp. 270–74) where he notes that for the Fang same-sex intercourse between adults is considered *widernatürlich* (against nature) and *unerhört* (unheard of). But he adds that it is there nonetheless, yet hidden under a *Stachelkleid* (prickly cover) that is none other than the *biang akuma* (wealth medicine) mentioned before.[17] In his later publications he developed this idea of a *Stachelkleid* covering same-sex practices in a more flowery style:

> A casual traveler must get the impression that *Homosexualität* does not at all exist among the untouched Negroes. However, whoever stays longer on the spot and gets to know the land and the people [*Land und Leute*] knows under which heading homosexuality can be found. Among the Pangwe it is called "wealth medicine." Such a wealth medicine offers release to same-sex drives next to many mystical instincts. People believe that through the close connection mystical forces are passed on that make both partners rich. (Tessmann 1919, 133; translation by Geschiere; see also Murray and Roscoe 1988, 156)

When Tessmann tries to explain why the idea of homosexuality was hidden under such a prickly cover "that protected against the attacks of *Andersgeartete* [people of different inclination] whose mouth and sharp tongue would be bloodily torn by it" (p. 271), he recounts one of the Pangwe stories that play such a key role in his work. This one is about the link between *biang akuma* and same-sex intercourse, and it acquired the status of a locus classicus in queer studies on Africa because it was translated and published in the Murray and Roscoe collection (1998) on traces of "African homosexualities" in earlier literature. Murray and Roscoe chose to translate a shorter version of this story that Tessmann published in one of his first articles (in Karsch-Haak's 1911 collection on *Das gleichgeschlechtiges Leben der Naturvölker*). Here follows the fuller version as published in Tessmann's *Die Pangwe*.

Das Reichtumsmedizin (the medicine of wealth)

There once was a man called *bongo-be-ntuu-duomo* who had a daughter called *Akukebedanga* who was very beautiful, as her name indicated. Now it happened that on the road to the village of Bongo [Tessmann abbreviates the name] four young men met who were all going to see the girl. They asked each other where they wanted to go and they all said: "To Akukebedanga." So they agreed to go there together and see whom the girl would prefer.

The four young men, from different families, were called Schok-bo-schaua (meaning? [question mark Tessmann]); Schok-bö-ng-onne-ma-kö-makö (means: I go and will come back later); Schock [*sic*]—bö-kama-jem-bodscho-melang (do not know evil talk); Schok-bo-num-e-kub-b'pghuale-ba-jem-e'kidi-ma-lënne (the cock and the francolin know the morning is coming).

I [that is, Tessmann] will abbreviate their names as Schok I, II, III, and IV.

So the four young men arrived at the village and introduced themselves to Bongo, the girl's father, who said: "Oh, here we have four men but only one girl. But we will see." He led them into his house where they found the girl's mother who also said, "Oh . . . four men. Until now this or that lover would come and when the girl loved him she slept with him and when she did not love him, she did not sleep with him, and then he would return home. But this—four men at once." But the young men replied, "Let us see whom the girl will love."

But she loved Schok IV. However, the mother loved Schok III, *while the girl's brother loved Schok II and her father loved Schok I* [Tessmann's emphasis].

When night came, the guests were put up in the girl's house. She slept with Schok IV in one bed; the others slept on other beds. When Schok IV wanted to embrace her, one of the others called, "Oh, this girl is really horny [*geil*]; she gives herself to her lover already in the first night." So the girl said to Schok IV, "Hear this guy talking! Leave it and let us wait for another night."

But when the others had fallen asleep, Schok IV said softly to the girl, "Do you want to marry me?" The girl accepted and they agreed to flee together the next day.[18] In case they met someone they would say that they went for a bath.

The next day Schok IV pretended to go for a bath; the girl followed him unnoticed. Then both walked to the village of Schok IV.

However, when both had not returned in the afternoon of the same day and it became evident that Schok IV had stolen the girl, Schok III went to the mother—who liked him—and made her heavy reproaches because the girl had escaped. But the mother answered, "Well, this is not my fault, I am not in her skin!" Then Schok III became angry, grabbed his bushknife, and hacked into her. She died on the spot. Then he went home.

Schok I, who loved the father, addressed him, and also made heavy reproaches, asking how the girl got it in her mind to run off. Thereupon the father said, "Oh, I cannot help it. If I were the girl, I would not have done this[19] but I am not in the girl's skin." Schok I was not satisfied with this reply. Therefore, the father went to the village of Schok IV who had abducted his daughter and demanded a bride price from him. Schok IV effectively paid it. Bongo returned with this and said to Schok I, "Here is all the money for the girl; I pay you with this." But Schok I told him, "No, I do not want the money." Then the father took one of his wives and the money and offered everything to Schok I as compensation. But again Schok I did not want to accept any payment. He said, "No, I do not want this—rather (and this should be the compensation) we will be together for ever. When you piss, I shall piss as well; when you have a shit, I will have a shit as well; when you sleep, I shall sleep with you in one bed."[20]

And thus it happened, and they slept together. But eventually they fell ill with frambesia and they both died.

Finally Schok II, who loved the brother, did the same with him, as Schok I with Bongo. As compensation for the girl he stuck to the brother and both slept together. But they fell ill also, in their case with leprosy, and they both died.

The story seems quite straightforward (albeit full of surprises), but it apparently lends itself to different interpretations, certainly for what it says about same-sex arrangements and their implications for enrichment. Striking is, for instance, that in their interpretation Murray and Roscoe conclude that the medicine of wealth is passed "from the receptive partner *to* the penetrating partner" (1998, 142). In Tessmann's own text (reproduced in their collection a few pages later; p. 156, and see also above) the latter insists on mutuality, *both* partners becoming rich. Another ambivalence that disappears in Murray and Roscoe's translation is the direction of the love that emerges so abruptly in the story between Schok I and the father, and between Schok II and the brother. In several passages Tessmann states that it is the father who loves Schok I, just as it is the brother who loves Schok II (and the mother who loves Schok III); but in other passages the arrow is reversed, Schok I loving the father and Schok II loving the brother. Of course this makes one wonder what the word "love" (in German *Liebe*) stands for in Fang. We will come back to Tessmann being quite vague about the practice of love and/or sex.

Another complication is that the story's message is equally ambivalent. One can read it as "proof" that same-sex behavior—even if it was often severely condemned by Tessmann's interlocutors—was imaginable in Pangwe society; this is the way Murray and Roscoe propose reading it. Yet the horrible punishment that followed for both same-sex couples also turns it into a severe warning against such behavior.[21] Indeed, Tessmann's comments on *biang akuma* betray both excitement at having found at least a trace of same-sex arrangements and disappointment that it is so deeply hidden under a *Stachelkleid* (this prickly cover). Enrichment is only indirectly addressed in this story (the father offering money and a wife to Schok I and the latter turning it down and claiming the father himself). But the *biang* (medicine) of same-sex intercourse is directly linked to *akuma* (riches); indeed, it seems to be this special form of doubleness that brings riches. Should we see the doubleness of the partners in same-sex practice then as providing a false basis for enrichment—hence their fatal ending?

Tessmann and the Bafia: *Gleichgeschlechtligkeit* as an Earlier Phase?

Tessmann's references to same-sex behavior among the Pangwe are colored by a sense of disappointment. The *Stachelkleid* hiding its traces was apparently quite discouraging. However, Tessmann's subsequent research among the Bafia (about 300 kilometers to the northwest of the Fang, on the border between forest and savanna) was in many ways a breakthrough for him—and apparently a most welcome one. It confirmed his premonitions during his research among the Pangwe about the existence of an earlier "phase" that might still be present elsewhere. In his book on Tessmann, Thomas Klockmann (1988, 154) suggests even that his research among the Bafia, and notably their tolerance of same-sex intercourse, became a turning point in Tessmann's thinking about human evolution and the key role of sexuality. He could only work for a few months with this group in its own habitat, since he started this project in the middle of 1914, just before the outbreak of the First World War. After the Germans had to evacuate South Kamerun in 1916 and Tessmann was interned with the remainders of the German army on Spanish Fernando Po (Bioko) he could still conduct a series of interviews with Bafia soldiers among the *Hilfstruppen* (auxiliaries) who had followed the German army.

From the beginning of his research with the Bafia Tessmann was struck by radical differences with the Pangwe, and again *Geschlechtlichkeit* was for him the obvious gauge of this. For the Bafia, Tessmann noted *eine stark ausgeprägte Gleichgeschlechtligkeit* (a marked homosexuality; 1934, 225): "For them is it completely the same for judging sexual exchange whether one loves a man or a woman . . . No one has to dissemble because there are no radical contrasts in sexual exchange." *Freundesliebe* (loving a male friend) was completely acceptable among the Bafia, even among adults. Once, when Tessmann asked an informant whether he also practiced this, the latter answered with a counter-question: "Should I give up my people's custom?"—to the clear satisfaction of the ethnologist (1934, 226). Moreover, as was to be expected in Tessmann's view, this open sexual attitude corresponded to a worldview that was again radically different from that of *die Pangwe*. For the Bafia, the figure standing at the beginning of everything was not a singular God who abandoned his people after their fall from grace but rather a *Zauberer* (sorcerer; in Tessmann's theories characteristic for an earlier phase) who moreover was mostly of good intentions. Hence there was none of the pressure of binary oppositions (good/evil, man/woman) that burdened his Fang friends. In his monograph about the Bafia (published in 1934) Tessmann generalized this difference as a contrast between an earlier phase, *Monismus*, and a later one, *Dualismus*—and to his great regret he had to conclude that the Fang were already in this later phase. But luckily, the Bafia were still "monist." Again, Tessmann deduced this from the Bafia creation myth—no fall of grace, no death, and therefore no afterlife, no obsession with good versus evil—but he illustrates the difference once more, and most emphatically, with the consequences for *Geschlechtsverkehr*. For the Bafia this was not at all associated with an original sin—on the contrary, Tessmann marveled at their very permissive attitude toward all forms of sexual intercourse.

An intriguing question is where Tessmann got these ideas of *Monismus* versus *Dualismus*. Since 1900 these had become current terms among German intellectuals. In 1906 several *Freigeister und Dissidenten* ("freethinkers and dissidents," as they called themselves) founded the *Monistenbund* in Jena with natural scientist Ernst Haeckel as its first president. The Monists were strongly influenced by Darwin's theory of evolution, which they saw as a clear victory over the dualism of the Christian vision of human history. Ernst Hirschfeld, with his third gender theories, found an interested audience in these circles. Freemasons were also well represented. However, during the First World War the *Monistenbund* rapidly lost its appeal. It seems that Tessmann applied the *Monismus/Dualismus* contrast in his own work when the movement was already in decline (Seeck 1996). Moreover, he used the terms in quite an original way. For the German *Monisten, Monismus* meant a surpassing of *Dualismus*, while Tessmann seems to see it as an earlier phase instead, one that was—unfortunately—to be superseded by increasing dualism (as it had been among the Fang).[22] It night be good to underline here that Tessmann's characterization of Pangwe society as having already passed into a "dualist" phase has nothing to do with the idea of the human as double, the central theme of this chapter. He may see the Bafia as "monists," but this does not preclude that with them as well there was (and is) a constant emphasis on the plurality of the person. Clearly, duality can be a confusing notion, since it lends itself to so many meanings.

But what to think of Tessmann's almost lyrical passages on the relaxed acceptance of same-sex intercourse among the Bafia? Thomas Klockmann (1988, 152) somewhat drily remarks that Tessmann's main informants on this aspect were Bafia soldiers in the German *Schutztruppen* (colonial army) when they were interned on Fernando Po after 1916. However, it would be wrong to assume that they were there without women. On the contrary, the German auxiliaries were accompanied by a large following of women and children when they were forced to leave Kamerun.[23] Moreover, Achille Mbembe (oral communication), who grew up in a neighboring society in Cameroon, remembers that in his youth people used to gossip about the Bafia and their readiness for sexual experiments. Can we say that Tessmann's cumbersome theoretical preoccupations—which so strongly marked his Bafia monograph—did not stop him from noting real variations in everyday behavior?[24]

Discourse and Sexual Realities

Geschlechtsleben (sexuality) and especially *Gleichgeschechtliches* (homosexuality) may have a central role in Tessmann's work, but he remains remarkably brief on what forms it takes in practice. Apart from one discreet translation of the Bafia term for the sexual act between young adults— *cohabitat [in] anum* ("intercourse into the anus"? Tessmann 1934, 229)— we did not find more detailed indications of the forms sexual intimacies take. Especially striking is that in Tessmann's other descriptions—all fairly open—there is little trace of any distinction between penetrating and being penetrated. Compare also the discrepancy between Murray and Roscoe's summary of Tessmann's ethnography—the by now familiar Fang medicine of wealth (*biang akuma*) supposedly being appropriated by an active partner from the passive lover—and the text of Tessmann's story itself in which all emphasis is on the bond between the two partners making them both rich, without any clear division of roles.[25] Indeed, even in the folktale about the *biang akuma* with the quite direct declarations of love by the rejected suitors to the father and the brother of the unattainable bride—"I will piss where you will piss," and so on—there is no clear sense of direction in their intercourse. For Tessmann same-sex practices seem to be something to be studied at the level of discourse and not of practice.

In general Tessmann's writing on sexuality—important as the topic was for him—was marked by considerable discretion. Especially in his personal writings—in his *Tagebücher* (diaries) and his 1940 autobiography—he wrote at length about his emotions in his contacts with his interlocutors without, however, addressing his sexual feelings (let alone practices). In these writings there are regular eulogies about the aesthetic pleasure the sight of beautiful "Herculean" boys—swimming naked and so on—offered to the author. And he was clearly much more interested in male than in female beauty (several times he notes in his diaries that a local headman offered him a woman for the night—a common form of hospitality in the forest societies—but apparently he did not accept such offers). Any reference to intimacies with his own "boys" is also lacking. On the contrary he describes them as fairly unattractive. Max and Mabale, the two "boys" to whom he genuinely became attached during his first trip to the Fang, are described as efficient and loyal but also as quite common in appearance (Tessmann 1940, 74). Only Boka, whom he also called Ajong, one of his youngest servants, is described with some tenderness (Tessmann 1940, 156–57). One morning, when Ayong was serving him his coffee, Tessmann noted that the latter's makeshift loincloth showed the contours of his penis, but this is not accompanied by any erotic reflections (Tessmann 1940, 148). Ajong was also allowed to accompany Tessmann on his daily bath in the river, when he swam naked (and Ajong also?—not exactly clear), but again this did not seem to lead to any further intimacies (Tessmann's only comment is how refreshing it was to swim in the river).[26] Only in his journal entry about the dramatic moment all at the end of his second expedition with the Fang (May 1909), when his Ntum boys revealed the betrayal of Schok, who had been his most trusted collaborator during the whole expedition, does Tessmann add a reference to things that had to remain unsaid (the "boys" also told him about "things that cannot be mentioned here"; Tessmann 2015, 151).[27]

The same discreteness marked Tessmann's writings about the Bafia and their sexual practices. In his 1919 article he mentioned (p. 129) that among this group some adults continued with same-sex relations, who can therefore be qualified as *die eigentlichen Homosexuellen* (real homosexuals). But he added that he never met one in person. Also compare a note at the very end of this 1919 article (p. 138) in which he commented very negatively on "degenerate same-sex practices" that were developing along the coast among *verchristlichten Küstenneger* (christened coastal Negroes).[28] Tessmann clearly saw this as a sign of degeneration without any link to *biang akuma*. Clearly his keen interest in *Gleichgeschlechtligkeit* among *Naturvölker* did not inspire him to a more activist attitude like some of his contemporaries in Germany (Hirschfeld and others).

Tessmann's Epigones: Doubleness and Occult Enrichment among the Beti

Tessmann's vagueness about sexual practices is problematic for our analysis since it is difficult to ascertain on what observation his references to same-sex intimacies were based, both among the Bafia and the Fang—all the more so since these references were later strongly contested, not only by people from these groups themselves but also in academic publications. Only in the final decades of the twentieth century was Tessmann's interest in binary oppositions, sexuality, and the doubleness of human beings picked up again by anthropologists writing about the Fang and related groups; a stream then followed. A brief overview gives an idea of differences and convergences.

Powerful statements came from Meinrad Hebga (1928–2008), a visionary thinker, anthropologist, and Jesuit, but also practicing as a healer cum exorcist; in 1976 he founded a charismatic brotherhood in Yaoundé (still inside the Catholic Church) called Ephphata. A constant theme in all these activities was Hebga's effort to reconcile *sorcellerie* (witchcraft), as a real force, to rational thinking (cf. notably Hebga 1979; Hebga 1995). Taking his ethnographic examples from his own Bassa group (which lives in the same forest area as the Fang, about 100 kilometers to the north), he offered original insights into the way *sorcellerie* can be related to an evil-versus-good binary. On the one hand, he emphasized the distortion caused by European terms like" witchcraft" as translations of local notions that had much broader associations (both destructive *and* constructive). On the other, he insisted on the evilness of *sorcellerie* in the present day as an unequivocally destructive force that had to be combatted by all means. Thus he seems to agree with Joseph Tonda's view, quoted earlier, that the *sorcellerie* as we know it has to be understood as a colonial creation turned inside out by the pejorative impact of the terms introduced during that period.[29] Another constant in Hebga's thinking is of more direct relevance to our theme. In his preoccupation about understanding what for him were clear manifestations of an all too real human capacity for metamorphosis—the topic of his first doctoral thesis (1968)—he kept opposing on the one hand Western thinking stuck in binaries, and, on the other, African thought capable of handling a much more complex plurality of the person as well as other forms of agency. Clearly Tessmann's complex scheme, quoted before, trying to capture the manifold aspects of the human being through a piling up of binaries, would not have satisfied Hebga, who remained closer to the idea of doubleness as constantly shifting.

Similar accents can be found in the work of French-Catalan anthropologist Louis Mallart, who worked in the 1960s among the Evozuk, another group of the large Beti (= Pangwe/Pahouin) conglomerate (see note 8 above). The enigmatic title of one of his books, *Ni dos ni ventre* (Neither back nor belly, 1981), in which the *evu* notion has central consideration, expresses the openness the *evu* notion had in his view and the dilemmas this poses for academic analysis, intent on creating clarity and unequivocalness. In contrast to Tessmann (whom he also does not quote), Mallart avoids any radical contrast between *religion* and *sorcellerie*. He situates *evu* at the interface of the two; therefore it can work negatively but also positively (for instance, in relation with healing). Thus the doubleness of the person is also central to his analysis—especially in relation to the more empowering side of *evu*—but nowhere in his writing is this linked to same-sex arrangements.

The work of Philippe Laburthe-Tolra (1929–2016) is of special interest for this chapter, not only because he produced a series of voluminous books (1977, 1981, and 1985) that are still considered authoritative ethnographic studies on the Beti (generally seen as closely related to the Fang) but also because he straightforwardly addressed Tessmann's analysis (Laburthe-Tolra did read German), notably Tessmann's emphasis on the link between *biang akuma* (the much-discussed medicine of wealth) and same-sex intercourse. Even more interestingly, while Laburthe-Tolra was in general deeply impressed by Tessmann's ethnography and analysis— especially where it concerned the great rituals of secret associations (Soo, Ngi, Schok) that were no longer held when Laburthe-Tolra did his fieldwork (1964–1972)—he flatly contradicted the old master on the link Tessmann saw between wealth and homosexuality. In Laburthe-Tolra's view, Tessmann was fooled by the stories of his informants (Laburthe-Tolra 1977, 912, 1243; 1985, 170–72). Laburthe-Tolra explicitly referred to the folktale quoted above about the four suitors and the same-sex escapades of two of them, but for Laburthe-Tolra the story's morale was instead to highlight how utterly foolish such behavior would be. Quoting also J.-F. Vincent (1969 and 1976) in this sense, Laburthe-Tolra stuck to his idea that any alternative form of sexuality—and certainly homosexuality—would be deeply shocking for the Beti since it would directly be equated with *evu/sorcellerie.* Laburthe-Tolra did mention the notion of *biang akuma* but only as a much broader category, in no way related to same-sex intercourse (1985, 93, 141, 154).

However, it is striking that elsewhere in his voluminous monograph, Laburthe-Tolra also insisted on the ambiguity of *evu*—basically evil but also a source of wealth and power (1985, 93, 141). Indeed, part 4 of his 1977 magnum opus on *Les relations avec le monde invisible* (reprinted in 1985 as *Initiations et sociétés secrètes au Cameroun: Essai sur la religion beti*) can be read as a drawn-out struggle with the ambiguity of *evu*. A whole chapter (and by far the longest) is about *evu* and offers an honest report on the ethnographer confronting this enigmatic notion, notably how it could be seen as basically evil and at the same time vital for both people and the wider social order (Laburthe-Tolra 1985, chapter 2, pp. 59–164). The following offers a striking example in this respect.

After quoting several interlocutors who insisted that, of course, the *evu* is evil, Laburthe-Tolra tells how one evening when he and his assistant were starting an interview with several village elders—"somewhat heated up by palmwine"—one of them suddenly turned the tables on their guests and started to interrogate them: "My father was a great *nganga* [healer]. When he initiated people, he placed two funnels in a bowl of water. The candidate had to take one of the funnels. If that one was empty, Papa knew the candidate's belly was empty. But if he picked the funnel with something in it, papa knew that he had something in his belly: the *evu*." Then the elders put, indeed, a bowl of water in front of Laburthe-Tolra and his assistant; in it for each of them were two funnels, rolled from leaves, and asked them to choose—adding, "you would not want to cheat on us."

Laburthe-Tolra continues in his flowery style: "We did as we were told, and anxious not to be identified as a *sorcier* [witch], I heaved a deep sigh of relief when my funnel was empty and the one of my companion as well. However, at the moment of my triumph, there was to my great surprise clear consternation among the elders: 'But then, if you do not have the *evu*, what can you understand then? We cannot tell you anything, you are like children.' We turned out to be *pauvres types* [poor blokes] because we did not have anything in our belly. How can one maintain then that the *evu* is only negative. Is he good? Is he bad? Our effort to define the *evu* ended in an inextricable aporia" (1985, 67–68).

Laburthe-Tolra's very balanced conclusion after this altercation can be summarized as accepting that the *evu* is basically an evil force but that it is also a condition for all forms of success. Among the Beti, healers (*nganga*) can only heal because they have learned to control their powerful *evu*; an elder needs his *evu* in order to control "his" young men; and so on.[30]

However, such a balanced view also raises the question of how Laburthe-Tolra could then be so categorical in his refusal of Tessmann's linking *biang akuma* as a mystic source of riches to same-sex intercourse. If such practices were indeed seen as manifestations of the *evu*, could not the very ambivalence of this notion give such transgressive sexual practices enticing aspects as well?

Laburthe-Tolra's rich ethnography evokes a world that is pervaded by doubleness and de-doubling. It is not only the *evu* that allows for a wide range of transformations. The spirits of the deceased (*bekon*) can also remain present in the human environment for quite some time.[31] His work certainly confirms that this tumbling world of the doubles is a source of riches and empowerment. But for him it is anathema to relate the idea of witchcraft-bringing-riches to same-sex practices. For Laburthe-Tolra, and also for Vincent, the severe condemnation of such practices by the Beti apparently excludes same-sex behavior as a real occurrence, let alone associating it with enrichment.[32]

Another anthropologist, Jean-Pierre Ombolo, himself a Beti, is as radical in his denial of any trace of male homosexuality among his people. In his *Société et sexualité en Afrique noire* (1990)—which is essentially a monograph on the Beti—he insisted, like Laburthe-Tolra, that *perversions sexuelles* (sexual perversions) are always equated with *sorcellerie*. In his chapter on such perversions (Ombolo 1990, 155ff.) he mentioned homosexuality as the first one, but he added that the Beti did not know homosexuality between men, only between women—and then it was seen as a cause of sterility. Ombolo did quote Tessmann (p. 163) but completely ignored the latter's statement that same-sex practices did exist between males, albeit under a prickly cover.

Sévérin Abega's Carnival of Doubles

A quite different outlook comes from Sévérin Cécile Abega, a brilliant anthropologist of a younger generation, also a Beti himself.[33] For him homosexuality certainly exists in Beti society. Indeed, it is more or less a given considering the centrality of doubleness in the Beti view of the person. In contrast to the authors cited above, Abega's writings date from the period (2000s) when homosexuality became a public issue in Cameroon. As said, his key publication on this issue (Abega 2007a; see also Abega 2002) was published in a special issue of the journal *Terroirs*, edited by Fabien Eboussi Boulaga as a reply to the explosion of homophobia after the 2006 *affaire des listes*.[34] For Abega homosexuality has a special place in Beti culture since it relates so directly to the conception of the person as double. Often, one's double would be of one's own sex. But for others the double is of the opposite sex. People's perception of homosexuality would be based on this conception of the person and this would also explain the general unease with "the" homosexual as a person who has the wrong double. So, here is a specific image of "the" homosexual, albeit one that is about as heteronormative as possible: in this view "homosexuality is rationalized as the heterosexuality of doubles" (Abega 2007a, 104; see also Abega 2007b; Abega and Abe 2005).

Interestingly this view leads Abega to a somewhat dazzling enumeration of all the different ways it allows for relating same-sex intimacies to wealth. As a *sexualité de luxe* it is generally attributed to the *Grands* who impose same-sex intercourse on less fortunate people. This is also Abega's explanation why, as said, for quite some time in Yaoundé homosexuals were called *francs-maçons* (Freemasons; Abega 2007a, 104). It also explains why young men who have success are generally suspected of selling their sexual services. The *Grands* who patronize them are often supposed to fortify their own doubles by "pumping the vital energy of the partner"

FIGURE 5.4. Bulu mask. Important in the material culture of the Fang, Bulu, and related groups were masks playing central roles in the rituals Tessmann observed. Such masks relate to Cameroonian anthropologist Abega's seminal emphasis on the person as "double"—very relevant to understanding African specificities in queering sexuality. State Museum of Ethnology, Munich. Photo: Origamiemensch/Wikimedia Commons, CC-BY-SA 3.0.

(Abega 2007a, 105). But the link can also be made in the inverse: such "pumping" can equally reinforce the passive partners, who will become slightly overweight (*embonpoint*) by absorbing the seed of their partners. Also, someone who gets involved with a homosexual can become atrophied if his partner gives him a blow job. Abega relates all these different variations to the general Beti perception of sexual intercourse as depleting one's vital energy. Striking in Abega's cascade of possibilities is that the only fixed point seems to be the link between same-sex intercourse and enrichment. There is no fixed division between penetrator and penetrated (or "top" and "bottom," to borrow from present-day jargon). Both partners can profit or lose through these intimate contacts. Just as in Tessmann's descriptions of *biang akuma* (medicine of wealth), the profile of "the" homosexual remains volatile and open, except for the link people make with enrichment in whatever form.

General Implications

Abega's inventory of all these different possibilities in the articulation of doubleness, same-sex behavior, and enrichment is all the more interesting because his text is a forerunner in the wider debate developing about the anus and its variable articulations with riches in Africa—so succinctly summed up in the Cameroonian notion of *anusocratie*. The emphasis on same-sex arrangements offering enrichment, or in any case "access," became a recurrent theme in our explorations in earlier chapters. Remember also the different views of Mbembe and Tonda on the idea of *anusocratie*. Such accents and differences fit in very well with Abega's overview of the varying possibilities that the basic doubleness of the person opens up for imagining what a *homosexualité de luxe* might be about. Mbembe's version of the *Grand* as a supreme "phallocrat," subjecting even people of his own sex to anal penetration and thus appropriating their life force, develops a common theme in witchcraft discourse (Mbembe 2006, 2010). But Abega's overview also relates to Tonda's view of anal intercourse as depletion of the active partner. Thus we seem to be back at the questions Tessmann's ethnography raises. His emphasis more than one hundred years ago on same-sex intercourse as a source of enrichment turns out to be prophetic for preoccupations that have recently acquired considerable force in many parts of Africa. However, how exactly this link is made remains quite open—remember what was said before about "homosexuality" therefore becoming a floating signifier.

Yet this chapter's focus on the various ways the link between same-sex behavior and enrichment fits in with ideas of "witchcraft" may have suggested some openings for further insight. Broadening the notion of "witchcraft" as standing for a vision of a *monde des doubles* (world of doubles)—to borrow the felicitous phrase of Sévérin Abéga—can help us understand the crucial role such a conception of the person plays in linking transgressive forms of sexuality to mystical enrichment. It also helps to realize how confusing the introduction and appropriation of Western notions like witchcraft or *sorcellerie* with their pejorative implications has been for an imaginary that sees human beings as always plural, so their potentialities are not that easily classified as "good" or "evil." This is also why Tessmann's courageous scheme of Fang personhood, piling up ever more local binaries upon a good/evil opposition—apparently for him universal and therefore self-evident—had to implode through its internal inconsistencies. Clearly we need more fluid approaches to understand the basic ambiguities in which people's abilities and actions are caught. Yet, as always, witchcraft's impact is also confusing in this respect: the term itself imposes a powerful moral evaluation of actions and notions that are basically amoral, in the sense that they can easily shift from one pole to the other. What seems to be good can turn out to be extremely evil and vice versa (see Geschiere 2013).

This discourse about doubleness is confusing in another respect. As said, the emphasis on the plurality of the person seems to fit in very well with the "posthuman" approaches that have recently become current in human science discourse in the West (see Mbembe 2016a). It is certainly true that emphasizing the basic doubleness of the person undermines any idea of "the" individual as a clearly outlined actor. Yet, as said, witchcraft discourse at the same time confirms—or even exaggerates—the idea of human agency. The recent outbursts of homophobia in several parts of Africa show how easily such outlining of a hidden human actor as responsible for the staggering accumulation of riches can lead to scapegoating. It becomes all the more important to try and further understand the conceptual link between transgressive sexuality and illicit enrichment. To what extent can the emphasis on the plurality of the person as it emerged in this chapter—on the ambiguities of kaleidoscopic combinations of doubles underlining the relativity of all binary oppositions—further provide solutions in this minefield?

Conclusions

Conspiracy thinking is kaleidoscopic, loosely assembling elements from widely different backgrounds into a whole that for the adepts becomes convincing precisely because everything seems to be adding up. The preceding chapters may have shown that popular indignation in Cameroon and Gabon about a supposed plot of Freemasons using same-sex practices as one way toward illicit enrichment is, indeed, a stew of widely different elements. A key factor is clearly the link people in Cameroon and Gabon make with the omnipresence in higher circles of Freemasonry and other esoteric associations of a global allure—as noted, an urgent topic in its own right, severely understudied despite its omnipresence throughout the continent. Moreover, linking homosexuality to such global associations is invoked as a powerful confirmation that it is a colonial imposition, introduced into these countries by depraved politicians, morally corrupted by their colonial mentors: "homosexuality" as a colonial conspiracy. But the secrecy surrounding these brotherhoods also makes them easily associated with that other pole of conspiracy thinking in these countries, what people nowadays label as *sorcellerie* (witchcraft); the same applies to any form of same-sex intercourse.

Other factors play a role of their own in this conspiracy kaleidoscope. For Cameroon there is the extreme violence of the decolonization process because of the special difficulties in retaining this country—so dear to de Gaulle because of the crucial role it played in 1940 in the constitution of his *La France Libre*—inside the *Françafrique* community. A crucial moment in this line was the "return" after 2000 of Dr. Louis-Paul Aujoulat, in the 1950s the architect of a cooperative elite to which France could give independence without losing its footholds there, but abruptly turned into a "homo-Masonic" figure. Another crucial turn in the genealogy of this narrative was President François Mitterand's determined choice—after the 1981 socialist victory in the

French elections—to work with Freemason networks (in contrast to preceding French governments), bringing the brotherhood back in the heart of France's neocolonial policies. A completely different line— but as important to balance the idea of homosexuality as a colonial imposition—is the link to the work of Günther Tessmann (1913) on the Fang notion of *biang akuma* (the magic of wealth). Tessmann, the first ethnographer to do in depth fieldwork in the interior, noted with some surprise that this *biang akuma* was associated with same-sex intercourse: sexual transgression already then seen as a source of enrichment and, more generally, empowerment. A similar theme is now—more than a hundred years later!—elaborated in the popular preoccupation with Freemasons and Rosicrucians as empowered by their practices of *anu-socratie*. But now this theme of magic, wealth, and same-sex intercourse is evoked to vent popular anger at the elite's habits of ostentatious consumption at a time when the country is thought to be in crisis and has lost belief in economic development. Clearly the epistemological knot we traced behind people's anger—condensing Freemasonry, homosexuality, and illicit enrichment into one powerful conspiracy narrative—has a long history, bringing together quite different strands into an explosive mixture. Indeed, in our different chapters both Freemasonry and witchcraft emerged as quite open historical assemblages, allowing for the inclusion of a variety of elements depending on time and space. No wonder that the articulation of such shifting assemblages in popular imaginaries in present-day Cameroun and Gabon turned "homosexuality" into a vibrant issue.

This brief summary already contains some answers to the questions raised by Steven Pierce that we took as points of departure in this book's introduction. For him an urgent challenge for understanding the homophobic tide that has swept over the African continent since the end of the last century is to go beyond general explanations, like emphasizing that homophobia rather than homosexuality is a colonial export. Such a "decolonizing" approach is of course very necessary, but Pierce pleads for more fine-tuned interpretations—and with good reason. As emphasized, it is a gross misunderstanding to take homophobia as some sort of given in African contexts. As Patrick Awondo (2012a, 2019) has shown most convincingly, the recent "politicization" of the issue follows very different trajectories and takes on different forms in various countries. We have shown that even in Cameroon, at the outbreak of this moral panic after 2005, when the most gross fantasies about same-sex intercourse circulated in the media, there were other voices who spoke up against such discrimination and disrespect of privacy. The above suggests, indeed, quite surprising answers for Cameroon and Gabon to Pierce's first question: What do people mean when they use a term like "homosexuality"? People seem to target two quite different groups with the term. It is used for men and women who conform to the global profile of LGBTQ people: marginalized and discriminated, increasingly victimized by the police. But "the homosexual" who plays such a prominent role in popular conspiracy theories is of a very different caliber—remember Ateba Eyene's 2012 book about "the dictatorship of the lodges" and "the magico-anal." In such a context "the" homosexual is a so-called *Grand*, submitting youngsters, eager to get a job, to anal humiliation. Our brief comparisons suggest that such linking of same-sex intercourse to enrichment gets heavy emphasis in many African contexts. But again, this general aspect is articulated across the continent following different trajectories. In Cameroon it became intertwined with the leftovers of the particularly violent decolonization trajectory that enabled the French to give independence (1960) to a "cooperative" elite—already at the time ridiculed by more radical nationalists as *les femmes des Blancs*, an accusation that subsequently made notions like *anusocratie* appear self-evident. In Gabon the prowess of presidents father and son Bongo at combining ostentatious involvement in secret associations of both local and global provenance encouraged a magical climate that Gabonese anthropologist Joseph Tonda (2015a) aptly captured with the notion of *la société des éblouissements* (dazzlement).

Such special backgrounds can also provide answers to Pierce's second question: Why now? An obvious link is that homosexuality became a hot issue when people gained more regular access to the internet beginning at the end of the twentieth century. But the Central African cases show with particular sharpness the ambiguous implications of this general fact. On the one hand the internet was received as a most welcome liberation by many people involved—remember the relief that older self-identifying gays among our interlocutors felt when internet access showed them that they were not the only ones to nourish such desires. But for others the internet brought the confirmation that the West was, indeed, exporting its depravities to Africa, as another way to corrupt the nation. Growing access to the internet coincided with completely novel campaigns of human rights missions and other interventions—mostly of Western provenance—to promote LGBTQ rights, which met with sympathy by some but also triggered fierce reactions among African populations at large. Indeed, the switch in the conspiracy theories about Dr. Aujoulat—from a neocolonial strategist to a homo-Masonic figure—occurred at the same time. But other contextual factors gave special twists. For Cameroon, access to the internet coincided with a dramatic depoliticization of young people. In the early 1990s the *Opération villes mortes*—a complete lockdown of the major cities as a protest against President Biya's stubborn refusal to organize a national conference and his blatant rigging of the crucial 1992 presidential elections—mobilized a political protest that seemed to spell the end of his regime. However, Biya was saved by unfailing support from Mitterand, and since then his regime has been very effective in dampening people's political involvement. Remember Eboko and Awondo's salient characterization (2018a) of the Cameroonian state as *l'État stationnaire*, only interested in its own survival. What we called President Biya's spiritual pluralism—his trajectory, after having been almost killed during the 1984 coup, from a faithful Catholic through the kabbalah and Freemasonry to Raymond Bernard's OSTI (Ordre souverain du temple initiatique, an obscure form of Rosicrucianism)—added to the mystification of state power. A short ethnographic vignette can illustrate the effects in everyday life.

In 2014 Jean-François Bayart, ever since his 1978 book *L'État au Cameroun* a leading scholar on Cameroon, returned to the country after thirty years of absence (he had good reasons to fear for his personal safety). To celebrate this occasion the Alliance française in Doula organized a lecture. The room was packed, particularly with people of younger generations who were eager to see and hear the man whose writings had been discussed for so long in the country. Bayart's lecture met with enthusiastic applause followed by a most animated discussion. But it was striking that nearly all the questions concerned the mystic backgrounds of the state's power in Cameroon—the role of esoteric associations, secret deals, and magic backgrounds in the exercise of power. This was notable since Bayart's talk had not focused on these aspects. The perspicacious comment of our good friend and colleague Basile Ndjio—quoted extensively above on the impact of popular notions like *les pédés de la République* or *anusocratie*—was "You see, this is exactly what the regime wants: make people speculate about the secrets behind its power rather than focus on the failures of its policies."

In Gabon, Bongo *père et fils* had (and have), as said, their own ways of shrouding their power in mysteries. Here also it seems to have the same effect of encouraging a proliferation of ugly conspiracy theories—remember people's obsession with "spare parts" of innocent bodies killed by "butchers" to produce fetishes for *les Grands*—to confound any form of more regular opposition. Historicizing conspiracy theories means patiently disentangling the different strands adding up to what seems to be a convincing assemblage in specific contexts.

General Relevance: LGBTQ, "Witchcraft," and Enrichment

Yet precisely our focus on the specificities behind homophobic conspiracy theories raises points of more general relevance. A practical point of considerable urgency is the association, omnipresent in the preceding, of same-sex intercourse with "witchcraft" and illicit enrichment, condensed in the idea that it provides "access" (but access to what exactly?). Indeed, one of the surprises of our comparative explorations was how strongly the link with enrichment kept coming back in quite different contexts. Of course associations of homosexuality with wealth and consumerism occur all over the world. However, in Africa this link seems to get particularly strong emphasis, and invariably the supposed link with "witchcraft" (or whatever term people use for occult aggression) plays a key role in this. This makes it all the more important to note that such links get very little attention in the general literature on LGBTQ rights and homophobia, budding topics in African studies over the last decades. Of course there are good reasons for this; such associations easily confirm stereotypes that legitimize nasty forms of sexual discrimination. The above may nonetheless have shown how important it is to take homophobic discourse seriously in its often confusing articulations: as Michael Taussig (1987) taught us, epistemological "murk" is often the secret of discursive power.

Apparently the powerful image of the nightly meetings of "witches" as a place for the enactment of transgressive forms of sex in many parts of Africa shapes people's reactions to "homosexuality"—a word that only became common with the impact of the internet at the end of the twentieth century. But in this respect it is also important to stress the ambiguity of these images depending on local contexts. In general such occult forces are seen as highly dangerous and basically evil. Yet they are associated also with daring, unknown challenges and talents for improvisation, just like the *biang akuma* that Tessmann stumbled upon among the Fang: basically transgressive but because of this also empowering. However, the very labelling of these notions as "witchcraft" during colonial times confirmed the increasingly pejorative perception of them, with its starkest expression the recent Pentecostal equation of these forces with the devil, and homosexuality as one of the most blatant manifestations of such evil. But local equivalents (like the *evu* among the same Fang) do retain some of their challenging fascination, and this also affects people's perceptions of same-sex practices as shameful but also in unexpected ways empowering.

Also important is that the image of such nightly meetings relates directly to the idea of special "access." Just as initiation into the secrets of "witchcraft" gives access to the hidden networks of the witches that reach out beyond the frame of kinship communities, same-sex intercourse is supposed to offer access to new opportunities. This applies to both avatars of the popular idea of "the" homosexual in Cameroon despite their apparent differences: to *les Grands* but also—albeit in a more hidden way—to the unhappy victims of police raids and popular discrimination. The two groups are different in every respect, yet just as *les Grands* are supposed to profit from access to global networks, for the more marginal figures same-sex practices also seem to bring special openings.[1] Vinh-Kim Nguyen used this image of "access" as a powerful notion in his 2010 analysis of gay circles in Abidjan. In this case it was also often not exactly clear what kind of access, or to what. In Günther Tessmann's ethnography of *biang akuma* among the Fang in the forest of southern Cameroon around 1900, it remained equally unclear how exactly same-sex intercourse was supposed to make such couples rich (a powerful caveat was that it was supposed also to bring a horrible death—a warning that such riches were transgressive?). For present-day Africa we met this idea of special "access" in all sorts of variations (see chapter 3): gay hairdressers in rural South Africa attracting clients because of their modern taste; same-sex escapades protecting the success of Congolese music stars; marabouts in Senegal imposing such transgressive forms of intercourse on rich clients in order to protect their wealth. Remember also the converging conclusions by Christophe Broqua (2009) and Charles Gueboguo (2009), working on quite different parts of Africa, that "homosexuality" for Africa is becoming "a privileged site" for domination and enrichment. If we want to understand the more flamboyant forms of homophobia that have erupted over the last decades in many parts of Africa—and such understanding might be essential for dealing with them—it is important to take such darker associations seriously. Certainly academics should not try to gloss over such aspects, even if they seem to be less politically correct.

The Person as Plural—Africanizing Queer Theory

Our probing of what "homosexuality" means in postcolonial Africa suggests, as another point of general relevance, similarities and differences with queer studies and its imaginative takeoff in the West over the last decades. One point of convergence is clearly the anus, again an object often shrouded in secrecy. Popular expressions like *anusocratie* (Cameroon) or *anustocratie* (Gabon)—the rule of the anus—highlight the special role it is playing in the postcolonial imaginary around Freemasonry, homosexuality, and illicit enrichment. It is also notable that this focus has lent itself to quite different interpretations. In the introduction we opposed Achille

Mbembe's (2010, 213) interpretation of the way *les Grands* supposedly submit young men, eager to find a job, to anal penetration as a supreme form of phallocracy (in line with witchcraft horrors of elders draining the life force from their younger victims) to Joseph Tonda (2016, 132) linking this image to the Fanonian nightmare of an "impotent" African bourgeoisie. In Tonda's examples are elite persons who allow themselves to be penetrated, thus being robbed of their life force. This recalls the central role the anus played in queer studies as it developed in the West in the 1970s and 1980s. Remember Leo Bersani's classic "Is the Rectum a Grave?" (1987) and Mario Mieli's earlier *Towards a Gay Communism* (1977) with his flamboyant battle cry of "I keep my treasure in my arse, but it is open to everybody"; or Quentin Dubois's recent plea (2021) for a "desublimation of the anus" as a condition to save its destabilizing charge. At first sight the interpretations of the anus in African studies and queer studies seem to be miles apart—small wonder since the African contexts are so different from the Euro-American one. Yet the African idea of the multiple person, coming back in the above time and again, suggests interesting convergences.

This idea relates to a recurrent theme in the growing stream of studies of same-sex arrangements in everyday life in present-day Africa: the ease with which people combine different sexual roles. In the above as well, roles that Western discourse has come to distinguish seemed to shade into each other—not only top/bottom in same-sex intercourse[2] but also homo/hetero distinctions. This variability runs counter to the homophobic discourse quoted above in which in Africa as well "the" homosexual is seen as a specific and well outlined type. But studies of the everyday give a strikingly different profile. In Graeme Reid's study (2010) of an explicitly gay Pentecostal church in Johannesburg the pastor claimed that people had to follow their same-sex preferences because clearly God made them so. However, the church was embarrassed by members (both young men and women) who strayed away by falling occasionally for the charms of the opposite sex—thus, in the church's version of the Gospel, "sinning" against God's intentions for them. In Donald Donham's fascinating *The Erotics of History: An Atlantic African Example* (2018), West African men lodge their Euro-American lovers (male) on an upper floor added to their family house, with the wife and the kids living downstairs; this author also quoted examples of social pressure on the wife to accept such an arrangement. Apostolos Andrikopoulos (forthcoming) describes a young man living in a same-sex liaison in Nairobi who joked about his role as a "housewife" there, but also mentioned that it was only thus that he could maintain his wife and kids in the village. Ndeye Gning (2013), in her study of young men in Senegal experimenting with same-sex arrangements, characterized them as "men of multiple sexualities." In the Kenyan anthology *Stories of Our Lives*, compiled by the Kenyan art collective The Nest in 2012–13 and bringing together life stories by 250 LGBTQ Kenyans, participants talk of sleeping with both men and women; characteristically many of them are therefore reluctant to identify as gay or lesbian (Van Klinken 2019).[3] Of course this recalls Tessmann's stories (1934) about Bafia (one of the groups he studied in Cameroon) taking it as self-evident that they had sex with both women and men.

In many of these stories economic enrichment—the aspect of same-sex intercourse that was strongly emphasized above—certainly plays a role. But often there seems to be more at stake: enjoyment, a taste for diversity, and a talent for playing different roles. In a certain sense this diversity is reminiscent of the "multiple self-realization" principle that Jane Guyer (1993) highlighted as characteristic for political-economic performance in many parts of Africa. Guyer noted this talent for combining different forms of "knowledge" as an asset for Africans in playing into new opportunities for enrichment.[4] In his Abiola Lecture, Achille Mbembe (2016a) referred to this characteristic in a more general sense, as a talent allowing Africa's "animist" heritage to open up new possibilities in the present global crisis. Africans combining various sexual roles in the examples above can be seen as performing their sexuality in a similarly multiple and enriching way.[5] This may be a special kind of enrichment. Yet a similarity is that this view of sexuality-as-enriching makes fixed boundaries—in his context homo/hetero, as clearly delimited sexual "identities"—seem to evaporate. In this sense the African examples concur with Mieli's call for celebrating intercourse as bringing a liberation of Eros beyond a homo/hetero divide.

Confronting African realities with queer theory thus helps to look beyond the homophobic discourses we mostly quoted in our chapters; it can also help bring back the desire surrounding anal penetration in African contexts as well. But what about the reverse? In what respects can these African imaginaries help queer theory to further loosen itself from its Western moorings? Over the last decade there has been an ongoing debate on "Africanizing" queer theory (see Hendriks and Spronk 2020 for an overview) in line with the points touched upon above—that is, liberating same-sex relation from its association with fixed identities and hard binary oppositions.

In this respect our examples are ambiguous. The central discourse about a conspiracy of the *Grands*—whether Freemasons, Rosicrucians, or Illuminati—spoiling the nation by imposing anal penetration on youngsters refers, indeed, to a same-sex *act*, not necessarily to an

identity. Yet we saw (chapter 4) that Woungly-Massaga in his new identification of Louis-Paul Aujoulat as a homo-Masonic figure uses the word
"homosexuality"—thus referring to an identity. In general, in rumors
about the *Grands'* perversions it is the *act* that is central. But the victims
of the Yaoundé Eleven police raids themselves felt that their *identity* was
under attack. We also saw how deeply they were affected by their access
to the internet, which showed them they were not that exceptional by
putting them into contact with the global discourse on homosexuality as
an identity. However, we also noted that many Africans involved in same-
sex arrangements have a tendency to dodge the usual terms—like "gay,"
"lesbian," "homosexual," "LGBTQ," and even "queer"—precisely because
such labels suggest a fixed identity while they want to keep things open.
The Cameroonian police in their witch hunts against "homosexuals" have
a similar double attitude: according to the law same-sex acts are what
constitute a crime, but in their arrests they often follow neighbors' de-
nouncements that so-and-so *is* a "homosexual."

In the West there is a tendency to understand the passage from same-
sex intercourse as an *act* to same-sex behavior as an identity as a teleolog-
ical development. The African examples instead suggest that all sorts of
combinations remain possible, and that various alternatives might have
a future of their own. Is Africa showing the way for overcoming the link
between sexual acts and specific identities that has become so self-evident
to many in the West? The homophobic discourses that got a new lease of
life in many parts of Africa around the turn of the twenty-first century
may still sanction the homo/hetero demarcation. But they are balanced
by everyday examples, like those cited above, of "multiple self-realization"
in sexualibus as a common practice, highlighting a talent for everyday conviviality that is liberating.

Historicizing Conspiracy Thinking:
The Precarity of the Nation-State

What about conspiracy thinking as the other axis of more general relevance for our case studies? What are the implications of the above for
academics all over the world increasingly challenged by the proliferation
of ever wilder assemblages of suspicious conspiracy thinking with people's
increasing access to new social media? In our introduction we proposed, as
an inspiring starting point for confronting this challenge, Luc Boltanski's
analysis of the tension between the nation-state's effort to create its own
reality and the growing transnationalization of capitalism. Bayart's "triangulation" added identity as a disturbing ominous third pole for efforts

to solve this tension between national closure and transnational flux. We also signaled how the conspiracy narrative around Freemasonry, homosexuality, and illicit enrichments managed to bring together the two main popular preoccupations in present-day Central Africa: (post)colonial dependency and "witchcraft." Different as these two seem, they both feed, indeed, on this tension between closure and "extraversion."

We earlier emphasized that linking homosexuality to Freemasonry automatically turned it into a transnational issue. For Cameroon, the first president after independence, Ahmadou Ahidjo, with his unrelenting emphasis on unity, made a serious effort in the 1960s and 1970s to create a closed national space. But his opponents could easily denounce him as some sort of mole, pointing out that he had been a creature of the French, who put him up to keep Cameroon within *Françafrique*. Later, identifying him (after 2000) as a "homo-Masonic" figure from Aujoulat's stable made him appear to be doubly dependent on the former metropolis: homosexuality as a betrayal of the nation. But the same tension between closure and extraversion marks the other pole of conspiracy thinking, "witchcraft." In a comparative analysis, one of us (Geschiere 2013) showed that witchcraft attacks are often seen as coming from inside, while delivering the victims to outsiders.[6] Remember the haunting image of the nocturnal meetings where witches are supposed to betray their relatives to henchmen from elsewhere. Also in this sense the reference in present-day conspiracy thinking to Freemasonry and other transnational associations seems to give a new turn to an older imaginary of witchcraft being positioned at the interface of inside and outside—but now this ambiguous position is reproduced at a transcontinental scale. It is this strategic position at the crossroads of these two shibboleths of conspiracy thinking in Central Africa that can explain the mobilizing force of a narrative linking Freemasonry, homosexuality and illicit enrichment. It places (homo)sexuality, the private in *optima forma*, in a transnational register (secret brotherhoods reproducing global dependencies). In such a narrative new forms of riches become doubly illicit.

What then is the possibility of an ethnographic approach, proposed by Jaron Harambam and his colleagues as the best approach to confront the present-day challenge of conspiracy thinking (see our introduction), for disentangling such a doubly embedded conspiracy assemblage, organically relating the intimate to the transnational? The preceding may have shown the good sense of their advice to listen (as a good ethnographer always has to do) rather than to try to refute. But it showed also that, simple as this advice may seem, this required in this case (and probably in others as well in view of the inherent "kaleidoscopic" nature of conspiracy thinking) a laborious unraveling of many different strands in order to follow the genealogy of this epistemological knot: Freemasonry's trajectory via France into Africa, special itineraries of decolonization in these countries, the crystallization of "witchcraft' as interpellated by colonial presence, and "mystic" conceptions of riches and power. Such exuberance requires, indeed, the subtility of Bayart's "historical and comparative sociology of the political" (2022). However, a question then arises about where to stop.

Rather than giving in to the temptation of trying to select what is true and false in such a sea of rumors and allusions, we opted for trying to "historicize" this particular conspiracy assemblage. Our case offered special possibilities for this since we could follow it over a longer period of time and pin down some noteworthy turns: the revival of Freemasonry in the politics of *Françafrique*, the "return" of Louis-Paul Aujoulat after 2000 as a "homo-Masonic" figure. Such historizing, highlighting the changeability and shifting nature of what is presented as self-evident, may help contextualize conspiracy plots and unsettle their self-evident appearance for people without flatly contradicting them or entering into stubborn debates about truth. Historicizing can also help to explore what links and which contexts make such narratives so persuasive, and when they may lose their cogency. Or, to put this in terms used earlier: when the articulation does or does not "fit."[7] For instance: the long history of (anti-)Masonism in France can help to explain why in francophone Africa there was a certain fit with rumors about same-sex practices (while this hardly seems to work in anglophone parts of the continent).

Historicizing can help also to highlight the abrupt turns in conspiracy narratives that are presented as timeless. In Cameroon, Freemasonry, homosexuality, and illicit enrichment had already been around for quite some time, but it was only after 2000 that their linking created a moral panic. Above (chapter 3) we spoke of a "sudden click" that created visceral popular indignation. Clearly a convergence of several factors—global gay identity coming in through the internet, but also the increasing presence of Freemasonry and Rosicrucianism in the circles around President Biya and human rights missions from abroad insisting on the decriminalization of homosexuality—set the stage for making such a "click" work. This idea of a sudden click might be useful to explain the often surprising mobilizing power of conspiracy narratives in general. Compare, for instance, the talent of QAnon in the West for revealing to the faithful that elements generally seen as separate are in "reality" closely linked. Working through "Q-drops," encouraging people to discover for themselves such links through the internet, has proven to be very effective in creating this sense of a revelation: what was hidden is suddenly made explicit, producing an "aha!" experience that makes the revelation all the more convincing. This makes it even more important to show that such a click is produced by an often quite accidental coincidence of factors.

Historicizing may therefore have its merits, but looking forward may be as urgent. A somewhat different challenge is to explore what kind of citizen the proliferation of conspiracy theory produces in these contexts, and how this affects the state. The above—notably chapters 3 and 4—already offers some answers to the last question. We saw that Boltanski's master trick—producing Kafka's *Process* as a spy story in reverse that suddenly shows that the state itself is the major conspirator—is certainly relevant to our examples. In postcolonial Africa, and certainly in Cameroon and Gabon, the state is seen as the main force behind hidden conspiracies. In this sense conspiracy thinking is mostly a direct attack on the state as such. Yet, as one can expect, the result is still ambiguous. The effect is certainly not a one-sided weakening of the existing style of government or the state. As in the example above of Bayart's 2014 presentation on his return to Cameroon and the "mystic" questions he got, such rumors about secret conspiracies and hidden backgrounds reinforce the idea that there is so much power condensed at the political top. Elites' allusions to such occult backgrounds—remember father and son Bongo's ostentatious involvement with various secret associations (both global and local ones), or what we called Biya's "spiritual pluralism"—help to confirm such a sensation of power. Thus, all the indignation compressed in the rumors about the elite's scandalous behavior can at the same time contribute to the "stationary state" that for Eboko and Awondo (2018a) has become the hallmark of the regime in Cameroon. And it is precisely the channeling of people's indignation into quite fantastic accusations—often difficult to prove—that steers away attention from blatant forms of misrule and corruption.

It seems that such malpractice has become so current and obvious that stronger stuff is needed to raise people's moral indignation. Is this the background for the "sexualization of citizenship" signaled for Cameroon by Basile Ndjio (2013)? In both Cameron and Gabon adding the idea of a supposed proliferation of homosexuality to people's indignation about the elite's corruptive practices did create a true moral panic. And this has worrying consequences for the question as to what kind of citizen all this produces: apparently a citizen obsessed with tracing and excluding sexual minorities who can serve as convenient scapegoats for what Achille Mbembe called "politics of *l'inimitié*" (enmity; 2016b). It is all the more important to point out that even if the witch hunt for gays and lesbians—as an effort to "purify" the nation—seems to mobilize wide support from society in these countries, there are prominent countervoices trying to direct popular dissatisfaction into more productive channels.

This study has shown the volatility of the term "homosexuality" that has created such havoc across the African continent over the last few decades. It highlights how urgent it is to check for each context what people mean when they evoke the notion and, especially, who is targeted. As we saw above, widely different persons can be thus labelled, which makes it a panacea notion that can be used for any political argument. Of course, in view of its increasingly generalized appropriation by people involved, it is not feasible to discard "homosexuality" as a term. But it clearly can have distorting implications, giving it an apparent self-evidence that hides important variations.

For us the great discovery during this project was, originally, the link with Freemasonry hiding behind this societal obsession with a supposed proliferation of homosexuality in Cameroon and Gabon as a threat to the nation. We are still most grateful to the anonymous person who, as quoted earlier, confronted us with this link through the question at the 2010 Yaoundé symposium about when Europeans would stop exporting their forms of witchcraft—"Freemasonry, Rosicrucianism, homosexuality." For one thing, following up on this question (probably rhetorically meant) made us realize that the present-day role of Freemasonry and other global networks in Africa is a severely understudied topic; so are the fascinating transformations these global associations went through in their tortuous transnational history. It may be difficult to study them because of their hidden character (certainly still in Africa), but their omnipresence on the continent today makes them too important to leave the topic to journalists and general opinion leaders. Their central role in conspiracy thinking shows, moreover, that their shadowy presence does affect people in their everyday perceptions of ever more confusing realities. Certainly in Cameroon and Gabon they play a role as catalysts of outbursts of homophobia.

Another surprise for us was the emergence, in the course of our research, of special notions of the person, "double" and "incomplete," crucial for understanding how witchcraft imaginaries affected peoples' linking of Freemasonry, homosexuality, and enrichment; but also crucial for the way our interlocutors seemed to arrange their sexual life. Discourse on "the" homosexual—both the homophobic discourse that has exploded in Central Africa and the global LGBTQ discourse—is often in terms of a well-outlined individual (neoliberal?) whose acts correspond to an equally well-outlined identity. But the everyday in these countries seems to be pervaded by quite another notion. Remember Séverin Cécile Abega's emphasis that the perception of same-sex practices in Cameroon has to be seen in relation to people's general idea of the person as "double"; Francis Nyamnjoh's view of the African person as "incomplete"—constantly crossing borders; or Jane Guyer's celebration of "multiple self-realization" that we tentatively transferred from economics to everyday sexualities (see the introduction and chapter 5). In this line of thought there are clear bridges to the sophisticated ways in which Western queer theory seeks to overcome the boundary making that seems so deeply anchored in Western sexology (as in Western thinking in general). Africa as providing propitious starting points for arriving at a more open way of exploring sexuality, variation, and conviviality? The articulation of elements from very different backgrounds in an unstable conspiracy imaginary, produced by global encounters, may be a process that can bring deep suffering for the people directly involved, but it can also open up new possibilities. This might be a surprising ending for a book about homophobia as a moral panic. But it is important to underline that the very data on such panics, often terribly distressing, also contain starting points for overcoming them.

Acknowledgments

The present-day world is haunted by an eruption of conspiracy narratives, and Africa is no exception. As elsewhere, these narratives are like rhizomes forging hidden connections between elements that seem to be far apart. To understand the sudden moral panic about a supposed proliferation of homosexuality that took hold after 2000 in Cameroon—and to a lesser extent in Gabon—we had to follow unexpected links. As elsewhere in postcolonial Africa, this idea is propagated by a vision of homosexuality as a colonial imposition. But for understanding the special intensity of this panic in Cameroon, the link that people make with the strong presence of Freemasonry—and other secret associations of global allure—among the elite turned out to be of special importance. However, behind this vision of so-called *Grands* submitting young men (and also women), eager to get a job, to anal intercourse as a lurid initiation, a whole web of other, half-hidden links emerged: "witchcraft"; illicit practices of enrichment; a long history of anti-Masonism in France, the former metropolis; and also pent-up anger about the particularities of the French decolonization of Cameroon. Disentangling the complex genealogy of this particular conspiracy narrative—linking homosexuality, Freemasonry, and illicit enrichment as the root of the nation's corruption—demanded following a constantly further ramifying network. If historicizing is one way of rela-tivizing the apparent self-evidence of conspiracy narratives, the challenge clearly is to understand why its different elements could become con-densed in one story: the "click" that gave the narrative its visceral cogency.

The tendency of our topic to constantly lead us into new directions may be an excuse for the ramifying character of these acknowledgments. It made us in any case deeply in debt to a wide circle of people. In Cameroon, we would like to thank friends and colleagues who contributed directly or indirectly to our project. Some, in the media and Masonic lodges, cannot be named here, but we would like to register our gratitude to them. Others are well-known public figures, including Barrister Alice Nkom, who has shown exceptional courage in defending LGBTQ persons and their rights ever since the panic started; and Professor Daniel Abwa, who is a historian with deep insight into the political evolution of the country. In Gabon, we are grateful to a number of people who gave their time to talk to us about the rumors they had heard or their own experiences of public anxieties and suspicions. We are also grateful to our colleagues in Gabon, particularly Joseph Tonda, Georice Berthin Madebe, and other colleagues of the Laboratoire d'anthropologie at the Université d'Omar Bongo, for inviting us to Libreville.

All along the way Achille Mbembe has been a truly inspiring friend and colleague to us both, always ready to share his long experience with us, and indicating links we tended to overlook. We owe, moreover, a lot of thanks to Patrick Awondo, Robbie Corey-Boulet, Charles Guebogo, Basile Ndjio, and S. N. Nyeck, for their earlier work on the topic on which we could build. Special thanks also to George Paul Meiu for particularly insightful comments that helped to further open up our project. Apart from Achille Mbembe's, the work of Wale Adebanwi, Jean-François Bayart, and Jean and John Comaroff has served as beacons for us. Many colleagues were ready to read drafts of chapters, giving similarly stimulating critiques and comments; in order of appearance in the project we mention Birgit Meyer, Thomas Hendriks, Franck Beuvier, Joseph Tonda, Florence Bernault, Charles Piot, Rachel Spronk, Jean-Pierre Warnier, Apostolos Andrikopoulos, and Graeme Reid.

Additionally, we would also like to thank a long list of colleagues who helped us in all sorts of ways: Wale Adebanwi, Jean-Pierre Bat, Ayse Çaglar, Bambi Ceuppens, Kate Crehan, Lars Frühsorge, Divine Fuh, Francio Guadeloupe, Michael Guericke (formerly Schütte), Marloes Janson, Kriti Kapila, Thomas Klockmann, Guillaume Lachenal, Claudio Lomnitz, Bouna Mbaye, Brice Molo, Isaac Niehaus, Sarah Nuttal, Francis Nyamnjoh, Ebenezer Obadare, Pierre Petit, Deborah Puccio-Den, Katrien Pype, Ben Soares, Antoine Socpa, Rachel Spronk, Jojada Verrips, and Joshua Walker. Rogers Orock's research on Freemasonry in France was supported by a grant from the Fondation maison des sciences de l'hommes (FMSH) and a Fernand Braudel Postdoctoral Fellowship at the Center for International Studies (CERI) at Sciences Po Paris in 2015 for which Rogers is also thankful to Richard Banegas for being a wonderful host at the CERI; his research on these topics in Cameroon and Gabon was also supported by the African Humanities Program's postdoctoral fellowship awarded by the American Council on Learned Societies in 2017–18. Rogers also benefited from support for additional research travels from the Department of Anthropology at the University of the Witwatersrand; his colleagues there, particularly Hylton White, Julia Hornbergr, Eric Worby, Kelly Gillespie, Nosipho Mgnomezulu, and George Mahashe, were most helpful. At Louisiana State University, Rogers wants to express his thanks to a wonderful group of new colleagues, particularly Stephen C. Finley, Lori M. Martin, and Sarah Becker. The College of Humanities and Social Sciences at Louisiana State University also generously supported Rogers's writing on this project with the award of a Manship Fellowship (2023). Peter Geschiere was supported during this project by the research group Exploring Diversity in the Department of Anthropology, University of Amsterdam.

Limited and revised portions of some of the chapters of this book were previously published as articles in *Africa: The Journal of the International Africa Institute* (2020, vol. 91, no. 2) and *African Affairs* (2021, vol. 120, no. 478). We are thankful to the editors (notably Stephanie Kitchen at *Africa*) and the reviewers of both journals for helpful comments and suggestions. Additionally, various portions of this work were presented at a number of venues where we received stimulating responses. These include the African Studies Seminar at Lafayette College (2023), the LAIOS seminar at the EHESS in Paris (2023), the Oltramare seminar at the Graduate Institute in Geneva (2023), the seminar at the African Studies Center at the University of Oxford (2021), the seminar of the Department of Anthropology at University College London (2021), the Meriam Institute for Advanced Study in Africa (MIASA) at the University of Ghana (2021), the International Summer Program in Social Sciences (SPSS) at the Institute for Advanced Study at Princeton (2018), the Wits Anthropology Seminar at the University of the Witwatersrand (2018), and the WISH Seminar at the Wits Institute for Social and Economic Research (WISER). We are grateful to the many friends and colleagues who gave us the opportunity to talk about this project when it was still in its early phase, including Rob Blunt and Wendy Wilson-Fall at Lafayette College, Wale Adebanwi at the ASC Oxford (now at the University of Pennsylvania), Mark Anthony at UCL Anthropology, Susan Baller and Agnes Schneider-Musah at MIASA in Accra, Ghana, Didier Fassin and the participants of the IAS's SPSS (2018–19 cohort), Hylton White at Wits Anthropology, Keith Breckenridge at WISER, George Paul Meiu at the University of Basel, and Jean-François Bayart at the Graduate Institute (Geneva). Many thanks also to the Völkerkundesammlung Lübecker Museen (Dr. Lars Frühsorge) for giving us access to pictures and documents of Günther Tessmann.

We want to thank also the staff of the University of Chicago Press—David Brent, Priya Nelson, Mary Al-Sayed, Fabiola Enriquez Flores, and

Dylan Montanari. The involvement of Dylan in the project and the stimulating attention of Fabiola have been most encouraging. Moreover, Peter wants to express his special thanks to the people he lived with in the Maka region, in particular to Meke Blaise for teaching him to go beyond seemingly obvious binaries, especially modern versus traditional; unfortunately Meke died in 2018 after more than forty-six years working on the research Peter and he undertook together.

Our topic's propensity for evoking constantly new links made this project a true voyage of discovery for us, full of unexpected turns. We hope that our following these ramifying historical links will, indeed, help to relativize the visceral appeal of these conspiracy narratives.

Notes

INTRODUCTION

1. Patrick Awondo (2012) first applied the term "moral panic" to popular concerns about homosexuality in Cameroon after 2000. He borrowed the term from Gilbert Herdt (2009); see also Lancaster 2011.

2. This "homophobic tide" started earlier (already in the 1990s) in southern Africa with President Mugabe in Zimbabwe and President Nujoma in Namibia. In the rest of postcolonial Africa, similar reactions followed only in the course of the first decade of the twenty-first century.

3. The draconian antigay laws in Uganda and Nigeria attract the most attention in news accounts on Africa in the Western press and among LGBTQ activists. But especially since the 2006 *affaire des listes*, Cameroon became some sort of forerunner. The Ugandan law is clearly related to outside interventions (promoted by US Pentecostal missionaries, yet finding considerable support among Ugandan politicians and population). This makes the question all the more urgent as to why similar homophobic initiatives developed in Cameroon earlier.

4. See George Paul Meiu (2023) on the association in present-day Kenya of elites with diapers as a similar way of making them lose face.

5. Interestingly, some of the people who stormed the Washington Capitol on January 6, 2021, repeatedly alleged in their defense that Freemasons were among the main conspirators who sought to rob Donald Trump of his "legitimate" victory in the 2020 presidential election. See, for example, Tom Dreisbach and Barbara Van Woerkom, "Former Police Chief Turned Yoga Teacher Sentenced to 11 Years over Jan. 6 Riot," *NPR*, December 7, 2023.

6. See, for example, Lancaster (2011), who analyzes the easy shift from "moral panics" to "sexual panics" in general terms and also in relation to a recent case in the United States. Compare also Halperin (2017) on *The War on Sex* as a general trend in the present-day world. See Herdt 2009 about how a "moral panic" can easily slide into a "sex panic."

7. Cf., for example, Bonhomme (2009/2016) *Sex Thieves* on the explosive spread of a different scare about "penis-snatchers" throughout West and West-Central Africa, mainly in the coastal zones.

8. Of course Western terms like *sorcellerie* or witchcraft are highly problematic translations of local notions. However, they have been appropriated on such a scale by African populations that it is difficult or even problematic to try to avoid them.

Any search for the "right" word in this field is challenging since translation is a productive process in which both imported terms and local ones acquire new meanings (see further Geschiere 2013).

9. Of course there are also many examples from precolonial Africa where same-sex practices did not have an explicit transgressive aura. See Evans-Pritchard (1970) on the Zande, to cite just one example. However, the close link with occult enrichment often reinforced the transgressive aspect, certainly where same-sex intercourse is associated with new forms of wealth.

10. Recall Foucault (1976, 79–80) on the idea of the homosexual as a product of subjecthood with an immutable interiority that he/she can "confess"; this idea also dominates much writing about LGBTQ issues in Africa. Many thanks to George Paul Meiu for directing our attention to the tension with other notions of the person involved.

11. Of course, such doubleness is not completely absent from Western notion of homosexuality. See Halperin (2000, 89) on "A genealogical analysis of homosexuality"; for him this means following "discourses [that] have been . . . elaborated over time. . . . [and] condense a number of crosscutting systems of thought at whose intersections we now find ourselves" (see also Murat 2007, note 2). Yet the present-day controversies in Cameroon, Gabon, and elsewhere in Africa are marked by clashes between an LGBTQ version of "the" homosexual as an individual with a clear identity versus more ambiguous conceptions of the person. Clearly both homophobic protagonists and self-identifying LGBTQ persons freely use these different conceptions in uneasy combinations.

12. See Nyamnjoh (2017, 2018), Meyer (2018), Mbembe (2016), and the discussions in Newell and Pype (2021); see also Jane Guyer's ideas about "multiple self-realization" (Guyer 2003). A question is whether such "plasticity" is particular to Africa; isn't there a danger of culturalism here? See below chapter 5 and Geschiere (2021).

13. Cf. Stuart Hall (1996, 142): "in England the term has a double meaning . . . 'articulate' means . . . to be articulate . . . but we speak also of an articulated lorry." See also Geschiere, Guadeloupe, and Obarrio (in preparation).

14. This *affaire des listes* has been extensively analyzed in the literature (see especially Gueboguo 2006; Awondo 2012a, 2019; Nyeck 2013, 2016; Ndjio 2012b; Machikou 2009). The summary above gives the current story, which is refined by these authors on several points. For a more detailed treatment, see chapter 1, below.

15. Like most former French colonies, Cameroon inherited French law, which since the French Revolution no longer criminalized nonreproductive forms of sex. This makes President Ahidjo's 1972 initiative to explicitly criminalize same-sex intercourse all the more noteworthy; see chapter 1, below.

16. Jean Bodin and Marc Perelman, "Cameroun, le calvaire des homosexuels," *France 24*, January 17, 2014, amended January 24, 2014, https://www.france24.com/fr/20140117-reporters-cameroun-homosexuels-prison-gay-asile-justice.

17. See Francis Bajeck, "Affaire du documentaire de *France 24* sur l'homosexualité: Issa Tchiroma Bakary donne la position du gouvernement," *AfricaPresse.com*, January 24, 2014, http://www.africapresse.com/affaire-du-documentaire-de-france-24-surlhomosexualite-issa-tchiroma-bakary-donne-la-position-du-gouvernement/ (accessed February 10, 2015, but no longer available). See also *Camernews.com*, "Zacharie Biloa Ayissi (Journaliste et ancien commissaire de police)," February 9, 2014,

https://www.camernews.com/zacharie-biloaayissi-journaliste-et-ancien
-commissaire-de-police-idriss-deby-itno-eu-loutrecuidance-detraiter-vertement-le
-president-biya-en-france-meme-si-cela-na-pas-ete-rendu-public/ (accessed June 10,
2017, but no longer available).

18. See Kevin Mwachiro et al., in *Boldly Queer: African Perspectives on Same-Sex Sexuality and Gender Diversity* (The Hague: HIVOS, 2015); Currier and Migraine-Georges (2016); van Klinken (2019); Hendriks and Spronk (2020); Dankwa (2021).

19. See chapter 4. Katrien Pype's and Sasha Newell's pioneering work on "connectivity" for highlighting the crucial role of new communication technologies (particularly the internet and social media) for young people in, respectively, Kinshasa and Abidjan, offering them "access" to new *reseaux* (networks), is relevant for the perception of male homosexuality in Cameroon and Gabon, both among the public in general and for the individuals involved. In this respect there may be significant differences with the perception of female homosexuality; see the second interlude below.

20. See Awondo, Geschiere, and Reid (2012); the notion of "politicization" was used earlier in this context by Patrick Awondo in his doctoral thesis (2012a); his work, like the present book, fits in with a more general current proposing to contextualize homophobia. Cf. Meiu (2023) insisting on the need to "de-essentialize" homophobia or Rao (2020) exploring its variable "political economy." (See also Murray 2009.)

21. Of course, Freud linked the anus to a desire for accumulation, but as far as we know he never related this to *Inversion* (homosexuality). Jojada Verrips alerted us to the association between feces and money in European folklore (especially in Germany). Feces seems to be less present in African stories about enrichment; rather, money is imagined as streaming from the vagina as in the Ghanaian film *Diabolo* (1992); see Meyer (2015). The stories that were shared with us about the anus as source of enrichment focus on penetration. Further research is needed here.

22. Of course, the conceptual link between "gay" and enrichment is present in many parts of the word. See, for example, Gevisser (2020) on "the pink line," where this aspect is present in different settings all over the world. Yet, it is striking that in Gevisser's two case studies from sub-Saharan Africa the issue of "gay money" comes to the fore very strongly, the main protagonists being told that they profit from their homosexuality as a source of enrichment; see also chapter 5, below.

23. See also Hendriks (2021) for a fascinating analysis of how a group of young gay men in Kisangani (DRC) are performing their own kind of modernity in a playful way but with quite serious undertones.

24. As one of the anonymous reviewers of an earlier version of this text remarked, "women have anuses too." Pornographic sites suggest that there is growing interest throughout Africa as well in heterosexual anal intercourse. George Paul Meiu (2023) published on women in Kenya complaining about men increasingly preferring anal penetration. For Cameroon, stories are circulating on the internet about women experimenting with anal penetration by male partners as an interesting alternative. In 2013 a social media scandal broke out over this question. A group of Cameroonian immigrant women in Maryland (United States) created a WhatsApp chat group in which they shared stories of sexual escapades, including experiences of anal sex, but their chats were leaked. Apparently the women felt they could not discuss anal penetration with their husbands. Anusocracy as a path to riches, however, is most often associated with intercourse between men. Hence the unfortunate gender bias of our project. In the second interlude below we briefly explore possible gender differences

between emerging gay and lesbian spaces in Africa, notably in relation to "connectivity" and the handling of secrecy.

25. Remember Mbembe's famous passage on "the aesthetics of vulgarity" in the postcolony as "an obsession with orifices, odors and genital organs in political speech and humor" (2001, 103–4).

26. In a more recent article, Placide Ondo (2021, 121) signals both possibilities as alternate patterns for the Gabonese elite.

27. See, for instance, Sokari Ekine and Hakima Abbas (2013) and Adriaan van Klinken on Kenya (2019) and subsequent discussion in *HAU* (Meiu 2020a); see also Gevisser (2020).

28. "Il mio tesoro lo conservo in culo, ma il mio culo è aperto a tutti."

29. The focus on the anus and on anal penetration is common to many texts from queer studies. See, for example, Hocquenghem (1972), Edelman (2004), and Kemp (2013).

30. As examples of such "displacement," Bersani (2009 [1987]: 27–28) criticized Jeffrey Weeks for reducing sexual roles to social inequalities and Michel Foucault for advocating sadomasochistic rituals as a way of circumventing concerns about sexual promiscuity because of risks associated with AIDS.

31. Clearly, the idea of an "anusocracy" is not completely foreign to Western thinking. Cf. also Mieli's reference (2018 [1977], 179) to the title of an anonymous text *Les culs énergumènes* (The demonic assholes) published a few years earlier in *Trois Milliards de Pervers: Grande encyclopédie des homosexualités* (Three billion perverts: Major encyclopedia of homosexualities), a special issue, edited by Felix Guattari, of the journal *Recherches* (published by Guy Hocquenghem and René Scherer, Paris, 1973).

32. Nyamnjoh (2017, 2018). Compare also the earlier texts by Cameroonian anthropologist Séverin Cécile Abega (2007a, 2007b) on the person as "double." See further note 12 above.

33. See Hofstadter (1964); see also Boltanski (2012, 265). On the recent escalation of conspiracy thinking, see also British philosopher Quassim Cassam (2019) and the magazine *Jacobin*'s special issue on conspiracy theories (no. 49, Spring 2023).

34. The interest in conspiracy thinking relates to more general themes in Boltanski's work, notably to his plea that sociologists take people's own interpretations more seriously, and to his distinction between *monde* (the irregular world of events or "what is") and *réalité* (reality as a socially constructed framework). But it is only in his 2012 book that he explicitly addresses the sociology of conspiracy thinking as an emerging field.

35. Cf. Boltanski (2012, 276) on "seasoned intellectuals" being shocked by the forms of conspiracy thinking that circulate on the internet but nonetheless eagerly consulting it. See also Boltanski's analysis of a common nightmare for sociologists who want to analyze "conspiracy theories": Karl Popper's haunting critique that much sociology is itself is a conspiracy theory (formulated in Popper's memorable 1948 paper for the Tenth International Congress for Philosophy in Amsterdam). For Popper (see also Popper 1963) it was especially sociology's tendency of attributing intentions and agency to wider social phenomena—as some sort of shorthand for the individuals of which these phenomena consisted—that would turn the discipline into a scientific justification for unwarranted conspiracy thinking ("capital," "the Jewish lobby," etc.). This inspires Boltanski (2012, 325, 332) to an original overview of subsequent schools in sociology, all trying to deal in their own way with "Popper's curse."

36. Boltanski's emphasis on the nation-state's precarious struggle to impose a uniform social reality relates in interesting way to German historian Reinhardt Koselleck's well-known analysis of Freemasonry as an important factor behind the crisis of "bourgeois" politics in Europe in the twentieth century. See his *Kritik und Krise* (Critique and crisis, 1959). In this short but passionate text, the German historian—getting over his terrible experiences as a German soldier on the eastern front, and subsequently as a prisoner in a Russian camp—tries to come to terms with the implosion of the Weimar Republic, which paved the way for the Nazi regime in the 1930s. Important for Koselleck is that the Enlightenment created spaces for moral conscience outside the state; he speaks of a *Spaltung* (separation) of *Moral und Politik* (1954, 8). His main example for such dualism is Freemasonry, with its emphasis on secrecy and the *arcanum* (the sacred/secret); he warns that it is precisely its claim to be outside politics that makes it ultrapolitical (Koselleck 1954, 49, 67). Inspired by the ideas of Nazi ideologue Carl Schmitt, Koselleck sees this duality as the cause of the constant crisis of politics in Europe since the eighteenth century (civil wars, the French Revolution, the collapse of the Weimar Republic). This interpretation seems to lay the blame for the ongoing political crisis in Europe with the Enlightenment as such. A more concrete problem is that Koselleck's view of Freemasonry is surprisingly partial. As we shall see, the relation of Freemasonry to the state is highly variable in time and space. Sometimes the two are nearly coinciding (as in the Third Republic in nineteenth- and twentieth-century France), but mostly the relationship is half-hearted: Freemasons inside the state but also in opposition to it. For us the main challenge will be to understand the variability of Freemasonry's relations to the state.

37. See, for example, Bayart (2000). Compare also Goody's emphasis, already in 1971, on such extraversion as typical for processes of state formation in precolonial Africa.

38. See the special issue of *Journal for Cultural Research* 25, no. 1 (2021), edited by Elżbieta Drążkiewicz Grodzicka and Jaron Harambam; see also Harambam (2020, 2021).

39. See note 8 above on the use of this term. On "witchcraft" as a challenge to academic research, see also Geschiere (2013) and Puccio-Den (2022).

40. See Tonda (2003, 2005).

41. Cf. also Sanders and West (2003), who in a pioneering exploration of conspiracy thinking in Africa and elsewhere in the Global South conclude that the occult is so important that they prefer to speak of "occult cosmologies" rather than of conspiracy theories (see also Kroesbergen-Kamps 2023).

42. See, for a general overview on QAnon, Harambam (2020, chapter 3). For details, see Aliapoulos et al. (2021) and Hannah (2021); see also the BBC documentary *QAnon: The Cult of Conspiracy* (2021), https://www.bbcselect.com/watch/the-cult -of-conspiracy-qanon/.

43. Interestingly, at the moment we are writing this (July 2022) QAnon is suddenly back on his preferred website (8kun), after more than a year's silence (roughly since the January 2021 invasion of the Washington Capitol where QAnon followers were conspicuously present). On June 24, 2022, the mysterious Q suddenly published another of his enigmatic "drops"—followed by two more on subsequent days—exhorting people "to play the game again." Stuart A. Thompson, "The Leader of the QAnon Conspiracy Theory Returns," *New York Times*, June 25, 2022.

44. Yagé is a weed with strong hallucinatory effects, used by Colombian shamans from the First Peoples group.

45. Harambam (2021, 112, 116); see also Harambam (2020).

46. Many thanks to George Paul Meiu for raising these questions in relation to an earlier version of this text.

CHAPTER ONE

1. See Guebogo (2006); Ndjio (2012b, 2020); Nyeck (2013); Awondo (2012b, 2019); Awondo, Geschiere, and Reid (2012); Machikou (2009). Monseigneur Bakot's 2005 Christmas sermon was followed soon after by a similar statement by a prominent imam (Olinga 2006).

2. Awondo points to the case of the "Yaoundé Eleven" arrested earlier (see chapter 3)

3. *L'Effort Camerounais* no. 421, January 9, 2006; also *La Nouvelle Expression*, January 4, 2006.

4. See, for a parallel analysis, Ludovic Lado, himself a priest, who speaks of "popular homophobia" as a way of expressing people's anger at the regime in power (Lado 2011).

5. *La Metéo* 99, January 11, 2006; *L'Anecdote* 254 and 255, January 24 and 31, 2006; *Nouvelle Afrique*, January 26, 2006.

6. The circulation of *L'Anecdote*, until then a minor journal, grew rapidly after the publication of these lists, becoming the center of a multimedia and financial conglomerate directed by this Amougou Belinga (see Awondo 2012b). See also Machikou (2009).

7. See also Olinga (2006).

8. Minister Grégoire Owona lodged complaints against both Amougou Belinga (*L'Anecdote*) and Biloa Ayissi (*Nouvelle Afrique*), who were sentenced in March 2006 to, respectively, four and six months in jail plus damages. See Nine MSN, "Cameroon gay list publisher jailed," March 4, 2006, https://web.archive.org/web/20060312102548/http://news.ninemsn.com.au/article.aspx?id=89686; and Ifex, "Un deuxième journaliste condamné dans l'affaire de 'listes d'homosexuels,'" March 29, 2006, https://web.archive.org/web/20060312102548/http://news.ninemsn.com.au/article.aspx?id=89686 (both accessed March 21, 2023). Of course this further increased the popular attention for their newspapers. For Amougou Belinga in particular the whole affair proved to be a boost for his spectacular rise in Cameroon's nebulous web of media and politics; see below, chapter 3.

9. Even in 2015, Cameroonian cardinal Christian Tumi declared that "homosexuality is a crime against humanity; it is not only a plot to destroy the family but also the existence of the human race" (*L'Effort Camerounais*, March 25, 2015, 6–7; June 6, 2015). See also Awondo (2019, 165).

10. The book's subtitle was equally ominous: *De véritables freins contre l'émergence en 2035—La logique au coeur de la performance*. The book became difficult to obtain since its sale was banned by judicial order as early as 2012. We managed to acquire an edition of the book that is dated 2012. However, on p. 76, the author notes that this is already the third edition (apparently from January 2013). In this edition the author has decided, in consultation with his lawyers, to remove the list of *des présumés francs-maçons du Cameroun les plus en vue* (the most prominent, presumed Freemasons in

Cameroon). This is why we choose to refer to this edition of the book as 2012/13. Apparently the author decided to excise the list in the revised edition in the hope that the book would not be banned (it was nonetheless in 2013; see below).

11. Scores2000 Blog, http://scores2000.over-blog.com/article-charles-ateba -eyene-paul-biya-est-comptable-des-crimes-rituels-119335506.html.

12. See also Orock (2015).

13. See below (chapter 2) about the link between Freemasonry and the medieval order of the Templars being often evoked in relation to supposedly homosexual initiation rites.

14. In his subsequent book Ateba Eyene (2013, 92) also quotes Geschiere's book on "witchcraft" (1995); he seems to be especially interested in the idea that witchcraft imaginary can have both levelling and accumulating dimensions. Apparently Ateba Eyene signals mostly the accumulative side of witchcraft, promoting inequalities.

15. The author goes into salacious detail. A secretary of the presidency told him how she surprised her *patron* in the washroom with one of his colleagues "en plein l'un dans l'autre" (the one deeply into the other). As for the army, Ateba Eyene wonders, "what kind of military men do we have with their anus completely destroyed" (2012/13, 104, 105).

16. "Ritual crimes, lodges, sects, powers, drugs, and alcohol in Cameroon— Citizens' reactions and weapons for the struggle"; also published by Editions St. Paul.

17. However, even in chapter 10 on this "plebiscite," the author is vague about the circumstances of this election.

18. Ateba Eyene on Canal 2, https://www.youtube.com/watch?app=desktop&v =vD2HQM1ksm4 (accessed January 20, 2024).

19. Conversation with a former grand master of the Grande Loge Unie du Cameroon (GLUC), October 15, 2021 (Douala).

20. See an excerpt of the interview/debate posted on Facebook here: https://www .facebook.com/watch/?v=342593289873771.

21. 2008, MPS Records—album with the same title.

22. General Valsero, "Ce Pays Tue les Jeunes," *Politikement Instable* (2008, MOG Records). *Rio dos Cameroes* (literally, "the river of shrimps") is the name the first Portuguese explorers gave to the Wouri (the river of Douala); subsequently the name spread to the whole area.

23. Released on YouTube, September 7, 2014, https://www.youtube.com/watch?v =PuLvx90u0WQ (accessed March 2, 2015, but no longer available).

24. Translation of this and other French phrases done by the authors.

25. Cf. Mgr. Tonye Bakot's 2011 protest against "the forces from outside," such as the European Union (EU) offering 200 million CFA Francs (approximately 305,000 Euros) in support of sexual rights activism in the country, http://www .leffortcamerounais.info/2011/04/mgr-victor-tonye-bakot-archeveque-de-yaounde -aucune-société-ne-se-bâtit-sur-lhomosexualité-mais-sur—1.html (accessed March 2, 2015, but no longer available).

26. At independence (1960) Cameroon mostly adopted French law, from which articles against nonreproductive sex (implicitly also homosexuality) had been removed since the time of the Revolution. As in most formerly French colonies, homosexuality was not criminalized in this country (however, Awondo [2019, 123] signals that already the 1965 Cameroonian code contained some articles that permitted judicial actions against homosexuals). In 1972 President Ahidjo explicitly criminalized same-sex acts

by a special presidential decree. Only in 2016 was this decree formalized in a formal law approved by the Parliament. It is not clear why Ahidjo took this step in 1972 since homosexuality was not a contentious issue at the time. The date coincided with the transition from a federal state (with anglophone and francophone Cameroon as more or less separated states) to a "United Republic." Under British law, mostly prevailing in anglophone Cameroon, homosexuality was criminalized. So, Ahidjo may have profited from the unification to make this criminalization prevail throughout the republic. However, another explanation might be that by that time there were already rumors about him having a special relation with Louis-Paul Aujoulat, his political guru during the days of decolonization in the 1950s (see Corey-Boulet 2019, 67; see also below, chapter 4).

27. Mbembe (2001, 106; 2006, 3); see also *Le Messager*, December 27, 2005, 11; Geschiere (1997); Roxburgh (2019, 91).

28. Gielessen (2012). He published this complaint just after REHFRAM, the most important network of Masonic lodges in Francophone Africa (see below, chapter 2), organized their annual meeting in Libreville (Gabon's capital), which was of course chaired by Ali Bongo himself.

29. Gielessen (2012). At the time Gielessen was *secretaire exécutif* of the URDP (Union républicaine pour la démocratie et le progrès), which supported Jean Ping, Ali Bongo's chief rival. The 2012 article voices, indeed, a radical condemnation of Bongo's regime. But in 2017 Gielessen founded the Mouvement priorités citoyennes, taking a more moderate position and supporting Bongo's regime at least in some respects.

30. See chapter 2 below for the rivalry between the Grand Orient, the older French lodge, and the more recently founded Grande Loge Nationale Française—the latter specializing in postcolonial Africa in rapid initiations "from above" (presidents and prime ministers being initiated—as in Ali Bongo's case—in a few days and/or jumping several ranks).

31. However, Ali Bongo's position as *grand maître* for the Grande Loge du Gabon remained contested. In 2015 supporters of Jean Ping forcefully opposed Ali Bongo's candidacy for a second term as *grand maître*; yet Bongo was reelected in 2016 (see Gabonreview, https://www.gabonreview.com/a-moins-dun-an-de-la-presidentielle-du-rififi-chez-les-franc-macons, November 18, 2015).

32. Gielessen (2012). A moving letter by a certain Obiang Émile, published by *Gabonscoop*, an online newsletter, shows the other side of the coin. On January 21, 2017, Obiang applied in clear desperation for admission into "Alliance," a Masonic lodge in Libreville, complaining of his life as "miserable" and telling the Alliance Lodge, "You are my only hope" (https://gabonscoop.com/frappe-par-la-pauvrete-un-jeune-gabonais-decide-dintegrer-la-franc-maconnerie/).

33. Alix-Ida Mussavu, "Homosexualité: Le nouveau Code pénal sanctionne la pratique," *Gabon Review*, October 29, 2019, https://www.gabonreview.com/homosexualite-le-nouveau-code-penal-sanctionne-la-pratique/ (accessed March 28, 2023).

34. See France 24, "Gabon: la dépénalisation de l'homosexualité divise l'opinion," July 2, 2020, https://www.youtube.com/watch?v=sGhrd-U-YpU, accessed July 21, 2021; Gabon News Info, "Code Pénal: Réactions sur la dépénalisation de l'homosexualité," 2020, https://www.youtube.com/watch?v=kVQXQKB1WBk, accessed June 24, 2021.

35. The population was less than a million people at independence in 1960; it is a little more than two million today; the nation has the third-highest GDP in continental Africa.

36. See Ngolet (2000); Bernault and Tonda (2009); Tonda (2015b).

37. See Ngolet (2000) and also Cinnamon (2012).

38. See Bernault (2019, 65, 117, 168).

39. Interview with members of the Ancien et Mystique Ordre de la Rose-Croix (AMORC) in Gabon, Marché Banane, PK 8, Libreville, June 27, 2019.

40. Indeed, the sheer strength of the "spare parts" frenzy in Gabon raises with particular force the issue—also familiar from witchcraft studies in general or our analysis of the association of Freemasonry and homosexuality—of how to distinguish "imaginary" from "real." In a fascinating study, anthropologists André Mary and Mebiane Zomo (2015) set out to check the "spare parts" accusations—vague and circumstantial—that brought down prominent Libreville senator Gabriel Ekomié in 2012/13. But even their detailed analysis does not produce a definitive truth; the problems remains that elements that are clearly "imagined" can take on a reality of their own. Bernault's seminal analysis of "colonial interactions" as developing between "conversant and congruent imaginaries"—i.e., French and Gabonese imaginaries of cannibalism and "eating" in general, not as opposed but rather as convergent, and thus producing new realities—suggests how a long-term historical analysis (along similar lines as we are trying to develop) can help overcome the imaginary/real dilemma.

41. See Warnier (2023) for a seminal study of the force of a *Catholicisme antimoderne* in France until far into the twentieth century. A good example is also the *Revue Internationale des Sociétés secrètes*, published from 1910 until 1939 by an association that called itself Ligue anti-judéomaçonnique (Anti-Jewish-Masonic League); typical is also this league's short name, Le Franc-Catholique (the Free-Catholic). Special thanks to Jean-Pierre Warnier for the reference. There is a striking continuity with, for instance, a recent pastoral letter by bishops in Cameroun titled *La Franc-maçonnerie, le roses[sic]-croix et la croyance à la sorcellerie* (Freemasonry, Rose-Croix and the Belief in Witchcraft, 2019). This letter starts with a long enumeration of formal condemnations by the Catholic Church of Freemasonry (ever since 1738, and repeated throughout the nineteenth and twentieth centuries). In their 2019 letter, the Cameroonian bishops warn of the changeability of Freemasonry, and its being prepared to accept "depenalization of drugs, homosexuality, marriage against nature and in general *la destruction de la famille voulue par Dieu*" (the destruction of the family instituted by God; p. 12). Thus, they are picking up anti-Masonic arguments that have a long history in France.

42. Barruel (1797). We quote here from the American edition of a translation that came out only two years later (1799).

43. Barruel's name for the Illuminati, a late eighteenth-century spin-off from Freemasonry in Bavaria, led by Adam Weishaupt (see chapter 3 below). In the American translation from which we quote here *arrières-loges* is translated as "occult lodges" (Barruel 1799, iv).

44. Compare Hasquin (1993, 170) who emphasizes also that in the eighteenth century opposition to Freemasonry expressed itself in France mainly in the form of "mockery" but that Barruel's negative image of the brotherhood in his 1797 book brought a decisive turn in this respect.

45. Think of the sudden emergence in 1989 of General Boulanger as a popular leader and as a possible alternative to the Republic with its endless scandals and rapidly rotating cabinets.

46. We do not know who came up with the name *affaire des listes* for the 2006 affair in Cameroon with newspapers publishing list of "homosexuals." So we cannot

check whether there is a conscious word play involved. But the parallel with *l'affaire des fiches* of 1904 in France is interesting.

47. After the war Faÿ was sentenced to life imprisonment on the accusation that as a Vichy officer he had been instrumental in sending 989 Freemasons to concentration camps. However, he escaped to Switzerland, helped by his good friends Alice B. Toklas and Gertrud Stein. They also supported his request for amnesty with President Coty in 1959 (Coy 2007).

48. Nay Olivier, "La propagande antimaçonnique sous le régime de Vichy," *Mots* 43 (June 1995): 76–89.

49. The film was directed by Jean Mamy (a pseudonym of Paul Riche, himself a former Mason), who was executed after the war (also for betraying people of the Résistance and because of his journalism in the service of Vichy France and the Nazis). The film's scenario was written by Jean Marques-Rivière, again a former Mason, who was also condemned to death after the war but escaped to Spain. The principal actor, Maurice Rémy, went into self-imposed exile after the war (Coy 2007).

50. See Gervais et al. (2012) who recently argued that a homosexual affair between a German and an Italian officer, also involved in spying activities that regarded Dreyfus, may have confirmed the military courts in their anti-Dreyfus stance.

51. See Denis Quinqueton (2022) with the subtitle "Après son café au lait et sa tartine, Pétain réprima l'homosexualité" (After his morning coffee and his sandwich Pétain suppressed homosexuality).

52. An author like Jason W. Earle (2013, 77) refers to "popular representations of homosexuality as a form of Masonry." French author Sophie Coignard (2009, 209), a journalist with some expertise on French Freemasonry and its political role, refers to the "convergence of homosexuality and Freemasonry." See also Dickie in *The Craft* (2020, 102): "in France, where it was widely believed that homosexuality was the Craft's notorious secret, and that the rituals were a naked initiation into sodomy"; also an article on Freemasonry in *The Encyclopedia of Homosexuality* (1990, Routledge) quoting nineteenth-century French literary critic Charles Sainte-Beuve about "a freemasonry of pleasure."

53. Murat consequently puts this term in quotation marks—but unfortunately it is not clear whether she quotes here her sources or uses it as her own metaphor. Cf. also Sainte-Beuve's reference (in note 52, above) to "a Freemasonry of pleasure."

54. See also Pastorello (2010).

55. See also Willy's book *Le troisième sexe* (1927).

56. Bertier (1979); Mack (undated).

57. See a telling picture in *L'Obs* (May 24, 2015, https://www.nouvelobs.com/politique/mariage-gay-lesbienne/20130524.0BS0632/mariage-homo-les-anti-en-guerre-contre-les-francs-macons.html). The name Manif pour tous (Demonstration for all people) is a play on words on the slogan of LGBTQ activists in France: Marriage pour tous (Marriage for all people). The 2013 demonstration in front of the Grand Orient was notably attributed to Printemps français, a spinoff from Manif pour tous initiated by Béatrice Bourgeois and especially associated with Catholic networks.

58. See Luc Rosenzweig, "Richard Descoings, prince noir du gay pouvoir," *Causeur*, April 17, 2015, https://www.causeur.fr/richard-descoings-sciences-po-bacque-32397.

59. Jérôme Dupuis, "L'auteure de Richie, Raphaëlle Bacqué, gagne son procès," *l'Express*, September 25, 2015, https://www.lexpress.fr/societe/justice/1-auteure-de-richie-raphaelle-bacque-gagne-son-proces_1719670.html.

60. This collection (Dierkens 1993) was edited at the Free University of Brussels—long a Masonic stronghold.

61. Dierickx (1993, 109): "de l'indulgence amusée à une mise en question, sinon même une sourde hostilité."

62. One may wonder whether such a terminological shift will have much effect. After all, secrecy has been a hallmark of Freemasonry ever since its beginning. It's striking that, for instance, Dickie notes also an apparent surprise among "English Masonic leadership" when they discovered "that even rank-and-file Masons thought that they were supposed to keep silent about their membership" (Dickie 2020, 409). In our experience this is not such a surprising idea: most Masons are still very "discreet" in everyday life about being a member.

CHAPTER TWO

1. See Wauthier (2003); Odo (2015, 2017); Rich (2017); Tchuisseu (2021). See also Badila (2004) on Congo-Brazzaville for a more personal testimony and Béresniak and Badila (2008) for a more activist approach, arguing that Freemasonry can offer the solution to Africa's problems; see further Akindes (2017, forthcoming) on Ivory Coast.

2. In a later study historian John Dickie (2020, chapter 3) further developed this "Scottish" line. He emphasized that in medieval times masons' guilds were weakly developed because they had an itinerant profession, traveling from one building project to the next one. This was also why they specialized in secret codes (handshakes and such) to recognize men of their profession in new surroundings. Dickie saw the court of Stuart King James VI of Scotland at the end of the sixteenth century as the biotope of Scottish Freemasonry (in 1602, James succeeded Elizabeth I and also became King of England as James I). For his many building projects, James recruited stone masons from everywhere, and his main building master, William Schaw, organized these masons in "lodges," for Dickie a crucial step; he adds: "the name [lodges] being borrowed from the temporary shacks set up at building sites. For the first time, 'Lodge' was ceasing to be the name of a shack and starting to be the name of an organization" (Dickie 2020, 35).

3. See J. C. Jansen (2015) on Freemason lodges in the new Atlantic colonies. See also Harland-Jacobs (2013) on Freemasons as "builders of empire."

4. The above is a summary from early Freemasonry history as presented in the museum of the Grand United Lodge of London (Queen Street). But on this point Dickie (2020, 61–62) offers again a different version of this history. He sees the 1717 founding of the Grand (later United) Lodge of London and the canon of history it developed as a kind of Whig conspiracy to erase the Scottish ancestry of the movement (suspect because of the Catholic leanings of the Stuart kings and other conservative tendencies).

5. For a very accessible overview of initiation ritual, see Dickie (2020, 15–26). *Forces occultes*, the anti-Mason movie by the Vichy regime, mentioned in chapter 1, also offers a quite correct version of Masonic initiation ritual—no wonder, since it was produced by two apostates.

6. See Brother Jonathan Dinsmore, "Who is the Son of the Widow?" *Masonic Articles and Essays*, May 6, 2019, https://www.universalfreemasonry.org/en/article/the-widows-sons (downloaded March 14, 2019).

7. Cf. also Wagner's *Parsifal* and its pathos in evoking this doubleness of anxiety and redemption (or Mozart's *Die Zauberflöte* and many other famous operas marked by Freemason ideas and symbolism).

8. Interestingly historian John Dickie (2020) gives a different explanation of the notion "free." He notes that a "free mason" was a mason who worked on "free stone"—they cut the stone into shape, and then the "setters" assembled the blocks into a wall. The formal address that Freemasons still use of "Free and Accepted Mason" refers to this meaning of "free" and to "the Acceptations"—historically a ritual among stone masons prefiguring Freemasons' later preoccupation with proper initiation ritual (Dickie 2020, 40; unfortunately this historian does not give any source for these terminological explanations).

9. Also in membership curves there are interesting differences. In numbers, the brotherhood is much stronger in the United States and Britain than in France. In the United States, membership peaked in 1959 at around 4.1 million Masons; by 2020 that number had fallen below 900,000, the lowest since 1924 (see Masonic Service Association of North America, n.d, "Total US Masonic Membership Statistics Since 1924," https://msana.com/services/u-s-membership-statistics/, accessed April 10, 2015). In Britain, the United Grand Lodge of England reported in 2014 that there were over 250,000 Masons affiliated with it and another estimated 150,000 Freemasons in the Grand Lodges in Ireland and Scotland, which makes a total of approximately 400,000 Masons in the United Kingdom (see Taverners Lodge No. 7442, n.d., "What is Freemasonry?" https://www.taverners7442.0rg.uk/an-introduction/, accessed December 10, 2022). Figures for France suggest a different curve. After declining membership in the 1960s and 1970s, at the end of the 1970s the ten largest Grand Lodges boasted only 38,120 Masons. But that number had grown to 65,035 Masons ten years later, then to 96,820 Masons by 1990, and to 127,476 Masons by 2000. By December 2010 these ten largest Grand Lodges accounted for 162,845 Masons. See François Koch, "Francs-maçons: comment ils manipulent les candidats," *L'Express*, January 4, 2012, 20.

10. Dachez (2016, 72); Mollier (2016b, 76).

11. *Templiers et Francs-maçons* (2016); De Gassicourt (1797), "Les Templiers dans la révolution française," published in the same year as Abbé de Barruel's attack on French Freemasonry, quoted in chapter 2 as still a beacon in anti-Masonism in France. As we have seen, Barruel evoked similar aims for the brotherhood (killing the king would be their secret aim) to expose them as terribly dangerous. See also Mollier (2016a) and *Templiers et Francs-maçons* (2016, 42) with a very evocative picture from the cover of De Gassicourt's 1797 book quoted above. Cf. also the memorial plaque in honor of Jacques de Molay attached to Le Pont Neuf in the very heart of Paris in 1969 by the "Molay Order" from Philadelphia.

12. Josserand (2016, 53).

13. Saunier (2016, 198); see further Furet (1978); Jacob (2006). Cf. a related debate on whether Freemasonry originated in Scotland or in England: Sophie Coignard and Roger Dachez, "'Il est incontestable que la franc-maçonnerie est née en Ecosse et non en Angleterre,'" *Le Point*, January 21, 2010, http://www.lepoint.fr/actualites -politique/2010-01-21/il-est-incontestable-que-la-franc-maconnerie-est-nee-en -ecosse-et/917/0/415656 (accessed March 31, 2015).

14. Jean-Jacques-Régis de Cambacérès, Napoléon's chancellor, mentioned in chapter 1 as having built a special reputation for his unabashed homosexual lifestyle, became vice–grand master.

15. Yet this was not only the case on the French side. In Masonic perspective Napoleon's final defeat at Waterloo (1815) was a battle between "brothers": brother Michel Ney and Emmanuel de Grouchy (both Napoleon's generals) on one side, and brothers

Arthur Wellesley of Wellington (British) and Gebhardt von Blücher (Prussian) on the other side (see "Freemasonry under the French First Empire," https://www.napoleon .empire.net/franc.macon.php, accessed February 15, 2022).

16. Another concern was (and still is) the suspicion among the British that the French were willing to accept women in their lodges. The British lodges remained steadfast in their view that women were not "free" and could therefore not be initiated as Freemasons. In France, already in the eighteenth century some lodges accepted women, mostly however under the special form of *rite d'adoption* (no full access to the masonic secrets). In the nineteenth century such *loges d'adoption* disappeared again. However, with the growing liberalization towards the end of the nineteenth century some Grand Orient lodges agreed again to initiate women. In 1906 another French Grand Lodge, la Grande Loge de France, created a separate lodge for women.

17. John Dickie interestingly remarks that in France the 1789 Revolution destroyed much of the old aristocratic networks, thus creating a void that could be filled by Freemasonry. This is in contrast to the United Kingdom, where older networks remained largely intact (Dickie 2020, 122).

18. There is a double irony here. The name of the *club des Jacobins* referred to the group that during the French revolution was the Freemasons' main persecutor. Moreover, the Grand Orient masons who lobbied for Mitterand for the 1981 election seemingly preferred to forget about Mitterand's initial choice for Vichy in 1940.

19. See the documentary movie from France 5, *Les Francs-maçons et le pouvoir*, by Gabriel Le Bomin and Stéphanie Khemis (2000). Notably Grand Orient masons and politicians participated in this documentary alongside several professional historians (Serge Berstein, Rogers Dachez) and journalists (Sophie Coignard, François Koch).

20. It has become standard to see the founding of Freemason lodge Ste Jacques des Trois Amis Rassemblés, rebaptized later as St. Jacques des Trois Vertus in St. Louis du Sénégal in 1781, as the first one in French Africa (Odo 2017, 9). However, in 1777 French colonists had already founded a lodge, La Parfaite Harmonie, on Île Bourbon (now Réunion); see Waquet (1981).

21. Harland-Jacobs (2013, 220, 241, 284) notes a similar shift in the British colonies. In the eighteenth century Freemason lodges in India were still quite progressive and willing to initiate Muslim princes. But in the nineteenth century these lodges became increasingly reluctant to give access to educated elements from the more numerous Hindu population, using similar tactics as the Senegalese lodges to withstand pressure toward more openness from the mother lodges in Britain.

22. Striking is that even Blaise Diagne, the Senegalese politician of the first half of the twentieth century who is often quoted as a shining example that Africans did have access to the lodges, was only member of lodges in France, Réunion, and Guyana, but not initiated in any lodge in Senegal itself (Odo 2017, 52).

23. Beuvier (2022). These Baptist missionaries seem to have followed earlier British explorers (Allen) and consuls (Hutchinson in Calabar) who already in 1848 and 1861 referred to local secret associations as "Freemasonries."

24. After the Vatican Council of 1963, the church initiated steps to open a dialogue with the Freemasons, but these were apparently more successful in anglophone countries (where most lodges had retained God in their charters). See Rich (2017).

25. See Rich (2017).

26. See Wauthier (2003).

27. See Carter (2014) and Glaser (2014); see also Bodila (2004).

28. See *Jeune Afrique*, April 19, 2013, "RDC: Les Francs-maçons à Kinshasa . . . discrets, mais pas trop." Also Pype (2012, 41, 51; 2017); and Thomas Hendriks, oral communication.

29. *Jeune Afrique*, March 2, 2016; the overview also highlights the aura of secrecy that still surrounds membership for several presidents—notably for the ones who maintain that they are not involved.

30. There is an intriguing contrast here with the Belgian lodges which, after Congo's independence in 1960, seemed to have lost much of their interest in the lodges in the former colony.

31. See Smith and Glaser (1992, 1997); Verschave (1998); Glaser (2014); Borrel et al. (2021).

32. See Caseley-Hayford and Rathbone (1992) on Gold Coast; Cohen (1981) on Sierra Leone.

33. See, for example, Absolute Ghana, "Ex Ghanaian President John Kufuor talks Freemason and his Highest Honor in the Lodge," December 22, 2017, https://www.youtube.com/watch?v=GMNBWF6gxdo.

34. When discussing a paper we presented at the Harvard symposium on "Religion and Public Life in Africa and the Americas" (April 17–18, 2019), historian Emmanuel Akyeampong, originally from Ghana, expressed some surprise at our image of Freemasonry in Africa. For him and his family it was the king's road to success in business, and therefore not proper for an intellectual. But there are also exceptions: some of the military rulers in Ghana in the 1970s would have been Freemasons.

35. Prince Hall lodges go back to the initiation of fifteen African Americans, among whom was a man called Prince Hall, as members of a British military lodge in Boston just before the War of Independence started in 1776. After US independence most American (white) Freemason lodges refused access to African Americans, so Prince Hall and his companions founded their own lodge. Despite constant pressure from London to respect the Masonic principle of being open to any free man, most white American lodges continued refusing to recognize Prince Hall lodges. Only toward the end of the twentieth century were there some changes in this respect (see Dickie 2020, 192–95).

36. See Smith and Glaser (1997, 182); Ellis (1999, 45, 250, 254, 258).

37. In 2012 François Stifani, the controversial grand master of GLNF, even claimed a membership in France of 50,000. However after the reorganization under the new grand master, Jean-Pierre Servel, the latter corrected this figure, giving in 2018 a membership of 29,000. See https://archive.wikiwix.com/cache/index2.php?url=https%3A%2F%2Fwww.lecercledesliberaux.com%2F%3Fp%3D26194#federation=archive.wikiwix.com&tab=url, accessed March 27, 2024. 2019 membership for the GOF was estimated to be around 53,000 (*L'Express*, August 26, 2019).

38. For the GLNF this "regularity" means that its initiates have to stick to Anderson's Charges, notably to the rule that there can be only one Grand Lodge for each country—which means that initiates have to avoid contact with all lodges from other obediences. Yet, we shall see that in practice many African members— and especially more prominent ones like Omar and Ali Bongo—did not adhere to this rule.

39. Important was also that Lissouba had antagonized ELF, then still the main French oil company, by announcing higher dues on exported oil (see Heilbrunn 2005).

40. See also Hélene Cuny in the same issue of *Franc-Maçonnerie Magazine* (2010, apparently only published June 26, 2011). In the same issue the magazine's editor, Nicholas George, warns that the prominent membership of such dictators will give Freemasonry a bad reputation.

41. Cf. also Jean-Moise Bratberg, "La franc-maçonnerie en Afrique: le dévoiement" (Freemasonry in Africa: The derailment), *Franc-Maçonnerie Magazine*, January 4, 2012. See also *Médiapart*, December 1, 2012, "Des dictateurs en tablier" (Dictators in apron); and *Mediapart*, October 24, 2013, "La GLNF doit chasser le dictateur Sassou Nguesso" (GLNF has to get rid of dictator Sassou Ngouesso); see also Carter (2014).

42. Some people even maintain that the manifestos were a playful hoax. Johann Valentin Andreae (1586–1654), the author of one of these texts, *Chymische Hochzeit Christiani Rosencreutz anno 1459* (Chymical wedding of Christian Rosenkreutz in 1459), published in 1616 in Strasbourg, declared toward the end of his life, in his auto-biography (published only in 1799), that he had written the text in his youth (between 1602 and 1604). It would have been a *ludibrium* (a lampoon) but "to my surprise the book was appreciated by certain people and explained through subtle interpretations, although it was a small and insignificant work." *Selbstbiographie Johann Valentin Andreæ*, Seybold (1799), quoted in Arnold (1990).

43. See for instance, https://spiritueleteksten.nl/rozenkruisers/amorc -rozenkruisers-ontstaan-groei-en-imperators-van-de-aloude-mystieke-orde-rosae -crucis/.

44. Cameroon Link, interview with Serge Toussaint, 2014, http://www.rose-croix -cameroun.org/index.php/amorc-et-media.

45. See above chapter 1 about our interviews at AMORC temple in Libreville, June 2019.

INTERLUDE ONE

1. A striking exception is of course Liberia with its Freemason lodge as a shining beacon in the middle of Monrovia, the capital (see figure 2.4).

2. *Le Lien* 4 (January 2012), 6–7.

3. However in an interview with Orock (October 10, 2021, in Douala) Denis Bouallo emphasized that his Masonic membership was no secret to his inner family circle.

4. "La Franc-maçonnerie ne recrute pas," *Le Lien* 4 (January 2012), 7.

5. However, these are not the Rosicrucian groups that attract so much attention in popular conspiracy theories in Cameroon (see chapter 4 about President Biya's being member of a quite marginal Rosicrucian group, CIRCES).

6. Cf. for instance Vincent Hugues in *L'Express*, April 14, 2008, 10.

7. See chapter 2 on Gabon President Ali Bongo's initiation on YouTube in 2009; see also https://fb.watch/eeOLlOaP4I/; for the enthronization of Sassou Nguesso see https://blogs.mediapart.fr/sissoko/blog/091210/intronisation-de-denis-sasssou -nguesso-la-franc-maconnnerie.

8. See Georges Dougueli, "Cameroun: Francs-maçons et francs-patrons," *Jeune Afrique*, March 2, 2016, https://www.jeuneafrique.com/mag/303985/politique/ cameroun-francs-macons-francs-patrons/; *La lettre du continent* 722, January 27, 2016 (at the time the total population of Cameroon was slightly over 18 million people). In 2013 Maxwell Bityeki Emmanuel ("De la Franc-maçonnerie du Cameroun à la Franc-Maçonnerie camerounaise," April 22, 2013) arrived at a much lower estimate

for Cameroun of only 300 masons, but he refers to *Maçons réguliers,* so probably only brothers from the Grande Loge Nationale du Cameroun (GLNF affiliated), http://les-batisseurs-du-cameroun.over-blog.com/de-la-franc-ma%C3%A70nnerie -du-cameroun-%C3%A0-la (accessed March 12, 2022, but no longer available).

9. Memo, Ambassador Barrie Walker, Public Library of US Diplomacy, January 23, 2007, https://wikileaks.org/plusd/cables/07LIBREVILLE36_a.html (accessed March 12, 2022). But in 2016, François Soudan and Georges Dougueli arrived at a much higher estimate for Gabon: 1,500 initiated masons ("Gabon: les francs-maçons au Coeur de l'État," *Jeune Afrique,* March 2, 2016, https://www.jeuneafrique.com/ 306750/politique/gabon-au-coeur-de-letat/) (accessed March 12, 2022).

10. See Bityeki Emmanuel, "De la Franc-maçonnerie du Cameroun à la Franc-Maçonnerie camerounaise," 5, 6; and G. Solle, "Hommage du Grand Orateur au très illustre frère Théodore Koule Njanga," *Le Lien* 4 (January 2012): 10–13.

11. Even though after 2005 ever more people in Cameroon became convinced that President Ahmadou Ahidjo, like his successor Paul Biya, had been initiated into a "homo-Masonic" network by Louis-Paul Aujoulat, their mentor during the days of decolonization (see below, chapter 4), it is probable that Ahidjo, with his obsession with unity, had problems with accepting the existence of Freemason lodges outside the control of his singular party.

12. *La lettre du continent* 643, September 27, 2012.

13. The GLCAM's presence on the ground in Yaoundé is still precarious. This lodge was formally founded in 2001, but in 2018 an internal coup seemed to be brewing against its grand master, Pierre Moukoko Mbonjo, minister in several cabinets under the Biya regime. According to a strongly worded motion by an anonymous brother, this grand master had not achieved anything since his nomination in 2001, except arranging to be reelected for a third term by meetings where only his allies attended. For the rest hardly any *convents* (meetings) had been organized. The complainant notes that for seventeen years now any initiative toward the construction of the GLCAM's own temple has been blocked, so that the brothers have to do their work in "insalubrious" places, rented from *des profanes* (Hiram-be, June 12, 2018, "Au Cameroun, Grand Maitre débarqué ou pas?" https://www.hiram.be/au-cameroun-grand-maitre -debarque-ou-pas, accessed July 12, 2022).

14. Dougueli, "Cameroun: Francs-maçons et francs-patrons."

15. Bayart noted in 1989 the central role Freemasonry had acquired in Gabon (Bayart 1993/1989, 203).

16. Memo, Ambassador Barrie Walker, January 23, 2007, 2; see also *L'Express,* February 4, 2009; Péan (1983).

17. Cf. Heilbrunn (2005). All this made Omar Bongo and his role in *Françafrique* a striking illustration of the subtitle of Antoine Glaser's 2014 book (*Quand les dirigeants Africains deviennent les maîtres du jeu*).

CHAPTER THREE

1. *L'Anecdote* no. 255, January 25, 2006—see also chapter 1 on *l'affaire des listes.* A problem with the term *anusocratie* is the "o" in the middle, which makes no sense grammatically. Clearly the word is meant as a pun on *démocratie,* since 1990 a much-discussed concept in Cameroon. Cf. also the Gabonese notion of *anustocracie*—a pun on *aristocratie*?

2. See chapter 2; remember also the intriguing parallel with the term *l'affaire des fiches* denouncing a Freemason intervention to block Catholics in the French army around 1900.

3. See Bernault (2019); Bubandt (2014); Ceriana Mayneri (2014); Geschiere (2013); Siegel (2006).

4. We base this especially on a series of ten asylum cases for which Geschiere was asked to give advice by Dutch and British lawyers. Other elements in these stories were police harassment and pressure from the family (especially for lesbians). See also Awondo (2012a, chapter 7).

5. https://rsf.org/en/cameroonian-journalist-martinez-zogo-s-murder-was-state-crime-official-confesses (accessed April 2, 2023).

6. For instance, in Uganda the newspaper *Red Pepper* only did this in 2014.

7. In 2000 another Yaoundé sociologist Jean-Marie Essomba published master's thesis on the "phenomenon of homosexuality" in Cameroon. Unfortunately we did not manage to retrieve this unpublished thesis, but Gueboguo (2006, 81) criticizes Essomba for following the dominant homophobic attitude in the country. Neither did we manage to get a copy of Sévérin-Cécile Abega's unpublished 1995 report for the WHO (*Aprentissage et vécu de la sexualité chez les jeunes Camerounais de 15 à 30 ans*).

8. S. N. Nyeck, oral communication.

9. In those days it was common among expatriates to compare things to Dakar and Abidjan, where there was a gay scene; supposedly nothing of this was then to be found in Douala and Yaoundé.

10. Achille Mbembe, oral communication.

11. This might refer to the bar where the Yaoundé Eleven were arrested in 2005 (see below).

12. Cf. also Basile Ndjio's 2005 article, by now a classic, on *le carrefour de la joie* as a place for civil disobedience and sexual bravado—mostly heterosexual, but Ndjio also mentioned some queer elements.

13. In the 1970s, *franc-maçon* (Freemason) was used as a popular slang for "homosexual" (see Geschiere 2017; Abega 2007a, 104).

14. International Commission of Jurists, AVIS No. 22/2006 (CAMEROUN), "Communication: Adressée au Gouvernement 23 January," cited in https://www.hrw.org/reports/cameroon1010Web.pdf.

15. Of interest is, though, that several of Corey-Boulet's main interlocutors gained increasing respect from their relatives after they attracted more international attention.

16. In 2015, the IGLHRC changed its name to OutRight Action International.

17. Cf. also the sad ending of the case of Roger Mbede, arrested in 2011 because he had sent an email to an official at the presidency, saying "I am attracted by your beauty" (again the pattern of someone getting in trouble after threatening to compromise *un Grand*). His case was also adopted by the IGLHRC, which helped to get him free but did little to prevent his sad death in 2014 (Corey-Boulet 2019, 89, 97). After 2006, Lambert Lamba became a creative gay activist, both nationally and internationally respected. Sadly he suddenly died from a stroke in August 2019 at only forty-five years old.

18. Cf. also chapter 4 below on the "return of Dr. Aujoulat" around the same time.

19. See also Newell and Pype (2021); and on connectivity in general, de Bruijn and van Dijk (2012).

20. Our interlocutors (who prefer anonymity) also mentioned two other emerging organizations, founded in 2003 but both short-lived because of police interventions (apparently the police were already intervening then).

21. In several cases Nkom's judicial interventions had success, for instance because of her insisting on the fact that the law requires two witnesses who could testify that the sexual act had actually taken place. Interestingly Basile Ndjio (anthropologist at the University of Douala, who has worked since 2000 on growing homophobia in Cameroon; see the bibliography) qualifies in his recent work the importance of Ahidjo's 1972 presidential decree as a turning point in the criminalization of homosexuality in Cameroon. Ndjio's recent work on legislation in Cameroon and other French colonies after independence suggests that the French laws that were taken over by the newly independent African governments already contained articles criminalizing homosexuality that were included by the Vichy regime and maintained by successive French regimes after 1945 (only abolished for France by Mitterand in 1982); see the book Ndjio is preparing on this topic.

22. In 2016 the Dutch Ministry of Foreign Affairs gave a substantial subvention to the COC (the main LGTBQ organization in the country) to make an inventory of LGBTQ organizations in a number of African countries (a main argument for the Dutch immigration service to refuse asylum to LGBTQ refugees was—and still is—that the refugee concerned could find proper protection inside their own country). In 2017 this project counted 26 LGBTQ organizations for Cameroon alone! (See Nemande and COC Netherlands 2017, 14). Cf. also Neville Hoad's warning (2007) that the possibility of international financial support would multiply both the number of such organizations and their rivalry.

23. For instance, when in 2011 Alice Nkom's ADEFHO received an important EU subvention for organizing seminars that could sensitize people to gay and lesbian rights, these seminars were regularly physically attacked by angry youths of the ruling party.

24. See also Célime Metzger's documentary film *Sortir du Nkuta* (2009), a moving report on the everyday fears of self-identifying gays, lesbians, and trans people in Cameroon and Alice Nkom's courageous interventions.

25. On May 11, 2021, she was condemned to five years in prison, but two months later she was released pending an appeal in her case. But a few days after she was set free she was beaten up by a crowd of young men. The latest news is that she currently lives in Belgium.

26. See below and Nguyen (2010, 163); also Corey-Boulet (2019, 2).

27. See, for instance, Toulou (2007).

28. Quoted through Gueboguo (2006, 79, 141); cf. Abega (2007a, 2007b). As said we did not succeed in getting access to Abega's 1995 report—which in many respects must be a forerunner in the Cameroonian debate on homosexuality.

29. Cf. Pype (2017) and Newell (2021) on "connectivity" to capture what they see as a powerful drive among young urbanites in Africa. See also below about Vinh-Kim Nguyen's very sensitive analysis of how same-sex networks in Abidjan are associated with special possibilities for "access" in a vaguely defined sense (Nguyen 2010, 160ff.)

30. Colloque international sur l'œuvre de Joseph Tonda, Université Omar Bongo, February 16–17, 2017; Colloque, "L'Afrique dans le XXe siècle," organized by Éditions Oudjat, June 26–28, 2019.

31. We follow the summary of the story by Nguyen (2010) and Corey-Boulet (2019), who both did research on the spot some years later, talking to several of the people involved in this drama.

32. See above for the confusion the French term *pédé* can create because of its double meaning ("pederast/pedophile" and "homosexual"). In this case the supposed victim claimed to be underage (even though this was later doubted), so here pedophilia and homosexuality coincided.

33. See Vidal 1977. Cf. also Corey-Boulet's fascinating life story of Ibrahim, an Ivorian man whom he follows through a long series of love affairs with both men and women, which brought him to Cameroon. People's comments on Ibrahim were mixed, but everybody agreed that he knew how to dress; the Cameroonians' comments in particular expressed some jealousy. Ibrahim was quite disappointed in how "backward" Cameroon still was around 2000 (Corey-Boulet 2019, 107ff.).

34. Cf. Francis Akindes's pioneering work on Freemasonry in Ivory Coast (2017, 2022).

35. Akindes (2017, 332) explains Kutwa's spectacular step as stemming from the Catholic Church's worries about being infiltrated by Pentecostal movements and a wide array of "spiritualities without God"; apparently the Ivorian clergy thought it time to draw a firm line.

36. https://fr.sputniknews.com/afrique/201910071042226233-la-profanation-de-la-tombe-de-dj-arafat-revele-les-conflits-de-generations-en-cote-divoire/; see also https://www.theguardian.com/world/2019/sep/02/dj-arafat-fans-who-forced-open-coffin-and-took-photos-held-by-police (accessed February 28, 2022).

37. "Arafat DJ s'est-il 'donné la mort' pour dire non à la franc-maçonnerie?" May 26, 2020, https://www.yeclo.com/arafat-dj-sest-il-donne-la-mort-pour-dire-non-a-la-franc-maconnerie. See also some reactions to these rumors from the Freemasons in Ivory Coast: "Côte d'Ivoire: Mort de DJ Arafat, accusée de tout sur internet la franc-maçonnerie s'indigne," September 2, 2019, https://www.koaci.com/article/2019/09/02/cote-divoire/societe/cote-divoire-mort-de-dj-arafat-accusee-de-tout-sur-internet-la-franc-maconnerie-sindigne_134462.html.

38. "La manipulation obscène du cadavre de DJ Arafat par Hamed Bakayoko," https://www.youtube.com/watch?v=ZC_pYMB2ctQ.

39. *Le Figaro*, https://www.lefigaro.fr/flash-actu/2009/02/05/01011-20090205FILWWW00507-senegal-wade-a-ete-franc-macon.php, accessed February 9, 2022.

40. See *Jeune Afrique*, "Franc-maçonnerie droit de réponse de Macky Sall," April 9, 2013, https://www.jeuneafrique.com/171395/politique/franc-ma-onnerie-droit-de-r-ponse-de-macky-sall/; and Seneweb, "Démenti à l'Express-Abdoulaye Wade: 'Je ne suis plus franc maçon,'" https://www.seneweb.com/news/Societe/d-menti-l-express-abdoulaye-wade-je-ne-suis-plus-franc-ma-on_n_20963.html, accessed March 10, 2024. Indeed, *Jeune Afrique* notes that the presence of Freemasonry in Senegalese politics always remained rather limited compared to its prominent role in countries like Cameroon, Gabon, or Congo-Brazzaville (*Jeune Afrique*, August 27, 2018).

41. But cf. M'Baye (2019); Coly (2019); Berlot and Masse (2019); and Broqua (2017) about a "negative re-signification" of the *goorjigeen* notion when it became included in an emerging debate about homosexuality. What such a re-signification means in practice is powerfully conveyed in the courageous novel of Senegalese novelist Mohamed Mbougar Sarr, *Des purs hommes* (Dakar: Jimsaan, 2018).

42. Cf. Gning (2013, 159–60).

43. Compare similar impositions by *nganga* in Douala: obliging rich women to have intercourse with a madman in public, preferably on a crossroad (Ndjio, oral communication).

44. Gning (2013, 18, 184); she probably quoted this "Nabul-Lusi" through Khaled El-Rouhayheb's *L'Amour des garçons en pays arabo-islamique (XVIe-XVIIIe siècle)*. With many thanks to Ben Soares.

45. A special aspect of developments in Senegal was that the general rate of HIV infection remained relatively low, except among MSM. The consequence was that this group loomed large in projects for protection against the virus. The battle against AIDS therefore became the dominant context for emerging LGBTQ associations in Senegal. Jamra, the Islamic NGO, played a double role in this configuration, receiving subventions for working with MSM seropositive people but using these to combat homosexuality (see Broqua 2016).

46. Interview in *Jeune Afrique*, February 1, 2018; see also the *Guardian*, August 7, 2018. Interestingly one of Gning's interlocutors, who identifies as a *goorjigeen*, mentioned Rihanna as his model for dressing up for a night out (Gning 2013, 266). Could it be that, in choosing to attack Rihanna, Cheik Oumar Diagne knew about her role in the gay imagination?

47. See also Berlot and Masse (2019, 30) quoting a former Minister about "a link between these homosexuals and the Freemasons who hold the world. . . ." See also the popular singer Wally Seck, who in 2019 was severely attacked by Imam Ahmadou Makhtar Kanté—the latter denouncing the growing influence of both homosexuals and Freemasons in Senegal (with many thanks to Bouna Mbaye for this reference); https://senegal7.com/depenalisation-de-lhomosexualite-imam-kante-tacle-severement-les-imams-recus-au-palais/, accessed February 28, 2022.

48. *Jeune Afrique*, August 27, 2018. One can wonder whether the aforementioned rivalry between the Grand Orient de France and the Grande Loge Nationale Française (see chapter 2) did not play a role here as well. As said, since the end of the last century the GLNF had penetrated ever further into the continent (which used to be a GOF fief). Jamra's attacks on the GOF as atheist did not apply to the GLNF (since they reinstated the British clause on the veneration of God in their rules; see chapter 2).

49. Colleagues who prefer to remain anonymous suggest that Sassou Nguesso's control over "his" lodge is so strict that rumors like the ones in Cameroon or Gabon would never be allowed to circulate.

50. *Quality* ("Men with a Passion for Men" article by R. Egbi, June 16, 1988, 10–15, quoted in Johnson 2001, 139, 145). Epprecht (2006, 189) discusses a broad array of similar rumors, mainly from Southern and Eastern Africa, about chiefs trying to fortify their power against rivals; mine workers searching for protection against accidents; or boxers bracing themselves for their matches—all through acts of same-sex penetration. Compare also the common association in many parts of the continent of "homosexuals" with "modernity." This can again open up special alleys for success. Reid (2013), for instance, relates the success of gay hairdressers in small-town South Africa to the aura of modernity they have for their clients. Often it is "the ladies" (feminine gays) who have to maintain their "gents" (more masculine lovers).

51. See also Ihonvbere (1991, 616). Cf. also a recent audio from Nnamdi Kanu, the current leader of a separatist movement, the Independent Peoples of Biafra (IPOB), describing Governor Rochas Okorocha's ties to Babangida in similar terms (see Opejobi 2017). Also, in a quite different context Sulaiman and Adebayo (2002) write that

in "In Kano there was (and still is) the belief that the vitality and luck of man lurks in his anus."

52. See also Pierce (2016, 13) on the general worry in present-day Nigeria that the country is dominated "by an elite class of lawless and lewd wealthy malefactors. . . . whose religion is witchcraft. . . . [with, as the consequence] the prevalence of intertwined forms of immorality—crime, corruption, prostitution, homosexuality."

53. Corey-Boulet interlocutors emphasize that this was an attempt to gain moral respectability after all the cruelties he had committed during the war.

54. In a broader sense this theme has of course been around much longer. Cf. the 1991 film *Diabolo* from Ghana (see Meyer 2015, xi, 1).

INTERLUDE TWO

1. A particularity of the way Freemasonry developed in France was a tendency to create special openings for women (one of the reasons why the British mother lodge remained—and remains—suspicious of the French variants of the brotherhood; see chapter 2). However, this aspect was not transplanted to francophone Africa, where the lodges mostly remain the domain of men only.

2. Dankwa (2022); Oudenhuijsen (2021); Spronk (2018); see also Spronk and Nyeck (2021) and Andrikopoulos and Spronk (2023).

3. It is impossible to give a complete overview here, but the pioneering role of Ugandan lawyer Sylvia Tamale (2003, 2011) must certainly be mentioned.

4. Some authors note, for instance, that around 2000 francophone circuits of the internet had become overcrowded with women from Cameroon, Ivory Coast, and Madagascar in particular who were looking for European husbands (see Alpes 2017; Cole 2014; Ndjio 2008).

5. Rachel Spronk (personal communication) adds a more prosaic reason: the relative scarcity of ethnographies of intimacies between women in everyday life (compared to studies of gay men).

6. Another interesting difference is the emphasis Dankwa's women place on same-sex intimacies having to be "taught" (often in a relation between older and younger girls; see Dankwa 2022, chapter 2). The stories of our gay interlocutors are instead about their struggle to contain a very powerful drive toward having sex with men.

7. Spronk (2018); see also Andrikopoulos and Spronk (2023); Bakhuri, Spronk, and van Dijk (2020); Spronk and Nyeck (2021).

8. Again there is not a radical contrast with male same-sex intimacies. Cf. Joseph Massad's (2007) emphasis that the imposition of a global gay identity by "gay international" endangers existing niches in Arab societies where men can experiment with same-sex intimacies. See also Mbougar Sarr (2018).

9. Cf. Ndjio (2022) on the very public performance of Christine Manie, the captain of Les Lionesses (Cameroon's female football team). And of course for trans people like Shakiro an internet presence seems to be their reason for living (see above, chapter 3).

CHAPTER FOUR

1. Ndlovu-Gatsheni (2022); Stoler (2020); Mbembe (2020b, 2019); Wiener (2013).

2. See Kuoh (1991, 116–17).

3. See Olinga (2006).

4. ARCAM (Assemblée régionale du Cameroon), created in 1946, was transformed in 1952 into ATCAM (Assemblée territoriale du Cameroon).

5. See Lachenal and Taithe (2009); Nken (2014).

6. See Joseph (1978); Mbembe (2020b). The term *pré carré* was launched in the seventeenth century by Vauban, the fortification expert of Louis XIV. In principle, France's "*pré carré africain*" consists of the former sixteen French colonies in Africa. However cf. also France's increasing postcolonial presence in the former Belgian Congo, Rwanda, and Burundi.

7. *L'Echo rochelais*, September 20, 1940, 1.

8. "L'épopée africaine de la colonne Leclerc à la 2ᵉ DB," https://www.2edb-leclerc .fr/lepopee-africaine/.

9. We realize that the notion of *Françafrique* is contested. Bayart warned in 2011 that denouncing *Françafrique* had become an anachronism. (See also a more recent debate on the notion in *Politique Africaine 166*, no. 2 [2022]: 193–205, on Borrel et al. 2021 about the *Françafrique* notion). In Aujoulat's days the notion of *France-Afrique* was more current; *Françafrique* was around then but became common only in the 1990s when François-Xavier Verschave and others began to use it for denouncing the ongoing grip of metropolitan interests on the former French colonies in Africa (see also Borrel et al. 2021, 22). This is also the reason why the term is central in conspiracy narratives from postcolonial Africa and therefore relevant for our explorations.

10. See Foccart (1995, 1997), a series of interviews Foccart had toward the end of his life with Philippe Gaillard (for a long time the *Monsieur Afrique* of *Le Monde*); Bat (2012, 71).

11. See also Verschave (1998); Agir Ici et Survie (1996).

12. See Foccart (1995, 1997); and especially Bat (2012, 2015).

13. Orock (2019); cf. Pommerolle (2015).

14. See Lachenal and Taithe (2009); Nken (2014). Also Beti (1972, 42); Abel Eyinga (1984); Woungly-Massaga (2004).

15. See also Deltombe, Domergue, and Tatsitsa (2016); Joseph (1977); and Mbembe (1996). Furthermore the discussion in *Politique Africaine* (126, no. 2 [2012]: 185–205) of Deltombe, Domergue, and Tatsitsa (2011), which succinctly sums up different views of the war and its meaning for French colonial policies.

16. Deltombe, Domergue, and Tatsitsa (2011, 250). This concept of a *guerre révolutionnaire* was also applied by the French military in Algeria in 1957.

17. Deltombe, Domergue, and Tatsitsa (2011, chapters 15 and 16, notably p. 296).

18. Woungly-Massaga (2004); Beti (1972, 42); Eyinga (1984); Nyeck (2013); Deltombe, Domergue, and Tatsitsa (2011, 189).

19. See Deltombe, Domergue, and Tatsitsa (2011, chapter 26).

20. See Woungly-Massaga (1971, 1984).

21. Abwa (2005). Also, interview, Rogers Orock with Daniel Abwa, Yaoundé, November 25, 2019.

22. As noted in chapter 2 it was only in the 1980s that Foccart, apparently through his close contacts with Omar Bongo (president of Gabon, 1966–2009), began to see more possibilities for collaborating with Masonic networks in francophone Africa. All the more so since at this time another lodge, La Grande Loge Nationale Française—by reputation much more linked to the French right—began to make a determined effort to outdo the influence of Le Grand Orient in Africa (see chapter 2; also Verschave 1998, 290; Smith and Glaser 1997, 29, 179–205).

23. Cf. Foccart (1997, vol. 2, 303); Borrel et al. (2021, 64). Indeed, Mitterand's search for an alternative Franco-African network confirms that despite his emphatic statements to the contrary, the new government continued the highly personal and clientelist way of handling the continent, with of course a keen eye for the interests of French business (see Bayart 1984, who signaled this continuity at the very beginning of Mitterrand's rule; also Marches 1995; Chafer 2005; Glaser 2014).

24. Jean-Christophe Mitterrand—whose nickname in Africa became *Papa m'a dit* (Papa told me)—fell victim in the end to his own networking, serving various periods in jail because of a series of convictions for arms trafficking and similar criminal activities. See also Smith and Glaser (1995, 209).

25. See, for instance, Konde (2012). It is true that subsequently Ahidjo fell seriously ill. Moreover, Mitterand and his family continued to act as close allies to Biya, through all the crises to come. See Tesi (2017, 200), who adds that Mitterand also resented Ahidjo's outspoken support for Giscard d'Estaing (Mitterand's opponent in the 1981 elections in France).

26. See Ndzana Seme, a former bank director and journalist at *L'Effort Camer-oonais* (January 20, 2019), https://www.facebook.com/permalink.php?story_fbid =841020169384225&id= 755520261267550; also Angounou (2007) (the so-called *petit ami de Biya*—see below, note 41); Kuoh (1991, 116–17); Olinga (2006). These present-day rumors do not address the fact that two years later Ahidjo turned against his successor (the 1984 coup d'état); after the coup failed he had to go into exile; his family is still not allowed to bury him in Cameroon. All this is in glaring contrast to the idea of a "pact."

27. For many critics Biya "stability" is the main reason for Cameroon's stagnation over the last decades. Cf. Fred Eboko's and Patrick Awondo's special issue of *Politique Africaine* (2018, no. 150) under the telling title "Cameroon, L'État stationnaire"—that is, "a political organization which produces a system of clientelist allegiances that have as central objective the *perpétuation du pouvoir*" (7). In the same collection Machikou (2018, 116) adds that this "stationary state" realizes a displacement of the field of action *vers les cieux* (to the skies) and *un détour par l'invisible*. Belinga (2018, 53) speaks of "politics of suspicion" fed by an increasing lack of funding.

28. It is not clear whether Ahidjo had been involved in the preparation of the coup. He always denied this, as did the putschists. But Foccart, always happy to show how involved he still was with anything going on in France's *pré carré*, confirmed that Ahidjo was informed about what was going to happen (Foccart 1997, 340).

29. See Konde (2012), who emphasizes the resentment of Gaullist elements in the French army that Ahidjo had been marginalized so easily. Konde mentions as well that French soldiers in Yaoundé had been informed the day before the 1984 coup (see also Glaser 2014, 126).

30. Glaser (2014, 126). Mobutu's mediation is probable since Meyuhas, Biya's first Israeli henchman, also worked with Mobutu. Since the 1960s Israel has been quite present in Cameroon in the context of the Israeli policy of trying to raise support among newly independent African countries in order to balance the Arab vote in international organizations.

31. *African Arguments* is a series published by Zed Books and sponsored by both the Royal African Society and the International African Institute in London.

32. See Freudenthal and Van Der Weide (2020). See also Glaser (2014, 126); "Israeli security contractors making a killing in Cameroon," *The African Crime & Conflict*

Journal, https://theafricancriminologyjournal.wordpress.com/2022/01/27/Israeli
-security-contractors-making-a-killing-in-Cameroon/, accessed March 6, 2024; Cam-
eroonWeb, "Voici comment Mobutu a introduit Paul Biya en Israël," February 28,
2019, https://www.coupsfrancs.com/voici-comment-mobutu-a-introduit-paul-biya
-en-israel/, accessed March 10, 2024.

33. See Glaser (2014, 128); Pigeaud (2011).

34. Clarisse Juompan-Yakam, "Cameroon: Titus Edzoa, quaotrze ans de solitude,"
Jeune Afrique, March 14, 2018, https://www.jeuneafrique.com/191884/politique/
Cameroon-titus-edzoa-quatorze-ans-de-solitude/.

35. *Le Monde,* December 24, 1999; cf. also a second article by *Le Monde* (August 17,
2000) on this case. Cf. also *Le Dauphiné,* December 23, 2015, https://www.ledauphine
.com/faits-divers/2015/12/22/ordre-du-temple-solaire-il-y-a-vingt-ans-l-apocalypse
-dans-le-vercors; and the very interesting 2007 article by Lucien Toulou (to which
we will return below). See also Vallée (2010, 206–8) for other aspects of this case.

36. Wikipedia, https://en.wikipedia.org/wiki/Order_of_the_Solar_Temple; see
also Lewis (2008).

37. Subsequently there was still another case of collective suicide in Quebec in
1997 (five deaths) and another attempt in 1998 in Tenerife (where Luc Jouret had
been active).

38. Just before his suicide 1994 Di Mambro sent a letter (one of the many he sent
at that time) to Pasqua containing his passport and that of his wife. See, for instance,
Le Soir (Belgium), October 10, 1994.

39. See Camer.be, "Entretien Avec Serge Toussaint, Grand Maître De L'ancien Et
Mystique Ordre De La Rose-Croix," June 15, 2017, https://www.camer.be/60777/
11:1/france-entretien-avec-serge-toussaint-grand-maitre-de-lancien-et-mystique
-ordre-de-la-rose-croix.html (interview with Serge Toussant, *grand maître* of France
AMORC, accessed March 10, 2024); and Toulou (2007). See also AMORC, "Entretien avec Christian Bernard, Imperator de l'A.M.O.R.C.," http://www.rose-croix.org/
entretien-avec-christian-bernard-imperator-amorc and https://recherchestraditions
.blogspot.com/2012/12/raymond-bernard-1923-2006-raymond.html (official
chronology of Raymond Bernard's life).

40. It is telling that Geschiere left the newspaper in his hotel room. Clearly he had
no clue how important the topic of homosexuality was to become.

41. See also Daniel Angounou, *Paul Biya, le cauchemar de ma vie* (Paul Biya, the
nightmare of my life; Éditions Le Messager, 1992), who claimed to have been *le petit
de Biya* (Biya's lover boy) and who blames his terrible experiences in Yaoundé's Kon-
dengui prison on his courage to talk about homosexual practices and human sacrifice
in the president's surroundings.

42. Cf. Zacharia Biloa Ayissi's reactions to the France 24 documentary quoted in
the introduction to this book.

43. For a quite restrained summary of such rumors, see Deltombe, Domergue,
and Tatsitsa (2011, 189, note b). These authors also quote people who knew Aujoulat
at the time and confirm these rumors. Some of our interlocutors relate how in their
youth people would warn them about frequenting Aujoulat's place because "strange
things" were happening there.

44. For a very "technical" version of such same-sex intercourse—typical for the
mechanical way in which these rumors evoke such intercourse—see also the 2006 list
of Cameroon's "top homosexuals" in *La Nouvelle Afrique* (January 25, 2006) on how

politician Mayi Matip, invited for an audience at President Ahidjo's office, succeeded in circumventing the latter's apparent habit of submitting his underlings to anal penetration: "Mayi Matip . . . had taken the precaution to leave his 'backside dirty'" and this allowed him to return without being sodomized, "his backside's bad smell making Ahidjo utter a cry of disgust" (quoted in Awondo 2019, 69).

CHAPTER FIVE

1. Cf., for instance, his very complex schema of ramifying binary oppositions in the Pangwe worldview (Tessmann 1913, 2:126).

2. Abega is followed in this by more recent authors like Gueboguo (2006, 2009) and Awondo (2019).

3. See also Abega and Abe (2005).

4. See also Nyamnjoh (2017) and the introduction to this book on the "incompleteness" of the person.

5. See Mbembe's Abiola Lecture (2016a) and the debate on this in *African Studies Review* (Newell and Pype 2021).

6. See also Tonda (2015a) on the modern world being increasingly *ébloui* (dazzled) by an overproduction of images, and the suggestion that Africans have learned for quite some time how to live with such an overproduction because of the wild imaginary evoked by ideas of witchcraft and the person as inherently double. See also Geschiere (2021) and in the postface in Tonda (2015a).

7. The reverse question, even more difficult to answer, is of course to what extent such local conceptions influence African Masons' ideas of the self. In a series of lectures in February and March 2022 at the Chair Théodore Verhaegen, a budding center for Freemason studies at the Brussels Free University, Francis Akindes—one of the few academics in Africa working on Freemasonry—explored the problems for African Masons in finding a compromise between Western and local paradigms, notably between Masonic initiation ritual symbolizing the liberation of the individual versus "traditional" initiations aiming to integrate the person into a network of family obligations powerfully affirmed by "witchcraft threats" (see also Akindes 2017, 2022). It would be interesting to follow funeral rites for African Masons in more detail. In Europe Masonic funeral rites tend to emphasize the liberation of the Mason from other earthly obligations. But in Africa funeral rites are often a key moment of re-establishing kinship links, with "witchcraft" as their shadowy side (see Geschiere 2005).

8. Tessmann sees the Fang as one group within the wider Pangwe group. He also includes, for instance, the Bulu, Jaunde (Ewondo), Eton, Ntum, and many others in this group. See, on this now somewhat antique notion of Pangwe/Pahouin, Alexandre and Binet (1958) and Alexandre (1965), who also spoke of a Beti-Bulu-Fang group. Since the rise to power of present President Paul Biya (1982) the term Beti has become common for this ethnic bloc. These various groups share an oral tradition of a drawn-out migration (probably since the eighteenth century) from the savannah into the forest area of southern Cameroon and Gabon.

9. This expansion of German Kamerun was the result of the French-German agreement of 1912. Germany acquired Neukamerun in exchange for giving up its claims on Morocco.

10. Notably by people attached to the Völkerkundesammlung Lübecker Museen; see note 11 below.

11. Tessmann wrote this autobiography much later in Brazil. He concluded a first version in 1940 but kept rewriting and adding to it until 1960. It is written in a flowery style, clearly meant for publication, which never happened. We thank the Lübecker Museen, Völkerkundesammlung, especially Dr. Lars Frühsorge and Michael Guericke (formerly Schütte, PhD student in Göttingen), for helping us access a copy. Next to this more romanticizing autobiography Tessmann also continued working on his diaries that were based on journals he kept during his research trips. He finalized these much later than the period concerned (mostly during the 1920s and 1930s, but some even after 1950). Since 2012 Sabine Dinslage and Brigitte Templin have published these diaries in an impressive series (five volumes) for die Lübecker Museen/Völkerkundesammlung (the folk studies collection of the Lübecker museum, now also accessible on the internet). The first and the second volumes of this series concern the period on which we focus here; see Tessmann (2012, 2015). We thank Michael Guericke-Schütte for his comments on earlier versions of this chapter.

12. During his second expedition to the area (1907–9) this sound politicoeconomic model did not work so well. By this time more Europeans circulated in this area, the Fang had become more conscious of the value of the tusks, and Tessmann felt he regularly had to organize military expeditions (since this expedition was better financed, he had now some soldiers in service) in order to remain in control. His return in 1909 through Gabon had every appearance of a flight.

13. In his more down-to-earth *Tagebuch* (2012, 395) Tessmann gives a much simpler report on how he stumbled upon the interest of folktales for his research. When he is ill, Mabale, one of his first "boys," begins telling him folktales and this makes him realize that "these *schwarze Menschen* [black people] have stories like we do!"

14. See Geschiere (1997, 2013) for the generality of these conceptions.

15. In an earlier text (Mimche and Gueboguo 2006) these authors emphasize the difference between *biang akuma* (medicine of wealth) among the Fang in earlier days and present-day associations of same-sex intercourse and riches. It would now be more about the individual. However, in Tessmann's historical descriptions it also seems to concern individual ambition; that is the reason why it was punished by the Ngi secret association as asocial (see below).

16. In these passages this *Mekukmann* is unequivocally evil in his drive to kill kin and use their cranes for his sorcery. However Tessmann also translates *Mekukmann* as *Medizinmann*, and throughout the book—especially in chapter 11 on religion, in the sections on the great Panwge rituals (Soo, Ngi, and others) that made the book so famous—such medicine men play a crucial role: without them no ritual. Apparently evil and good are not so easily separated in the role of these experts.

17. Tessmann seems to use the two forms—*biang akuma* and *biang nkuma*—interchangeably.

18. Tessmann adds in a note "with the Pangwe this means that the lover would 'steal' the girl."

19. Tessmann adds: the father's *female* role seems to be signaled by this.

20. Tessmann (1913, 2:273); he adds that to the Pangwe this fairly straightforward approach amounted to a *grosse Liebeserklärung* (declaration of deep love) like in the German phrase "wo du hingehst will ich auch hingehen" (where you will go, I will go as well).

21. Cf. Tessmann (1919, 133), where he links the horrible illnesses that befell both couples to a revenge plot by the Ngi—the secret cult to which he attributes an anti-witchcraft role in Pangwe society.

22. In certain respects Tessmann's discovery of the Bafia as still in the monist phase rather reminds one of Bachofen, then already famous for his idea that *Mutterrecht* (matriarchy) preceded *Vaterrecht* (patriarchy) everywhere. But Tessmann seems to be more interested in the preceding transition to the one Bachofen imagined, the one from *Heterismus* (from *hetaere*, courtesan) to more regulated forms of reproduction. The Bafia, with their open attitude to all sorts of sexuality, still seem to be in this earlier phase. Yet, as far as we know Tessmann hardly quoted Bachofen. The only passage we found where he mentioned him was at the end of his unpublished biography (1940, 220), where he criticizes Bachofen's tendency to assume general stages in the evolution of human societies; for Tessmann such stages were too general and also too directly deduced from Western history. Tessmann was not against the idea of general stages but insisted that researchers had to pay due to attention to the original forms they take in varying contexts.

23. De Vries (2018).

24. This must remain an open question. There are now Bafia who also strongly contest Tessmann's views on their particularities.

25. However, in an earlier passage—in the chapter on *Medizin* (volume 2, chapter 13, page 158)—Tessmann offered the version Murray and Roscoe sketched: a passive partner having the medicine and the active one trying to appropriate it (but Tessmann gave no further details on how this was done).

26. Tessmann (1940, 177). Compare also Brigitte Templin's comment in her introduction to vol. 2 of Tessmann's *Tagebuch*: "also the prospect of being again near the Fang, most of whom he found quite attractive, pleased Tessmann, whose homoerotic inclinations are very present in his memories without being thematized in more concrete terms" (Tessmann 2015, 11, translation Geschiere).

27. Yet close reading suggests many layers in his writings. As said, Murray and Roscoe took the story of the two same-sex couples who died of frambesia/leprosy from a text Tessmann published earlier in Karsch-Haak's *Das gleichgeschlechtiges Leben der Nauurvoelker* (Karsch-Haak 1911, 152–54). In his later book on *Die Pangwe* (1913, 2:271–73) Tessmann abbreviates the complicated names of the four lovers in the story as *Schok*. But this was also the name of his most trusted "boy" who served him the longest during his stay in the forest with the Fang and by whom he felt so bitterly betrayed at the end of his stay. Deeply angry that all the faith he had put in this Schok had been shamed, he even had the man arrested and jailed, just before he took off on a steamer along the Ogowe on his way back. Yet he uses this name in one of his favorite stories! But another incident—Tessmann having a severe vertigo attack after climbing a mountain and having to rest his head in Schok's lap for fifteen minutes, which makes him comment on the unpleasant smell of Schok's body—does not suggest any erotic attraction (Tessmann 2015, 103). It seems Tessmann was playing all sorts of games in his complicated writings.

28. Tessmann (1919, 138). Interestingly this article was published in Magnus Hirschfeld's *Jahrbuch für sexuelle Zwischenstufen*.

29. Cf. also Ceriana Mayneri (2014) on the Central African Republic and Bernault (2019) on Gabon, both quoted before.

30. See for similar conclusions Geschiere (1997) on the Maka (neighbors of the Beti).

31. Striking is again that Laburthe-Tolra sees a complete separation between these *bekon* (spirits of the dead) and those of the witches. With the neighboring Maka such

a separation is always precarious: the term *djim* (spirit) is used for both witch spirits and those of the deceased. It is the capacity of *mindjindjamb* (witches) to contact the dead that makes them so powerful (Geschiere 1997). Laburthe-Tolra's highlighting of the fluidity of *le monde invisible* makes his insistence on such radical separations surprising.

32. A similar debate developed around the *mevungu*, the much-described Beti ritual for women. A central element in this ritual—secret in the sense that it was absolutely forbidden for men to observe it—seems to have been a celebration of the clitoris. Some authors—notably Marie-Paule Brochet de Thé (1985) but also Paul Alexandre and Jacques Binet in their classical study *Le groupe dit Pahouin* (1958)—suggested that the ritual enticed women to sexual intercourse. However this is strongly contradicted by others, notably by Jeanne-Françoise Vincent (1976, 2001, 2003) and Philippe Laburthe-Tolra (1985, 331), both emphasizing that the ritual was not so much about the clitoris but rather about the *evu* itself; for the Beti it would be unthinkable to link this to lesbian practices. Again one can wonder about the firmness of his denial. Even if the ritual was about the *evu*, it is clear that, in this context, *evu* manifested itself through the clitoris, and in light of the ambiguity of the *evu* it seems difficult to ascertain that its centrality in the *mevungu* would exclude sexuality playing a role. In his insightful overview of this *mevungu* debate Awondo (2019, 110) rightly relates it to Marc Epprecht's more general analysis of anthropologists' tendency to shy away from addressing same-sex practices even if there were clear indications in their material (Epprecht 2008). In the context of this chapter it is important to note that the *mevungu* ritual was in no way linked to occult enrichment; this association was apparently emerging only with same-sex practices among men.

33. See Abega (2007a, 2007b). Awondo (2019, 117) quoted an earlier article Abega published on the internet in 2002. Unfortunately we could not retrieve this text. However, Awondo's summary shows that on the point of relating the person's double to confusions about hetero- and homosexuality, this article was a prelude to Abega's 2007a text written when the debate on homosexuality was in full swing in Cameroon. Sadly, Abega died in 2008, only fifty-three years old.

34. Cf. also the challenging title of the special issue "L'homosexualité est bonne à penser" (Homosexuality is good to think with).

CONCLUSIONS

1. Cf. chapter 3 on Pype's and Newell's inspiring studies of the power of the idea of "connectivity" for young urbanites.

2. Cf. Hendriks (2017) about Congolese music stars who are supposed to play first the passive role as clients to earlier prominent singers and subsequently the active role in their relation to their younger successors. In chapter 4 above we sketched the same alteration of roles that people now construe between leading figures in Cameroonian politics (Aujoulat–Ahidjo–Biya).

3. Cf. also the recent studies of lesbian arrangements we referred to in interlude 2 (notably Dankwa 2022 and Spronk 2018) which suggest that in everyday practice homo/hetero binaries are particularly inadequate in these contexts.

4. In the article in which she introduced this notion, Guyer (1993) opposed "accumulation" (the same-on-the same) to "composition" (combining different assets). The first would be characteristic of capitalism (money-on-money); the second would

prevail, for instance, in big-men societies of West-Central Africa, where entrepreneurs could use all sorts of resources to profit from new contacts with the market economy.

5. It may seem a big step from Guyer's political-economic version of such "multiple self-realization" to people's experiments with sexual diversity, but Hendriks (2017) made a similar step—albeit with somewhat different implications—in his study of gay lifestyles in Kinshasa.

6. Compare also Thiranagama (2011) on treason from inside as particularly threatening.

7. In the terms of Bernault (2019): when a "transaction" does or does not work.

References

Abega, Sévérin Cécile. 2002. "Le sexe invisible." *Psy-cause*, no. 28. http://psycause .pagesperso-orange.fr/028_029/028_029_le_sexe_invisible.htm. No longer available; accessed November 26, 2018.

———. 2007a. "La presse et l'état: L'exemple des procès sur l'homosexualité au Cameroun." In "Dossier: L'Homosexualité est bonne à penser," ed. Fabien Eboussi Boulaga, special issue, *Terroirs* 1–2:95–110.

———. 2007b. *Les violences sexuelles et l'État au Cameroun*. Paris: Karthala.

Abega, Sévérin Cécile, and Claude Abe. 2005. "Approches anthropologiques de la sorcellerie." In *Justice et sorcellerie*, edited by Éric de Rosny, 33–47. Paris: Édition de l'université catholique de l'Afrique Centrale.

Abwa, Daniel. 2005. *Ngouo Woungly Massaga alias Commandant Kissamba: "Cameroun, ma part de vérité."* Yaoundé: Éditions Minsi DS.

Ageron, Charles-Robert, and Marc Michel, eds. 1995. *L'Afrique noire française: L'ère des décolonisations*. Paris: Karthala.

Agir Ici et Survie. 1996. *Dossiers noirs de la politique africaine de la France, no. 1 à 5*. Paris: L'Harmattan.

Airault, Pascal, and Jean-Pierre Bat. 2016. *Françafrique: Opérations secrètes et affaires d'état*. Paris: Tallandier.

Akindes, Francis. 2017. "La franc-maçonnerie en Côte d'Ivoire: Brève histoire des enjeux actuels." *Afrique contemporaine* 3–4:325–38.

———. 2022. "Y a-t-il des francs-maçons dans les loges en Afrique?" Leçon inaugurale de la Chaire Verhaegen, Université Libre de Bruxelles. February 16, 2022. https://www.youtube.com/watch?v=j3qAuBLn7DU.

Alexandre, Pierre. 1965. "Protohistoire du groupe Beti-Bulu-Fang: Essai de synthèse provisoire." *Cahiers d'Études Africaines* 5:503–60.

Alexandre, Pierre, and Jacques Binet. 1958. *Le groupe dit pahouin (Fang-Boulou-Beti)*. Paris: PUF.

Aliapoulios, Max, A. Papasavva, C. Ballard, E. De Cristofaro, G. Stringhini, S. Zannettou, and J. Blackburn. 2021. "The Gospel According to Q: Understanding the QAnon Conspiracy from the Perspective of Canonical Information." In *Proceedings of the of the 16th International AAAI Conference on Web and Social Media*. https://doi.org/10.48550/arXiv.2101.08750.

Alpes, Maybritt Jill. 2017. *Brokering High-Risk Migration and Illegality in West Africa: Abroad at Any Cost*. London: Routledge.

Andrikopoulos, Apostolos, and Rachel Spronk. 2023. "Family Matters: Same-Sex Relations and Kinship Practices in Nairobi." *Journal of the Royal Anthropological Institute* 29 (4): 899–916.

Angounou, Daniel St. Yves Ebalé. 1992. *Paul Biya, le cauchemar de ma vie; ou, Confession d'un "faussaire."* Yaoundé: Éditions Le Messager.

Arnold, Paul. 1990. *Histoire des Rose-Croix et les origines de la Franc-maçonnerie* Paris: Mercure de France.

Ateba Eyene, C. 2012/2013. *Le Cameroun sous la dictature des loges, des sectes, du magico-anal et des réseaux mafieux: De véritables freins contre l'émergence en 2035—La logique au cœur de la performance.* Yaoundé: St. Paul.

———. 2013. *Crimes rituels, loges, sectes, pouvoirs, drogues et alcools au Cameroun: Les réponses citoyennes et les armes du combat.* Yaoundé: St. Paul.

Aterianus-Owanga, Alice. 2012. "'L'Émergence n'aime pas les femmes!' Hétérosexisme, rumeurs et imaginaires du pouvoir dans le rap gabonais." *Politique Africaine* 126:49–68.

Awondo, Patrick. 2012a. "Homosexualité, sida et constructions politiques— Ethnographie des trajectoires entre le Cameroun et la France." PhD dissertation, École des hautes études en sciences sociales, Paris.

———. 2012b. "Médias, politique et homosexualité au Cameroun: Retour sur la construction d'une controverse." *Politique Africaine* 126:69–85.

———. 2019. *Le sexe et ses doubles: (Homo)sexualité, politique, santé et société en postcolonie.* Lyon: Presses de l'ENS Lyon.

Awondo, Patrick, Peter Geschiere, and Graeme Reid. 2012. "Homophobic Africa? Toward a More Nuanced View." *African Studies Review* 55, no. 3: 145–69.

Badila, Joseph. 2004. *La Franc-maçonnerie en Afrique noire: Un si long chemin vers la liberté, l'égalité, la fraternité.* Paris: Éditions Detrad aVs.

Bakhuri, Amisah, Rachel Spronk, and Rijk van Dijk. 2020. "Labour of Love: Secrecy and Kinship among Ghanaian-Dutch and Somali-Dutch in The Netherlands." *Ethnography* 21, no. 3: 394–412.

Barber, M. 1978. *The Trial of the Templars.* Cambridge: Cambridge University Press.

Barruel, Augustin. 1799. *Memoirs Illustrating the History of Jacobinism.* Philadelphia: Hudson & Goodwin. Originally published as *Mémoires pour servir à l'histoire du Jacobinisme*, Paris, 1797.

Bat, Jean-Pierre. 2012. *Le syndrome Foccart: La politique française en Afrique de 1959 à nos jours.* Paris: Gallimard.

———. 2015. *La fabrique des "Barbouzes": Histoire des réseaux Foccart en Afrique.* Paris: Nouveau Monde Éditions.

Bayart, Jean-François. 1984. *La politique africaine de François Mitterrand.* Paris: Karthala.

———. 1989/1993. *The State in Africa: The Politics of the Belly.* London: Longman.

———. 2000. "Africa in the World: A History of Extraversion." *African Affairs* 99, no. 395: 217–67.

———. 2005. *The Illusion of Cultural Identity.* Chicago: University of Chicago Press.

———. 2011. "Quelle politique africaine pour la France?" *Politique Africaine* 121:147–59.

———. 2022. *L'Énergie de l'État.* Paris: La Découverte.

BBC. 2021. *The Cult of Conspiracy: QAnon.* January 6, 2021.

Beetstra, Tjalling A. 2004. "Massahysterie in de Verenigde Staten en Nederland: De affaire rond de McMartin Pre-School en het ontuchtschandaal in Oude Pekela." In *Mediahypes en moderne sagen: Sterke verhalen in het nieuws*, edited by P. Burger and W. Koetsenruijter, 53–69. Leiden: Stichting Neerlandistiek Leiden.

Belinga, Patrick Dieudonné Ondoua. 2018. "Politique de la suspicion et de développement urbain au Cameroun." *Politique Africaine* 150:53–75.

Béresniak, Daniel, and Joseph Badila. 2008. *Les Francs-Maçons et l'Afrique: Une rencontre fraternelle*. Paris: Detrad aVs.

Berlot, Boris, and Léa E. J. S. Masse. 2019. "Mapping Political Homophobia in Senegal." *African Studies Quarterly* 18, no. 4: 21–39.

Bernault, Florence. 1996. *Démocraties ambiguës en Afrique centrale: Congo-Brazzaville, Gabon, 1940–1965*. Paris: Karthala.

———. 2019. *Colonial Transformations: Imaginaries, Bodies and Histories in Gabon*. Durham, NC: Duke University Press.

Bernault, Florence, and Peter Geschiere. 2022. "Joseph Tonda: The Social Sciences and the Vortex of City Life in Africa." *Africa* 92, no. 1: 152–60.

Bernault, Florence, and Joseph Tonda. 2000. "Dynamiques de l'invisible en Afrique." In "Pouvoirs sorciers," ed. Florence Bernault and Joseph Tonda, special issue, *Politique Africaine* 79: 5–17.

Bersani, Leo. 1987 [2009]. "Is the Rectum a Grave?" In Leo Bersani, *Is the Rectum a Grave? And Other Essays*, 1–30. Chicago: University of Chicago Press.

Bertier, Ph. 1979. "Balzac du côté de Sodome." *Année Balzacienne* 20:147–77.

Beti, Mongo. 1972. *Main basse sur le Cameroun: Autopsie d'une décolonisation*. Paris: Éditions des Peuples Noirs.

Beuvier, Franck. 2022. "La côte du Cameroun et ses mondes imaginaires. Chronique d'une barbarie annoncée (XVIIe-XIXe siècles)." *Journal des Africanistes* 91, no. 1: 6–37.

Bhély-Quenum, Olympe. 1979. *L'Initié*. Paris: Présence Africaine.

Biaya, Tsikata Keyembe. 2001. "Les plaisirs de la ville: Masculinité, sexualité et feminité à Dakar (1997–2000)." *African Studies Review* 44, no. 2: 71–81.

Boltanski, Luc. 2012. *Énigmes et complots: Une enquête à propos d'enquêtes*. Paris: Gallimard.

Boltanski, Luc, and Élisabeth Claverie. 2007. "Du monde social en tant que scène d'un procès." In *Affaires, scandales et grandes causes: De Socrate à Pinochet*, ed. L.Boltanski, E. Claverie, N. Offenstadt, and S. van Damme, 395–452. Paris: Stock.

Bonhomme, Julien. 2009. *Les voleurs de sexe: Anthropologie d'une rumeur africaine*. Paris: Seuil. Translated as *Sex Thieves: The Anthropology of a Rumor*, Chicago: HAU Books, 2016.

Borrel, Thomas, Amzat Boukari-Yabara, Benoît Collombat, and Thomas Deltombe, eds. 2021. *L'Empire qui ne veut pas mourir: Une histoire de la Françafrique*. Paris: Seuil.

Brochet de Thé, Marie-Paule. 1985. "Rites et association traditionnelles chez les femmes bëti du sud du Cameroun." In *Femmes du Cameroun: Mères pacifiques, femmes rebelles*, ed. Jean-Claude Barbier, 245–83. Paris: Karthala.

Broqua, Christophe. 2009. "Sur les rétributions des pratiques sexuelles à Bamako." *Canadian Journal of African Studies* 43, no. 1: 60–82.

———. 2016. "Islamic Movement against Homosexuality in Senegal: The Fight against AIDS as a Catalyst." In *Public Religion and the Politics of Homosexuality in Africa*, ed. Adriaan Van Klinken and Ezra Chitando, 163–79. London: Taylor & Francis.

———. 2017. *"Góor-Jigéen* : La resignification négative d'une catégorie entre genre et sexualité (Sénégal)." *Socio* 9:163–83. https://doi.org/10.4000/socio.3063.

Bubandt, Nils. 2014. *The Empty Seashell: Witchcraft and Doubt on an Indonesian Island*. Ithaca, NY: Cornell University Press.

Bureau, René. 1964. *Ethnosociologie religieuse des Duala et apparentés*. Douala: Institut des recherches scientifiques Cameroun.

Carter, Brett Logan. 2014. "Inside Autocracy: Political Survival and the Modern Prince." PhD dissertation, Harvard University.

Caseley-Hayford, Augustus, and Richard Rathbone. 1992. "Politics, Families and Freemasonry in the Colonial Gold Coast." In *People and Empires in African History: Essays in Memory of Michael Crowder*, ed. J. F. Ade Ajayi and J. D. Y. Peel, 143–61. London: Longman.

Cassam, Quassim. 2019. *Conspiracy Theories*. Cambridge: Polity Press.

Ceriana Mayneri, André. 2014. *Sorcellerie et prophétism en Centreafrique: L'imaginaire de la dépossession en pays banda*. Paris: Karthala.

Chafer, Tony. 2005. "Chirac and 'la Françafrique': No Longer a Family Affair." *Modern & Contemporary France* 13:7–23.

Chaffard, Georges. 1965. *Les secrets de la décolonisation*. Paris: Calmann-Lévy.

Cinnamon, John. 2012. "Spirits, Power and the Political Imagination in Late Colonial Gabon." *Africa* 82, no. 2: 187–211.

Cohen, Abner. 1981. *The Politics of Elite Culture: The Dramaturgy of Power in a Modern African Society*. Berkeley: University of California Press.

Coignard, Sophie. 2009. *Un État dans l'État: Le contrepouvoir maçonnique*. Paris: Albin Michel.

Cole, Jennifer. 2014. "Working Misunderstandings: The Tangled Relationship between Kinship, Franco-Malagasy Binational Marriage and the French State." *Cultural Anthropology* 29, no. 3: 527–51.

Coly, Ayo. 2019. "The Invention of the Homosexual: The Politics of Homophobia in Senegal." In *Gender and Sexuality in Senegalese Societies: Critical Perspectives and Methods*, ed. Babacar M'Baye and Besi Brillian Muhonja, 27–51. Lanham, MD: Lexington Books.

Combes, André. 2016. "La franc-maçonnerie au XIXème siècle (1814–1914)." In *La Franc-Maçonnerie*, ed. Pierre Mollier, Sylvie Bourel, and Laurent Portes, 215–19, 228–29. Paris: Bibliothèque nationale de France.

Corey-Boulet, Robbie. 2019. *Love Falls on Us: A Story of American Ideas and African LGBT Lives*. London: Zed Press.

Coy, Jean-Louis. 2007. "Un film français antimaçon en 1943: *Forces occultes*; Comment ont-ils pu?" *La chaîne d'Union* 3, no. 41: 46–53.

Currier, Ashley, and Joëlle M. Cruz. 2016. "Religious Inspiration—Indigenous Mobilization against LGBTI Rights in Post-Conflict Liberia." In *Public Religion and the Politics of Homosexuality in Africa*, ed. Adriaan van Klinken and Ezra Chitando, 146–62. London: Taylor & Francis.

Currier, A., and T. Migraine-George. 2016. "Queer Studies/African Studies: An (Im)possible Transaction?" *GLQ: A Journal of Lesbian and Gay Studies* 22, no. 2: 281–305.

Dachez, Pierre. 2016. "Les débuts de la franc-maçonnerie en France." In *La Franc-Maçonnerie*. ed. Pierre Mollier, Sylvie Bourel, and Laurent Portes, 72–76. Paris: Bibliothèque nationale de France.

Dankwa, Serena O. 2022. *Knowing Women: Same-Sex Intimacy, Gender, and Identity in Postcolonial Ghana*. African Identities. Cambridge: Cambridge University Press.

De Bruijn, M., and R. van Dijk. 2012. "Connectivity and the Post-Global Moment: (Dis)connections and Social Change in Africa." In *The Social Life of Connectivity in Africa*, ed. M. De Bruijn and R. van Dijk, 1–20. Basingstoke, UK: Palgrave MacMillan.

De Gassicourt, Charles-Louis Cadet. 1797 [2020]. *Le tombeau de Jacques de Molay*. London: Cubic Stone.

Deleuze, Gilles, and Félix Guattari. 1972. *L'Anti-Oedipe: Capitalisme et schizo-phrénie*. Paris: Éditions de Minuit.

Deltombe, Thomas, Manuel Domergue, and Jacob Tatsitsa. 2011. *Kamerun! Une guerre cachée aux origines de Françafrique*. Paris: La Découverte.

———. 2016. *La guerre du Cameroun: L'invention de la Françafrique, 1948–1971*. Paris: La Découverte.

De Rosny, Éric. 1974. *Ndimsi: Ceux qui soignent dans la nuit*. Yaoundé: Éditions Clé.

———. 1981. *Les yeux de ma chèvre: Sur les pas des maîtres de la nuit en pays douala*. Paris: Plon.

De Vries, Jacqueline. 2018. "Cameroonian *Schutztruppe* Soldiers in Spanish-Ruled Fernando Po during the First World War: A 'Menace to Peace'?" *War & Society* 37, no. 4: 280–301.

Dickie, John. 2020. *The Craft: How the Freemasons Made the Modern World*. London: Hodder & Stoughton.

Dierickx, Jean. 1993. "Aspects récents de l'antimaçonnisme en Grande-Bretagne: L'Effritement d'une position privilégiée." In *Les Courants antimaçonniques hier et aujourd'hui*, ed. Alain Dierkens, 109–21. Brussels : Édition de l'Université de Bruxelles.

Dierkens, Alain, ed. 1993. *Les Courants antimaçonniques hier et aujourd'hui*. Brussels: Éditions de l'Université de Bruxelles.

Dongmo, Jean-Louis. 1981. *Le dynamisme bamiléké (Cameroun)*. Yaoundé: CEPER.

Donham, Donald. 2018. *The Erotics of History: An Atlantic African Example*. Oakland: University of California Press.

Dosekun, Simidele, and Mehita Iqani. 2019. "The Politics and Aesthetics of Luxury in Africa." In *African Luxury: Aesthetics and Politics*, ed. Mehita Iqani and Simidele Dosekun, 1–16. Bristol: Intellect Books.

Drążkiewicz-Grodzicka, Elżbieta, and J. Harambam, eds. 2021. "What Should Academics Do about Conspiracy Theories? Moving beyond Debunking to Better Deal with Conspirational Movements, Misinformation and Post-truth." Special issue, *Journal for Cultural Research* 25, no. 1.

Dubois, Quentin. 2021. "Homosexualité et civilisation: Perspectives vitalistes à partir de l'anus." *Lundi matin* 269, January 4, 2021 https://lundi.am/Homosexualite-et-civilisation-perspectives-vitalistes-a-partir-de-l-anus.

Earle, Jason W. 2013. "Conspiracies and Secret Societies in Interwar French Literature." PhD dissertation, Columbia University.

Eboko, Fred, and Patrick Awondo, eds. 2018a. "Cameroun: L'État stationnaire." Special issue, *Politique Africaine*, no. 150.

———2018b. "L'État stationnaire: Entre chaos et renaissance." In "Cameroun: L'État stationnaire," edited by Fred Eboko and Patrick Awondo, special issue, *Politique Africaine*, no. 150:5–29.

Eboussi Boulaga, Fabien, ed. 2007. "Dossier: L'Homosexualité est bonne à penser." Special issue, *Terroirs* 1–2.

Edelman, Lee. 2004. *No Future: Queer Theory and the Death Drive*. Durham, NC: Duke University Press.

Edighoffer, Roland. 1998. *The Rosicrucians and the Crisis of European Consciousness in the 17th Century*. Paris: Editions Dervy.

Edzoa, Titus. 2012. *Méditations de prison*. Paris: Karthala.

Ekine, Sokary, and Hakima Abbas, eds. 2013. *Queer African Reader*. Dakar: Pambazuka Press.

Ellis, Stephen. 1989. "Tuning In to Pavement Radio." *African Affairs* 88, no. 352: 321–30.

———. 1999. *The Mask of Anarchy: The Destruction of Liberia and the Religious Dimensions of an African Civil War*. London: Hurst.

Epprecht, Marc. 2006. "'Bisexuality' and the Politics of Normal in African Ethnography." *Anthropologica* 48, no. 2: 187–201.

Evans-Pritchard, E. E. 1970. "Sexual Inversion among the Azande." *American Anthropologist* 72, no. 6: 1428–34.

Eyinga, Abel. 1984. *Introduction à la politique camerounaise*. Paris: L'Harmattan.

Falola, Toyin. 2003. *The Power of African Cultures*. Rochester, NY: University of Rochester Press.

Foccart, Jacques. 1995 and 1997. *Foccart parle: Entretien avec Phillipe Gaillard*. 2 vols. Paris: Fayard/Jeune Afrique.

Foucault, Michel. 1976. *Histoire de la Sexualité I: La Volonte de Savoir*. Paris: Gallimard.

Freud, Sigmund. 1905. *Drei Abhandlungen zur Sexualtheorie*. Leipzig: Deuticke.

Freudenthal, Emmanuel, and Youri Van Der Weide. 2020. "Making a Killing: Israeli Mercenaries in Cameroon." *African Arguments*, June 23, 2020. London: Hurst for International African Institute.

Furet, F. 1978. *Penser la révolution française*. Paris: Gallimard.

Gervais, Pierre, Pauline Peretz, and Pierre Stutin. 2012. *Le Dossier Secret de l'Affaire Dreyfus*. Paris: Alma éditeur.

Geschiere, Peter. 1997. *The Modernity of Witchcraft: Politics and the Occult in Postcolonial Africa*. Charlottesville: University of Virginia Press.

———. 2005. "Funerals and Belonging: Different Patterns in South Cameroon." *African Studies Review* 48, no. 2: 45–65.

———. 2013. *Witchcraft, Intimacy, and Trust: Africa in Comparison*. Chicago: University of Chicago Press.

———. 2017. "A Vortex of Identities: Freemasonry, Witchcraft and Postcolonial Homophobia." *African Studies Review* 60, no. 2: 7–35.

———. 2021. "Dazzled by New Media: Mbembe, Tonda and the Mystic Virtual." *African Studies Review* 64, no. 1: 71–85.

Geschiere, Peter, and Rogers Orock. 2020. "Anusocratie? Freemasonry, Sexual Transgression and Illicit Enrichment in Postcolonial Africa." *Africa* 90, no. 5: 831–51.

Geschiere, Peter, Francio Guadeloupe, and Juan Obarrio. In preparation. *Articulation as a Key Word to Overcome Binary Thinking*.

Gevisser, Mark. 2020. *The Pink Line: Journeys across the World's Queer Frontiers.* London: MacMillan.

Gielessen, Guillou Bitsutsu. 2012. "Gabon: Bienvenue chez les Francs-Maçons." *GL-9News.* https://www.gl9news.com/Gabon-Bienvenue-Chez-les-Francs-Maçons a18765.html. No longer available; accessed April 11, 2018.

Glaser, Antoine. 2014. *AfricaFrance: Quand les dirigeants africains deviennent les maîtres du jeu.* Paris: Fayard.

Gning, Ndeye Ndiagna. 2013. "Une réalité complexe: Sexualités entre hommes et prévention du Sida au Sénégal." PhD dissertation, Université de Bordeaux Segalen.

Goody, Jack. 1971. *Technology, Tradition and the State in Africa.* London: Oxford University Press.

Gorer, Geoffrey. 1935. *Africa Dances.* London: Penguin Books.

Gounin, Yves. 2009. *La France et l'Afrique.* Louvain-la-Neuve: De Boeck.

Gossman, Lionel. 2020. *The Passion of Max von Oppenheim.* Cambridge: Open Book.

Gueboguo, Charles. 2006. *La question homosexuelle en Afrique: Le cas du Cameroun.* Paris: L'Harmattan.

———. 2009. "Penser les 'droits' des homosexuels/les en Afrique: Du sens et de la puissance de l'action associative militante au Cameroun." *Canadian Journal of African Studies* 43, no. 1: 129–50.

Guyer, Jane. 1993. "Wealth in People and Self-Realization in Equatorial Africa." *Man* 28, no. 2: 243–65.

Hall, Stuart. 1996. "Interview with L. Grossberg." In *Stuart Hall: Critical Dialogues in Cultural Studies,* ed. D. Morley and K. Chens, 131–50. London: Routledge.

Halperin, David. 2000. "How to Do the History of Male Homosexuality." *GLQ: A Journal of Lesbian and Gay Studies* 6, no. 1: 89–91.

Halperin, David, and Trevor Hoppe, eds. 2017. *The War on Sex.* Durham, NC: Duke University Press.

Hannah, Matthew. 2021. "QAnon and the Information Dark Age." *First Monday* 26, no. 2. https://doi.org/10.5210/fm.v26i2.10868.

Harambam, Jaron. 2020. *Contemporary Conspiracy Culture: Trust and Knowledge in an Era of Epistemic Instability.* London: Routledge.

———. 2021. "Against Modernist Illusions: Why We Need More Democratic and Constructivist Alternatives for Debunking Conspiracy Theories." In "What Should Academics Do about Conspiracy Theories? Moving beyond Debunking to Better Deal with Conspirational Movements, Misinformation and Post-truth," ed. Elżbieta Drążkiewicz-Grodzicka and Jaron Harambam, special issue, *Journal for Cultural Research* 25, no. 1: 103–21.

Harland-Jacobs, Jessica. 2013. *Builders of Empire: Freemasons and British Imperialism, 1717–1927.* Chapel Hill: University of North Carolina Press.

Hasquin, Hervé. 1993. "L'antimaçonisme: Quelques réflexions en guise de conclusion." In *Les Courants antimaçonniques hier et aujourd'hui,* ed. Alain Dierkens, 171–73. Éditions de l'Université de Bruxelles.

Hausen, Karin. 1970. *Deutsche Kolonialherrschaft in Afrika: Wirtschaftsinteressen und Kolonialverwaltung in Kamerun vor 1914.* Zurich: Atlantis.

Hebga, Meinrad. 1968. "Le concept de métamorphose d'hommes en animaux chez les Basaa, Duala, Ewondo, Bantu du Sud Cameroun." Thèse de 3ième cycle, Université de Rennes.

———.1979. *Sorcellerie: chimère dangereuse . . . ?* Abidjan: INADES.

———. 1995. *Afrique de la raison, Afrique de la foi*. Paris: Karthala.

Heilbrunn, John. 2005. "Oil and Water? Elite Politicians and Corruption in France." *Comparative Politics* 37, no. 3: 277–87.

Hendriks, Thomas. 2016. "SIM Cards of Desire: Sexual Versatility and the Male Homoerotic Economy in Urban Congo." *American Ethnologist* 43, no. 2: 230–42

———. 2017. "Queer(ing) Popular Culture: Homo-Erotic Provocations from Kinshasa." *Journal of African Culture Studies* 31, no. 1: 71–88.

———. 2021. "'Making Men Fall': Queer Power beyond Anti-Normativity." *Africa* 91, no. 30: 398–417.

Hendriks, Thomas, and Rachel Spronk, eds. 2020. *Readings in Sexualities in Africa*. Bloomington: Indiana University Press.

Herdt, Gilbert, ed. 2009. *Moral Panics, Sex Panics, Fear, and the Fight for Sexual Rights*. New York: New York University Press.

Hoad, Neville. 2007. *African Intimacies: Race, Homosexuality and Globalization*. Minneapolis: University of Minnesota.

Hocquenghem, Guy. 1972. *Le désir homosexuel*. Paris: Fayard.

Hofstadter, R. 1964. "The Paranoid Style in American Politics." *Harper's Magazine*, November 1964, 77–86.

Ihonvbere, Julius O. 1991. "A Critical Evaluation of the Failed 1990 Coup in Nigeria." *Journal of Modern African Studies* 29, no. 4: 601–26.

Jacob, Margaret C. 2006. *The Origins of Freemasonry*. Philadelphia: University of Pennsylvania Press.

Jansen, J. C. 2015. "In Search of Atlantic Sociability: Freemasons, Empires and Atlantic History." *Bulletin of the German Historical Institute* 57:75–99.

Johnson, Cary Alan. 2001. "Hearing Voices: Unearthing Evidence of Homosexuality in Precolonial Africa." In *The Greatest Taboo: Homosexuality in Black Communities*, ed. Delroy Constantine-Simms, 135–49. Los Angeles: Alyson Publications.

Joseph, Richard A. 1977. *Radical Nationalism in Cameroun: Social Origins of the UPC Rebellion*. Oxford: Clarendon Press.

———. 1978. *Gaullist Africa: Cameroon under Ahmadou Ahidjo*. London: Fourth Dimension.

Josserand, Philippe. 2016. "Jacques de Molay: La fabrique d'un héros." In *Templiers et francs-maçons: De la légende à l'histoire*, ed. Roger Dachez et al., 53–56. Paris: Musée de la franc-maçonnerie. Exhibition catalog.

Karsch-Haak, Ferdinand. 1911. *Das gleichgeschlechtiges Leben der Naturvölker*. Münich: Ernst Reinhardt.

Kemp, Jonathan. 2013. *The Penetrated Male*. New York: Punctum Books.

Klockmann, Thomas. 1988. "Günther Tessmann: König im weissen Fleck; Das ethnologische Werk im Spiegel der Lebenserinnerungen." PhD dissertation, University of Hamburg.

Konde, Emmanuel. 2012. "Cameroon's Political Succession Schism of 1983 Revisited." *International Journal of Arts and Commerce* 1, no. 6: 25–27.

Koselleck, Reinhart. 1959. *Kritik und Krise: Eine Studie zur Pathogenese der bürgerlichen Welt*. Freiburg: Karl Alber.

Kroesbergen-Kamps, Johanneke. 2022. "Conspiracy Theories in Africa: A Continuum of Narratives about Evil Agents." *In Religious Dimensions of Conspiracy Theories: Comparing and Connecting Old and New Trends*, ed. Francesco Piraino, Marco Pasi, and Egil Asprem, 185–201. London: Routledge.

Kuoh, Christian T. 1991. *Une fresque du régime Ahidjo (1970–1982): Mon témoignage sur le Cameroun de l'indépendance*. Paris: Karthala.

Laborie, Pierre. 2019. *Penser l'évènement, 1940–1945*. Paris: Gallimard.

Laburthe-Tolra, Philippe. 1977. *Mínlaaba: Histoire et société traditionnelle chez les Bëti du Sud Cameroun*. Paris: Champion.

———.1981. *Les seigneurs de la forêt: Essai sur le passé historique, l'organisation sociale et les normes éthiques des anciens Beti du Cameroun*. Paris: Publications de la Sorbonne

———. 1985. *Initiations et sociétés secrètes au Cameroun: Essai sur la réligion Beti*. Paris: Karthala.

Lachenal, Guillaume, and Betrand Taithe. 2009. "Une généalogie missionnaire et coloniale de l'humanitaire: Le cas Aujoulat au Cameroun, 1935–1973." *Mouvement Social* 227:45–63.

Lado, Ludovic. 2011. "L'homophobie populaire au Cameroun." *Cahiers d'Études Africaines* 51, no. 204: 921–44.

LaFontaine, J. S. 1998. *Speak of the Devil: Tales of Satanic Child Abuse in Contemporary England*. Cambridge: Cambridge University Press.

Lancaster, Roger. 2011. *Sex Panic and the Punitive State*. Berkeley: University of California Press.

Le Bomin, Gabriel, and Stéphanie Khémis. 2000. *Les Francs-maçons et le pouvoir*. France 5. DVD.

Lewis, James R. 2008. *The Order of the Solar Temple*. London: Taylor & Francis.

Loiselle, K. 2014. *Brotherly Love: Freemasonry and Male Friendship in Enlightenment France*. Ithaca, NY: Cornell University Press.

Machikou, Nadine. 2009. "La liste des 'homosexuels de la République': Chronique d'une dépacification outrancière de la vie politique au Cameroun." Dixième congrès de l'Association française de science politique, Grenoble, 9 septembre 2009.

———. 2018. "Utopie et dystopie ambazonniennes: Dieu, les dieux et la crise anglophone au Cameroun." *Politique africaine* 150:115–39.

Mack, Robert W. Undated. "Honoré de Balzac's Gay Anti-Hero." http://rmack .com/balzac_with_footnotes.htm.

Mallart, Louis. 1981. *Ni dos ni ventre: Religion, magie et sorcellerie evuzok*. Paris: Société d'Ethnographie.

Marches, Philippe. 1995. "Mitterrand, l'Africain." *Politique Africaine* 58:5–24.

Mary, André, and Maixant Mebiame Zomo. 2015. "Épidémie de 'crimes rituels' au Gabon: Des affaires de sorcellerie au scandale de l'impunité." In *Penser la sorcellerie en Afrique*, ed. Sandra Fancello, 117–59. Paris: Éditions Hermann.

Massad, Joseph. 2007. *Desiring Arabs*. New York: Columbia University Press.

M'Bayé, Babacar. 2019. "Representations of the Gôr Djiguène [Man Woman] in Senegalese Culture, Films, and Literature." In *Gender and Sexuality in Senegalese Societies: Critical Perspectives and Methods*, ed. Babacar M'Baye and Besi Brillian Muhonja, 77–106. Lanham, MD: Lexington Books.

M'Baye, Babacar, and Besi Brillian Muhonja, eds, 2019. *Gender and Sexuality in Senegalese Societies: Critical Perspectives and Methods*. Lanham, MD: Lexington Books.

Mbembe, Achille. 1996. *La naissance du maquis dans le Sud-Cameroun (1920–1960)*. Paris: Karthala.

———. 2001. *On the Postcolony*. Berkeley: University of California Press.

———. 2006. "Le potentat sexuel: À propos de la fellation, de la sodomie et autres privautés postcoloniales." *Le Messager*, February 17, 2006. Translated as

"The Sexual Potentate: On Sodomy, Fellatio, and Other Postcolonial Privacies," in *Readings in Sexualities in Africa*, ed. Thomas Hendriks and Rachel Spronk, 283–96. Bloomington: Indiana University Press, 2020.

———. 2010. *Sortir de la grande nuit: Essai sur l'Afrique decolonisée*. Paris: La Découverte.

———. 2016a. "Future Knowledges." Abiola Lecture, presented at the African Studies Association Annual Meeting in Washington, DC, December 1–3, 2016.

———. 2016b. *Politiques de l'inimitié*. Paris: La Découverte.

———. 2019. *Necropolitics*. Durham, NC: Duke University Press.

———. 2020a. *Brutalisme*. Paris: La Découverte.

———. 2020b. "Les états voyous d'Afrique centrale sont les derniers avatars de la Françafrique: Organiser la grande transition." *Le Monde*, March 4, 2020.

Mbougar Sarr, Mohamed. 2018. *De purs hommes*. Paris: Livres de Poche.

Meiu, George Paul. 2020a. "Queerly Kenyan: On the Political Economy of Queer Possibilities." Review of *Kenyan, Christian, Queer: Religion, LGBT Activism, and Arts of Resistance in Africa*, by Adriaan Van Klinken. *HAU: Journal of Ethnographic Theory* 10, no. 2 (2020): 613–17.

———. 2020b. "Under-Layers of Citizenship: Queer Objects, Intimate Exposures and the Rescue Rush in Kenya." *Cultural Anthropology* 35, no. 4: 575–601.

———. 2023. *Queer Objects to the Rescue: Intimacy and Citizenship in Kenya*. Chicago: University of Chicago Press.

Meyer, Birgit. 2015. *Sensational Movies: Video, Vision, and Christianity in Ghana*. Oakland: University of California Press.

———. 2018. "Frontier Zones and the Study of Religion." *Journal of the Study of Religion* 31, no. 20: 57–78.

Mieli, Mario. 1977. *Elementi di critica omosessuale*. Turin: Einaudi. Translated as *Towards a Gay Communism: Elements of a Homosexual Critique*, London: Pluto Press, 2018.

Mimche, Honoré, and Charles Gueboguo. 2006. "Problématique de l'homosexualité en Afrique: L'expérience camerounaise." *L'Arbre à Palabre*, August 19, 2006, 18–59.

Mollier, Pierre. 2016a. "Chevaliers et Templiers aux débuts de la franc-maçonnerie/ Les Templiers dans la Révolution française." In *Templiers et francs-maçons: De la légende à l'histoire*, ed. Roger Dachez et al., 7–13, 43–45. Paris: Musée de la franc-maçonnerie. Exhibition catalog.

Mollier, Pierre. 2016b. "Premières loges, premiers grand-maîtres français" In *La Franc-Maçonnerie*, ed. Pierre Mollier, Sylvie Bourel, and Laurent Portes, 76–81. Paris: Bibliothèque nationale de France.

Mollier, Pierre, Sylvie Bourel, and Laurent Portes, eds. 2016. *La Franc-Maçonnerie*. Paris: Bibliothèque nationale de France.

Mollin, Jules-Henri. 2014. *La vérité sur l'Affaire des Fiches*. Paris: Hachette.

Muracciole, J.-F. 1996. *Histoire de la France libre*. Paris: PUF.

Murat, Laure. 2006. *La loi du genre: Une histoire culturelle du "troisième sexe."* Paris: Fayard.

———. 2007. "La tante, le policier et l'écrivain: Pour un protosexologie de commissariats et de romans." *Revue d'histoire des sciences humaines* 17, no. 2: 47–59.

Murray, Stephen D., and Will Roscoe, eds. 1998. *Boy-Wives and Female Husbands: Studies in African Homosexualities*. New York: Palgrave.

Ndjio, Basile. 2005. "Carrefour de la Joie: Popular Deconstruction of the African Postcolonial Public Sphere." *Africa* 75, no. 3: 265–94.

———. 2006. "'Feymania': Magic Money, Social Mobility, and Power in Contemporary Cameroon." PhD dissertation. Amsterdam: University of Amsterdam.

———. 2008. "*Évolués & feymen*: Old and New Figures of Modernity in Cameroon." In *Readings in Modernity in Africa*, ed. Peter Geschiere, Birgit Meyer, and Peter Pels, 205–14. Bloomington: Indiana University Press.

———. 2012a. *Magie et enrichissement illicite: La feymania au Cameroun*. Paris: Karthala.

———. 2012b. "Postcolonial Histories of Sexuality: The Political Invention of the Libidinal African Straight." *Africa* 82, no. 4: 609–31.

———. 2013. "Sexualities and Nationalist Ideologies in Postcolonial Africa." In *Sexualities and Modernity in the Global South*, ed. Saskia Wieringa and Horacio F. Sivori, 120–43. London: Zed Books.

———. 2022. "*Garçons manqués* and *Femmes Fortes*: Two Ambivalent Figures of Butch Lesbianism in Women's Football in Cameroon." *African Studies Review* 65, no. 3: 772–92.

Ndlovu-Gatsheni, Sabelo J. 2022. *Coloniality of Power: Myths of Decolonization*. Dakar: CODESRIA.

Nemande, Steve, with COC Netherlands. 2017. *Cameroun: Une analyse contextuelle de la situation des LGBT en lien avec les droits humains et la santé*. Amsterdam: COC Netherlands/New York: Hudson & Goodwin.

Newell, Sasha. 2021. "Decolonizing Science, Digitizing the Occult: Theory from the Virtual South." *African Studies Review* 64, no. 1: 86–105.

Newell, Sasha, and Katrien Pype. 2021. "Decolonizing the Virtual: Future Knowledges and the Extrahuman in Africa." *African Studies Review* 64, no. 1: 5–22.

Newell, Sasha, and Katrien Pype, eds. 2021. "Forum: Decolonizing the Virtual." *African Studies Review* 64, no. 1: 5–104.

Ngolet, François. 2000. "Ideological Manipulations and Political Longevity: The Power of Omar Bongo in Gabon since 1967." *African Studies Review* 43, no. 4: 55–71.

Nguyen, Vinh-Kim. 2010. *The Republic of Therapy: Triage and Sovereignty in West Africa's Time of AIDS*. Durham, NC: Duke University Press.

Nken, Simon, 2014. *L'empreinte suspecte de Louis-Paul Aujoulat sur le Cameroun d'aujourd'hui*. Yaoundé: Editions K2oteurs.

Nuttall, Sarah. 2004. "Stylizing the Self: The Y Generation in Rosebank, Johannesburg." *Public Culture* 16:430–52.

Nyamnjoh, Francis. 2017. "Incompleteness: Frontier Africa and the Currency of Conviviality." *Journal of Asian and African Studies* 52, no. 3: 253–70.

———. 2018. "Cannibalism as Food for Thought." In *Eating and Being Eaten*, ed. Francis Nyamnjoh, 1–99. Bamenda, Cameroon: Langaa.

Nyanzi, Stella. 2013. *Politicizing the "Sin of Sodom and Gomorrah": Examining the Christian Rightists' War against Homosexuality in Uganda*. https://ssrn.com/abstract=2295792.

Nyeck, S. N. 2013. "Mobilizing against the Invisible: Erotic Nationalism, Mass Media, and the 'Paranoid Style' in Cameroon." In *Sexual Diversity in Africa: Politics, Theory, Citizenship*, ed. S. N. Nyeck and M. Epprecht, 151–70. Montreal: McGill-Queen's University Press.

———. 2016. "Queer Fragility and Christian Social Ethics: A Political Interpolation of the Catholic Church in Cameroon." In *Christianity and Controversies over*

Homosexuality in Contemporary Africa, ed. Ezra Chitando and Adriaan van Klinken, 163–79. London: Routledge.

Odo, Georges. 2015. *La Franc-Maçonnerie dans les colonies, 1738–1960*. Montélimar: Éditions Maçonniques de France.

———. 2017. *La Franc-Maçonnerie en Afrique, 1781–2000*. Montélimar: Éditions Maçonniques de France.

Oestermann, Tristan. 2023. *Kautschuk und Arbeit in Kamerun under deutscher Kolonialherrschaft, 1880–1913*. Vienna: Böhlau.

Olinga, Luc. 2006. "Sex, mensonge et politique." *Jeune Afrique*, March 13, 2006. https://www.jeuneafrique.com/110446/archives-thematique/sexe-mensonge-et -politique/. Accessed August 10, 2015.

Ombolo, Jean-Pierre. 1990. *Sexe et société en Afrique noire*. Paris: L'Harmattan.

Omoigui, Nowa. n.d. "The Orkar Failed Coup of April 22, 1990." *Damodu.com*, https://dawodu.com/omoigui8.htm.

Ondo, Placide. 2021. "L'irrévérence politique ou le pillage symbolique du chef de l'État gabonais." *Politique Africaine* 163, no. 3: 107–27.

Opejobi, Seun. 2017. "Biafra: Okorocha in 'Homosexual Circle' with IBB, TY Danjuma—Nnamdi Kanu Audio." *Daily Post*, September 1, 2017. https:// dailypost.ng/2017/09/01/biafra-okorocha-homosexual-circle-ibb-ty-danjuma -nnamdi-kanu-audio/.

Orock, Rogers T. E. 2015. "Elites, Culture, and Power: The Moral Politics of 'Development' in Cameroon." *Anthropological Quarterly* 88, no. 2: 533–68.

———. 2019. "Rumours in War: Boko Haram and the Politics of Suspicion in French-Cameroon Relations." *Journal of Modern African Studies* 57, no. 4: 563–87.

Orock, Rogers, and Peter Geschiere. 2021. "Decolonization, Freemasonry, and the Rise of 'Homosexuality' as a Public Issue in Cameroon: The Return of Dr. Aujoulat." *African Affairs* 120, no. 478: 26–56.

Oudenhuijsen, Loes. 2021. "Quietly Queer(ing): The Normative Value of *Sutura* and Its Potential for Young Women in Urban Senegal." *Africa* 91:434–52.

Pagès, Alain. 2019. *L'affaire Dreyfus: Vérités et légendes*. Paris: Perrin.

Pastorello, Thierry. 2010. "L'abolition du crime de sodomie en 1791: Un long procès social, répressif et pénal." *Cahiers d'histoire* 112–13:197–208.

Paxton, Robert. 2001. *Vichy France: Old Guard and New Order, 1940–1944*. New York: Columbia University Press.

Péan, Pierre. 1983. *Affaires africaines*. Paris: Fayard.

Pesnot, Patrick. 2014. *Les dessous de la Françafrique*. Paris: Nouveau Monde Éditions.

Pierce, Steven. 2016. "'Nigeria Can Do without Such Perverts': Sexual Anxiety and Political Crisis in Postcolonial Nigeria." *Comparative Studies of South Asia, Africa and the Middle East* 36, no. 1: 3–20.

Pigeaud, Fanny. 2011. *Au Cameroun de Paul Biya*. Paris: Karthala.

Pommerolle, Marie-Emmanuelle. 2015. "Les violences dans l'Extrême-Nord du Cameroun: Le complot comme outil d'interprétation et de luttes politiques." *Politique Africaine*, 139:116–77.

Popper, Karl R. 1963. *Conjunctures and Refutations: The Growth of Scientific Knowledge*. London: Routledge.

Prier, Pierre. 2011. "Le Cameroun de Biya noyauté par les sociétés secrètes." *Le Figaro*, October 27, 2011.

Puccio-Den, D. 2022. *Mafiacraft*. Chicago: HAU Books.

Pype, Katrien. 2016. "Ethnographic Explorations of Rural-Urban Connectivity in and around Kinshasa's Phonie Cabins." *Mededelingen der Zittingen van de Koninklijke Academie Overzeese Wetenschappen/Bulletin des Séances de l'Académie Royale des Sciences d'Outre-Mer* 62, no. 2: 229–60. https://zenodo.org/records/3379983.

———. 2017. "Brahamist *Kindoki*: Ethnographic Notes on Connectivity, Technology, and Urban Witchcraft in Contemporary Kinshasa." In *Pentecostalism and Witchcraft: Spiritual Warfare in Africa and Melanesia*, ed. K. Rio, M. McCarthy, and R. Blanes, 115–45. London: Palgrave MacMillan.

Quinqueton, Denis. 2022. *Loi du 6 août 1942: Après son café au lait et sa tartine Pétain réprima l'homosexualité*. Paris: HES.

Ranger, Terence. 2007. "Scotland Yard in the Bush: Medicine Murders, Child Witches and the Construction of the Occult: A Literature Review." *Africa* 77, no. 2: 272–84.

Rao, Rahul. 2020. *Out of Time: The Queer Politics of Postcoloniality*. New York: Oxford University Press.

Reid, Graeme. 2010. *Above the Skyline: Reverend Tsietsi Thandekiso and the Founding of an African Gay Church*. Pretoria: UNISA Press.

———. 2013. *How to Be a "Real Gay": Gay Identities in Small-Town South Africa*. Scottsville, South Africa: University of Kwa-Zulu Natal Press.

Rich, P. 2017. "Freemasonry in Colonial Africa: Competing Allegiances of the Grand Orient of France and the Grand Lodge of England." https://afsaap.org.au/assets/1991_Paul-Rich_Freemasonry-in-Colonial-history.pdf.

Roussignol, Dominique. 1981. *Vichy et les Francs-Maçons: La liquidation des sociétés secrètes 1940–1944*. Paris: Jean-Claude Lattès.

Roxburgh, Shelagh. 2019. "Homosexuality, Witchcraft, and Power: The Politics of *Ressentiment* in Cameroon." *African Studies Review* 62, no. 3: 89–111.

Rueger, A. 1960. "Die Entstehung und Lage der Arbeiterklasse unter dem Deutschen Kolonialregime in Kamerun." In *Kamerun unter Deutschen Kolonialherrschaft*, vol. 2, ed. H. Stoecker, 149–242. Berlin: Deutscher Verlag der Wissenschaften.

Sanders, Todd, and Harry G. West. 2003. "Introduction: Power Revealed and Concealed in the New World Order." In *Transparency and Conspiracy: Ethnographies of Suspicion in the New World Order*, ed. Harry G. West and Todd Sanders, 1–37. Durham, NC: Duke University Press.

Sandfort, Theo, Fabienne Simenel, and Keven Mwachio, eds. 2015. *Boldly Queer: African Perspectives on Same-Sex Sexuality and Gender Diversity*. The Hague: Hivos.

Saunier, Éric. 2016. "Les francs-maçons et la Révolution française." In *La Franc-Maçonnerie*, ed. Pierre Mollier, Sylvie Bourel, and Laurent Portes, 198–206. Paris: Bibliothèque nationale de France.

Seeck, Andreas. 1996. "Wilhelm Ostwald, Monistenbund, Energie und Sexualwissenschaft." *Mitteilungen der Magnus-Hirschfeld-Gesellschaft* 22, no. 3: 67–97.

Sibalis, Michael. 1996. "The Regulation of Male Homosexuality in Revolutionary and Napoleonic France, 1789–1815." In *Homosexuality in Modern France*, ed. Jeffrey Merrick and Bryant T. Ragan, 80–101. New York: Oxford University Press.

Smith, Stephen, and Antoine Glaser. 1992. *Ces messieurs afrique.* Vol. 1, *Le Paris-village du continent noir.* Paris: Calmann-Lévy.

———. 1997. *Ces messieurs afrique.* Vol. 2, *Des réseaux aux lobbies.* Paris: Calmann-Lévy.

Spronk, Rachel. 2018. "Invisible Desires in Ghana and Kenya: Same-Sex Erotic Experiences in Cross-Sex Oriented Lives." *Sexualities* 21, nos. 5–6: 883–98.

Spronk, Rachel, and S. N. Nyeck. 2021. "Frontiers and Pioneers in (the Study of) Queer Experiences in Africa." *Africa* 91, no. 3: 338–97.

Starbensky, Alexandre. 2010. "Petite(s) Histoire(s) de l'antimaçonnisme(s) en France." https://amp.agoravox.fr/actualites/societe/article/petite-s-histoire-s -de-l-75742.

Stevenson, D. 1988. *The Origins of Freemasonry: Scotland's Century, 1590–1710.* Cambridge: Cambridge University Press.

Stoler, Ann Laura. 2016. *Duress: Imperial Durabilities in Our Times.* Durham, NC: Duke University Press.

Sulaiman, Tajudeen, and Bamidele Adebayo. 2002. "The Nation's Homosexuals." *The News* (Lagos), April 22, 2002. Accessed through AllAfrica, https://allafrica .com/stories/200204220488.html.

Tamale, Sylvia. 2003. "Out of the Closet: Unveiling Sexual Discourses in Uganda." *Feminist Africa: Changing Cultures,* no. 2. https://awdflibrary.org/index.php?p =show_detail&id=485.

Tamale, Sylvia, ed. 2011. *African Sexualities: A Reader.* Cape Town: Pambazuka Press.

Taussig, Michael. 1987. *Shamanism, Colonialism, and the Wild Man: A Study of Terror and Healing.* Chicago: University of Chicago Press.

Tchuisseu, Ghislain Youdji. 2021. "Franc-maçonnerie: Le joker de la Francafrique." In *L'Empire qui ne veut pas mourir: Une histoire de la Françafrique,* ed. Thomas Borrel, Amzat Boukari-Yabara, Benoît Collombat, and Thomas Deltombe, 505–16. Paris: Seuil.

Templiers et francs-maçons: De la légende à l'histoire. 2016. Paris: Musée de la franc-maçonnerie. Exhibition catalog.

Tesi, K. 2017. *Balancing Sovereignty and Development in International Affairs: Cameroon's Post-Independence Relations with France, Africa, and the World.* Lanham, MD: Lexington Books.

Tessmann, Günther. 1913. *Die Pangwe.* Berlin: Wasmuth.

———. 1919. "Die Homosexualität bei den Negern Kamerun." *Jahrbuch für sexuelle Zwischenstufen* 1, no. 2: 121–38.

———. 1934. *Die Bafia und die Kultur des Mittelkemerun-Bantu.* Stuttgart: Strecker & Schröder.

———. 1940 [and 1960]. *König im Weissen Fleck.* Unpublished manuscript in the Lübecker Museen/Völkerkundesammlung.

———. 2012. *Günther Tessmann, Mein Leben: Tagebuch.* Vol. 2, ed. Sabine Dinslage and Brigitte Templin. Lübeck: Schmidt Rönhild.

———. 2015. *Günther Tessmann, Mein Leben: Tagebuch.* Vol. 3, ed. Brigitte Templin. Lübeck: Schmidt Rönhild.

Thiébot, Emmanuel. 2008. *Scandal au Grand Orient.* Paris: Larousse.

———. 2021. *Le scandale oublié de la IIIe République: Le Grand Orient et l'affaire des fiches.* Paris: Dunod.

Thiranagama, Sharika. 2011. *In My Mother's House: Civil War in Sri Lanka*. Philadelphia: University of Pennsylvania Press.

Tonda, Joseph. 2003. *L'Afrique des guérisons*. Paris: Karthala.

———. 2005. *Le souverain moderne*. Paris: Karthala. Translated as *Modern Sovereign: The Body of Power in Central Africa*, Delhi: Seagull, 2020.

———. 2015a. *L'impérialisme postcolonial: Critique de la société des éblouissements*. Paris: Karthala.

———. 2015b. "L'impérialisme postcolonial du corps sexe à Libreville." In *Le féminin, le masculin et les rapports sociaux de sexe au Gabon*, ed. Esseng Abaá and J. Tonda, 21–38. Paris: L'Harmattan.

———. 2016. "Fanon au Gabon: Sexe onirique et Afrodystopie." *Politique Africaine* 143:113–37.

Toulou, Lucien. 2007. "Des scènes dignes de Sodome et Gomorrhe? Occulte, pouvoir et imaginaire de changement politique." In "Dossier: L'Homosexualité est bonne à penser," ed. Fabien Eboussi Boulaga, special issue, *Terroirs* 1–2:77–98.

Tutuola, Amos. 1952. *The Palm-Wine Drinkard and His Dead Palm-Wine Tapster in the Dead's Town*. London: Faber and Faber.

Valade, Jean-Michel. 2000. "La lutte contre les Francs-Maçons sous le régime de Vichy (1940–1944): L'exemple de la Corrèze." *Guerres mondiales et conflits contemporains* no. 197: 117–28. Paris: Presses Universitaires de France.

Vallée, Olivier. 2010. *La police morale de l'anticorruption: Cameroun, Nigéria*. Paris: Karthala.

Van Klinken, Adriaan. 2019. *Kenyan, Christian, Queer: Religion, LGBT Activism, and Arts of Resistance in Africa*. Philadelphia: Pennsylvania State University Press.

Van Klinken, Adriaan, and Ezra Chitando, eds. 2016. *Public Religion and the Politics of Homosexuality in Africa*. London: Taylor & Francis.

Verschave, François. 1998. *La Françafrique: Le plus long scandale de la république*. Paris: Stock.

Vidal, Claudine. 1977. "Guerre des sexes à Abidjan: Masculin, féminin." *Cahiers d'études africaines* 17, no. 65: 121–53

Vincent, Jeanne-Françoise. 1969. "Morts, revenants et sorciers d'après les proverbes des Beti du Sud-Cameroun." *Cahiers d'études africaines* 9, no. 34: 271–89.

———. 1976. *Traditions et transition: Entretiens avec des femmes Beti du Sud-Cameroun*. Paris: ORSTOM/Berger Levrault.

———. 2001. *Femmes beti entre deux mondes: Entretiens dans la forêt du Cameroun*. Paris: Karthala.

———. 2003. "La ménopause, chemin de la liberté chez les femmes beti du Sud-Cameroun." *Journal des africanistes* 73, no. 2: 121–36.

Waquet, Claude. 1981. "Les débuts de la Franc-Maçonnerie à la Réunion." In *Problèmes religieux et minorités en océan indien*, 23–30. Institut d'Histoire des Pays d'Outremer, Université de Provence, Aix.

Warnier, Jean-Pierre. 1993. *L'esprit d'entreprise au Cameroun*. Paris: Karthala.

———. 2023. *Dix ans de bonheur: Un couple bourgeois à l'âge des extrêmes*. Paris: Karthala.

Wauthier, C. 2003. "L'essor de la franc-maçonnerie africaine." *Géopolitique africaine* 10:281–93.

White, L. 2000. *Speaking with Vampires: Rumor and History in Colonial Africa*. Berkeley: University of California Press.

White, Owen. 2005. "Networking: Freemasons and the Colonial State in French West Africa." *French History* 19, no. 1: 91–111.

Wiener, Martin J. 2013. "The Idea of 'Colonial Legacy' and the Historiography of Empire." *Journal of the Historical Society* 13, no. 1: 1–32.

Willy [Henri Gauthier-Villars]. 2014 [1927]. *Le troisième sexe.* Montpellier: Gaykitschcamp.

Woungly-Massaga. Nguo. 1974. *La revolution au Congo: Contribution à l'étude des problèmes politique d'Afrique centrale.* Paris: Maspero.

———. 1984. *Où va le Kamerun?* Paris: L'Harmattan.

Index

Page numbers in italics indicate figures.